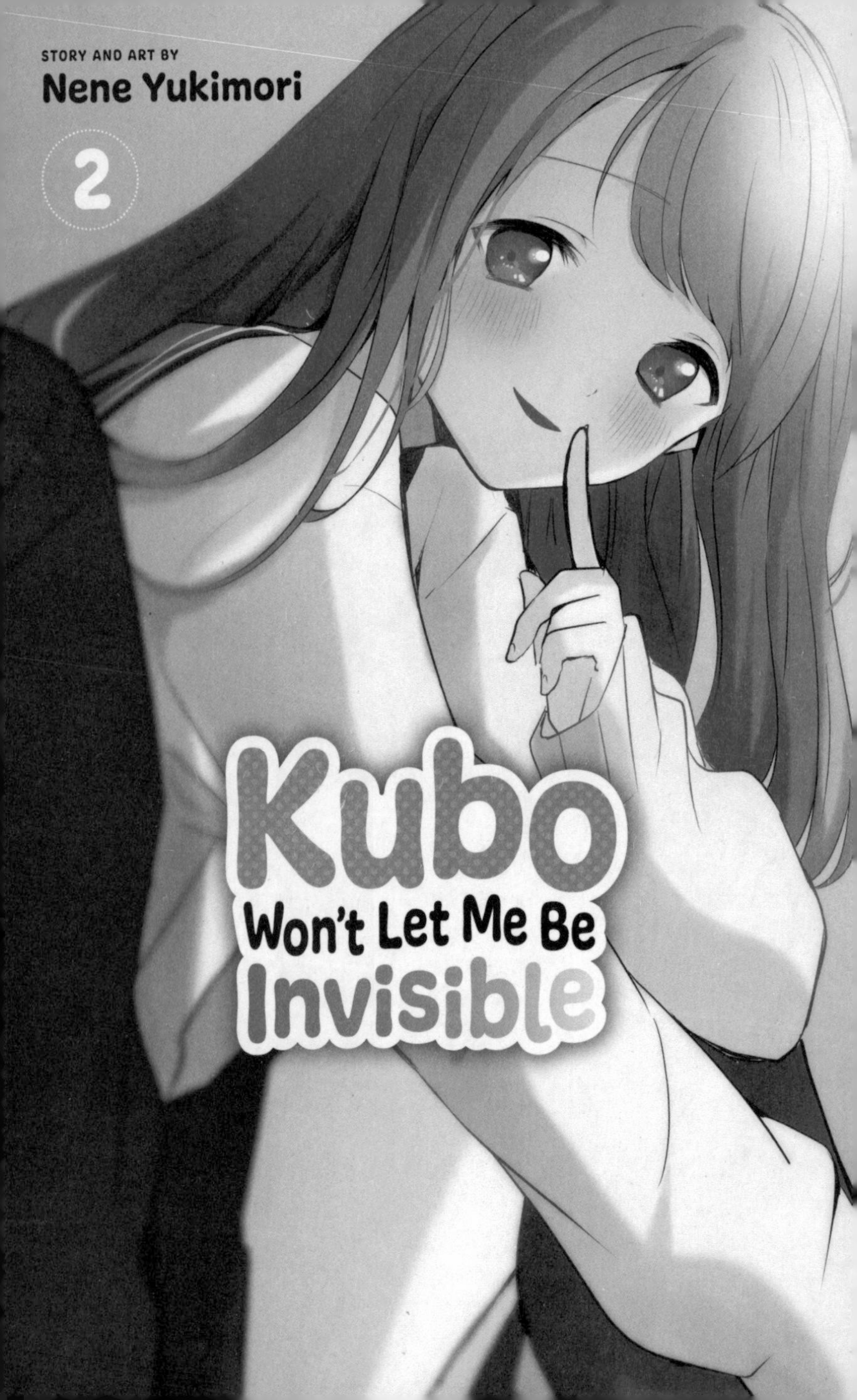
STORY AND ART BY
Nene Yukimori
2
Kubo
Won't Let Me Be
Invisible

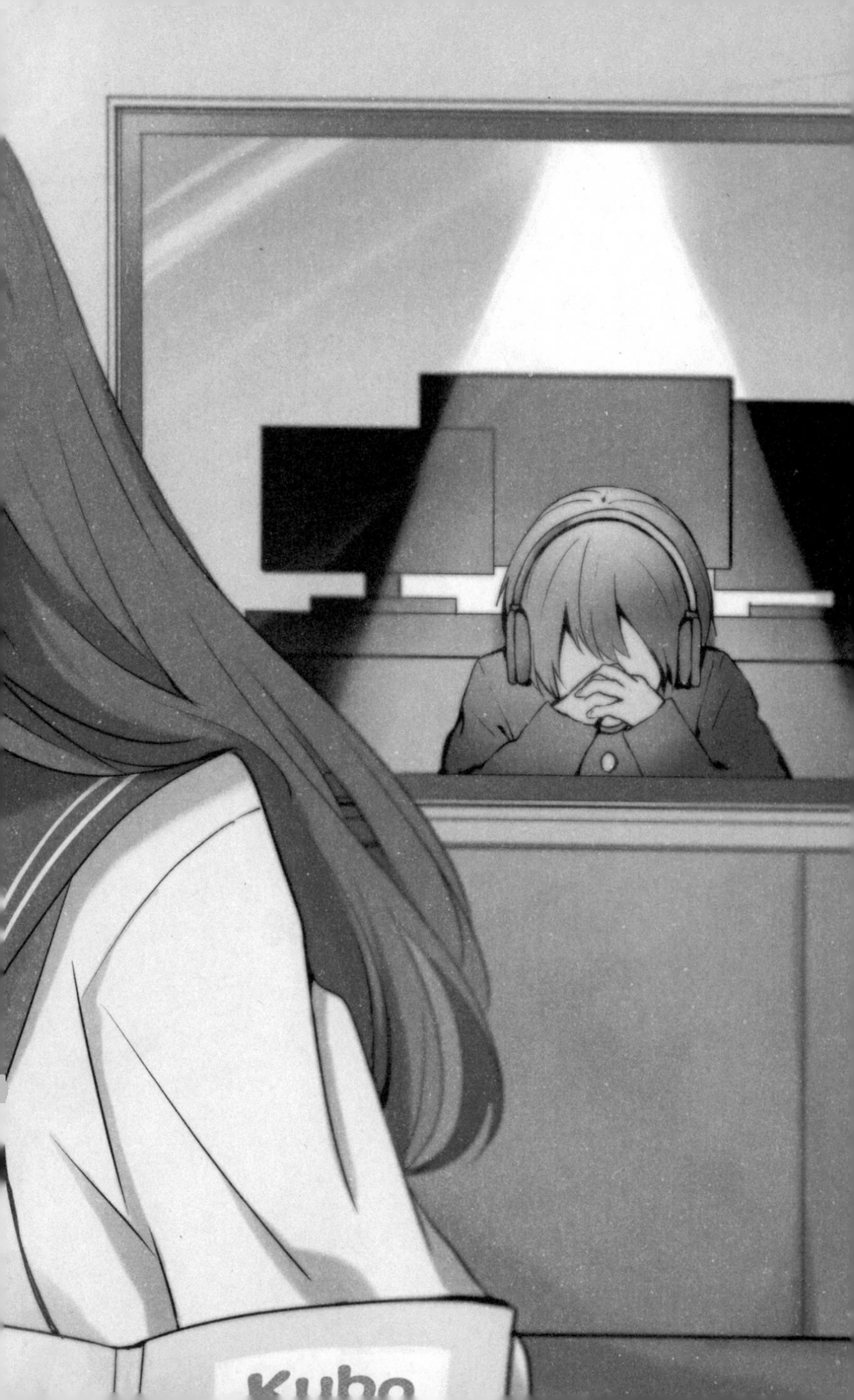
Kubo

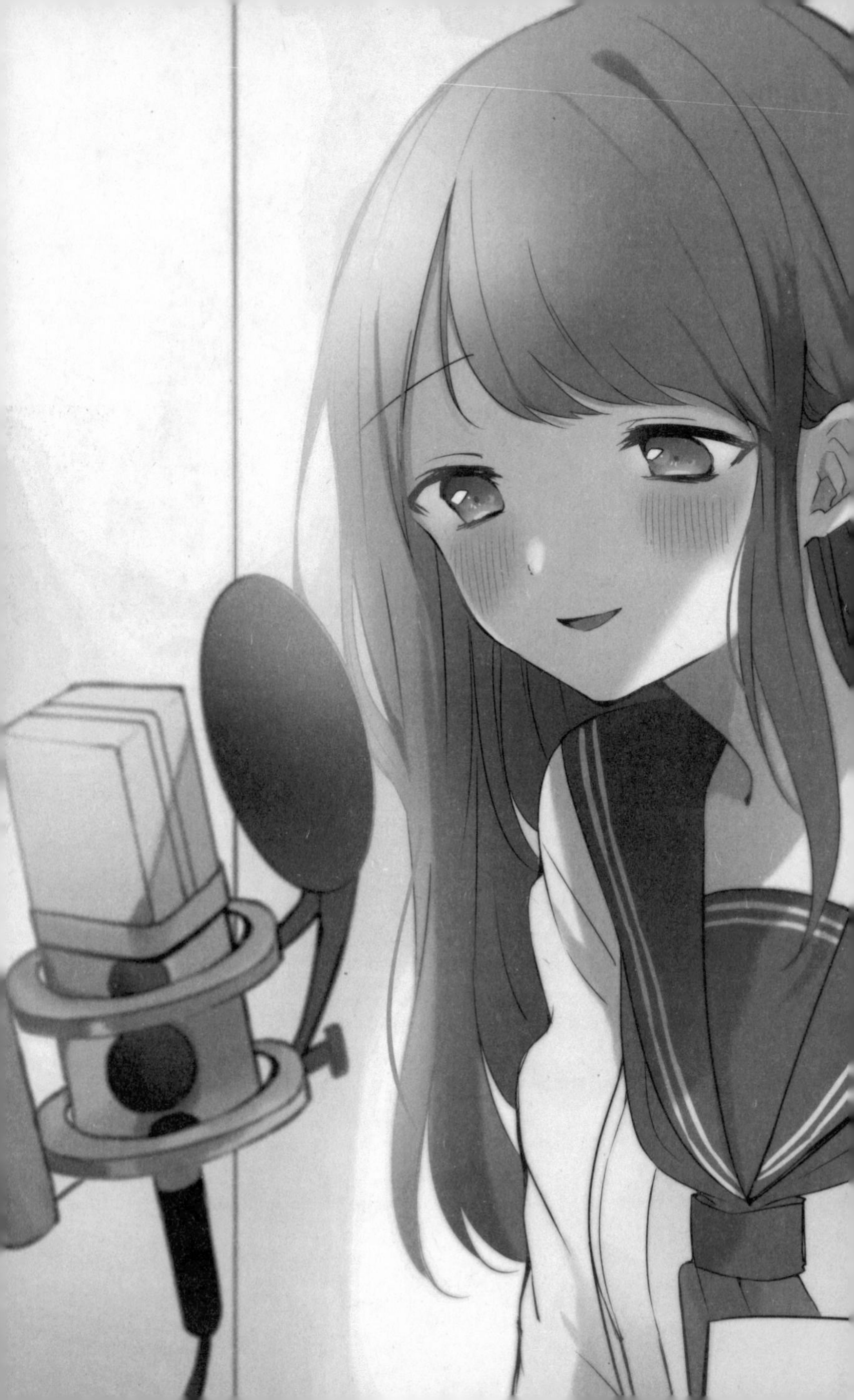

To me ten years from now—
Who are you smiling beside?
Are you happy?

CONTENTS

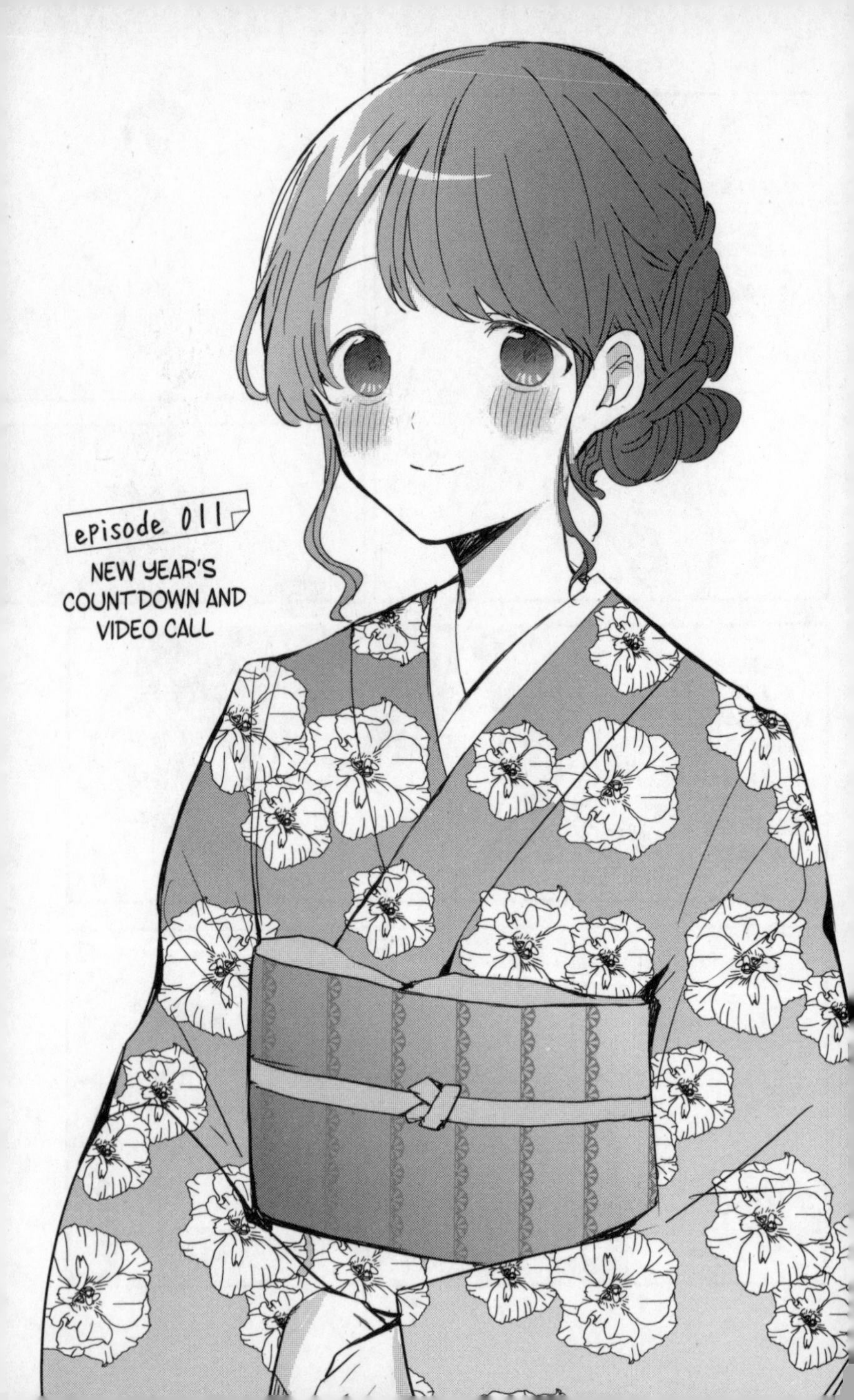
episode 011
NEW YEAR'S COUNTDOWN AND VIDEO CALL

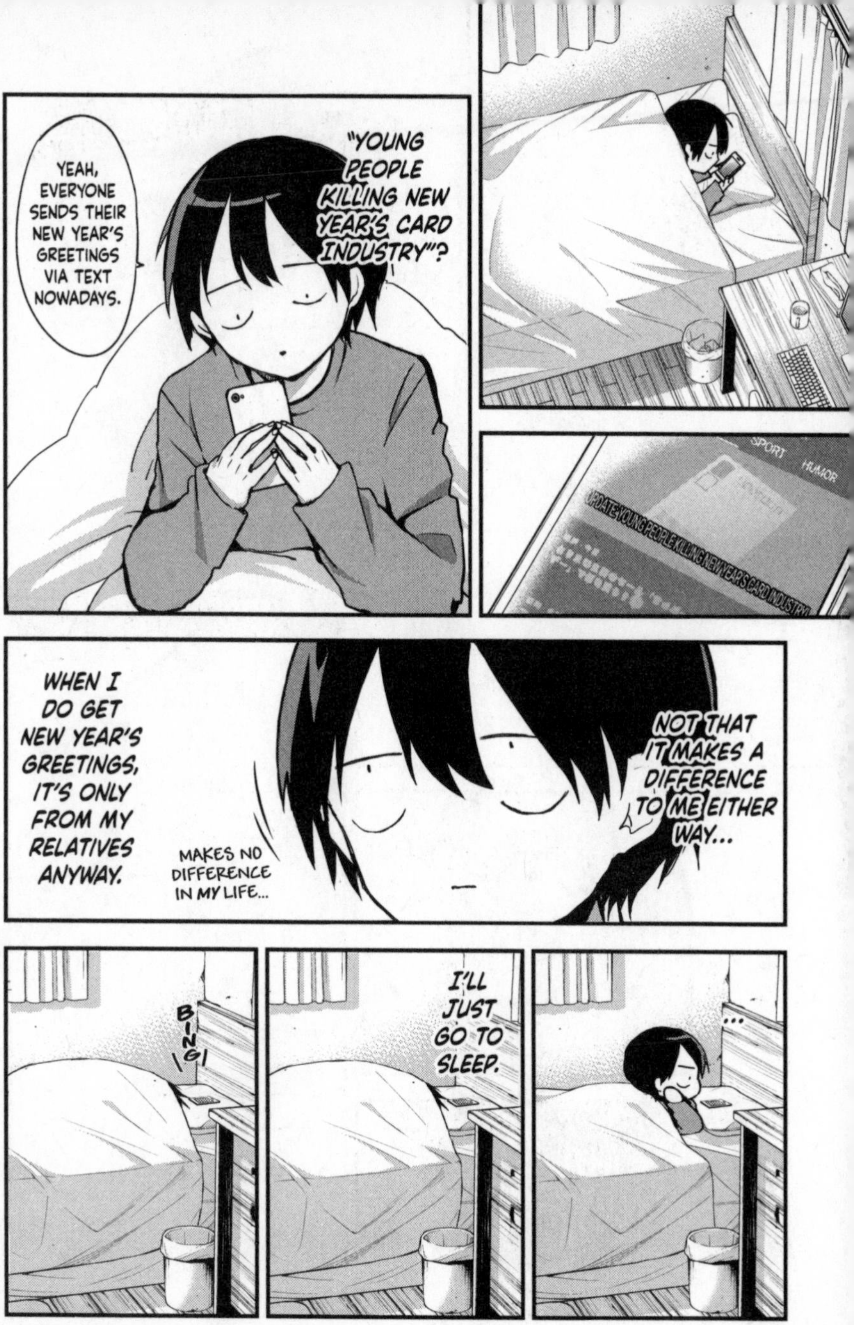
SPORT
HUMOR
UPDATE: YOUNG PEOPLE KILLING NEW YEAR'S CARD INDUSTRY!
"YOUNG PEOPLE KILLING NEW YEAR'S CARD INDUSTRY"?
YEAH, EVERYONE SENDS THEIR NEW YEAR'S GREETINGS VIA TEXT NOWADAYS.
NOT THAT IT MAKES A DIFFERENCE TO ME EITHER WAY...
WHEN I DO GET NEW YEAR'S GREETINGS, IT'S ONLY FROM MY RELATIVES ANYWAY.
MAKES NO DIFFERENCE IN MY LIFE...
...
I'LL JUST GO TO SLEEP.
BING!

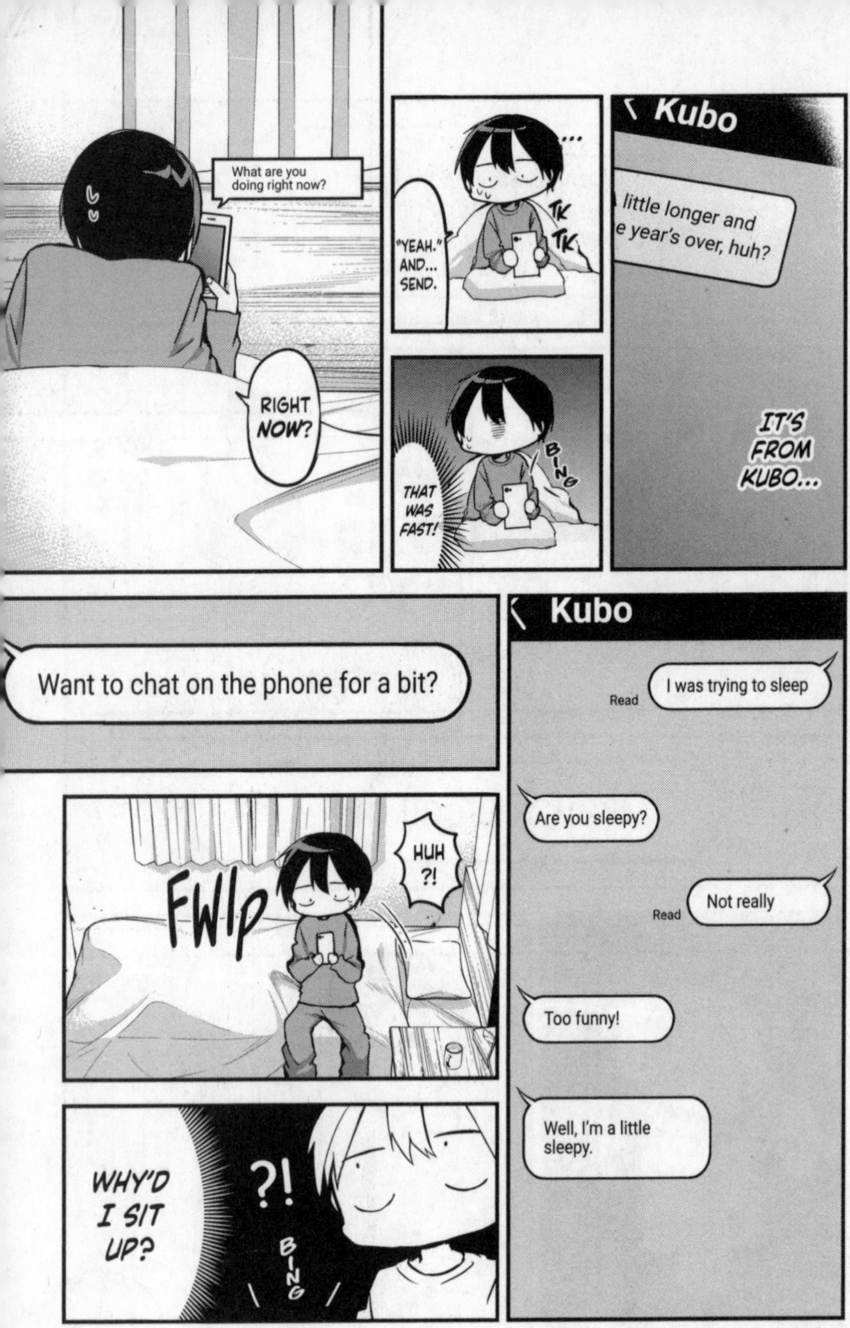
Kubo
little longer and
e year's over, huh?
IT'S FROM KUBO...
...
TK TK
"YEAH." AND... SEND.
BING
THAT WAS FAST!
What are you doing right now?
RIGHT NOW?
Kubo
I was trying to sleep
Read
Are you sleepy?
Not really
Read
Too funny!
Well, I'm a little sleepy.
Want to chat on the phone for a bit?
HUH ?!
FWIP
?!
BING
WHY'D I SIT UP?

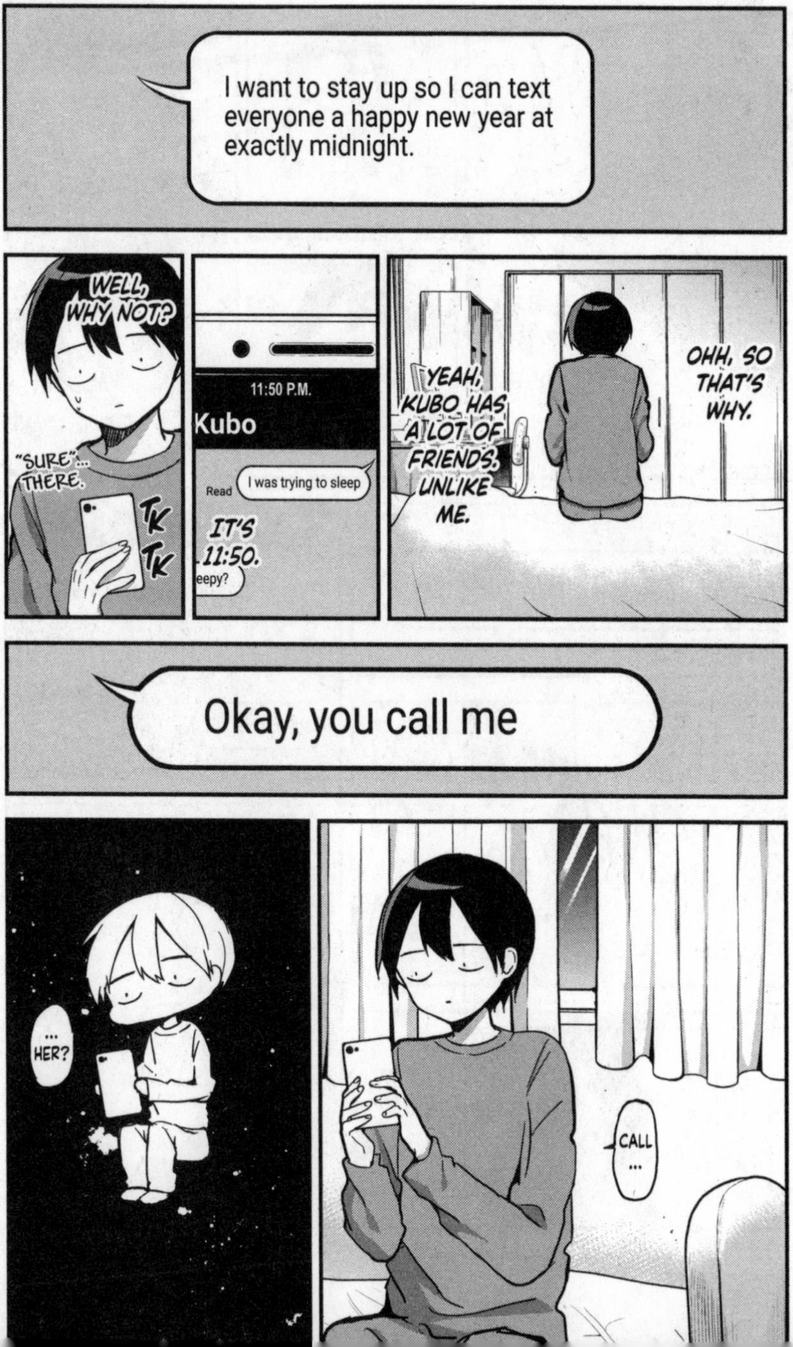
I want to stay up so I can text everyone a happy new year at exactly midnight.
OHH, SO THAT'S WHY.
YEAH, KUBO HAS A LOT OF FRIENDS. UNLIKE ME.
11:50 P.M.
Kubo
Read
I was trying to sleep
IT'S 11:50.
eepy?
WELL, WHY NOT?
"SURE"... THERE.
TK TK
Okay, you call me
CALL ...
... HER?

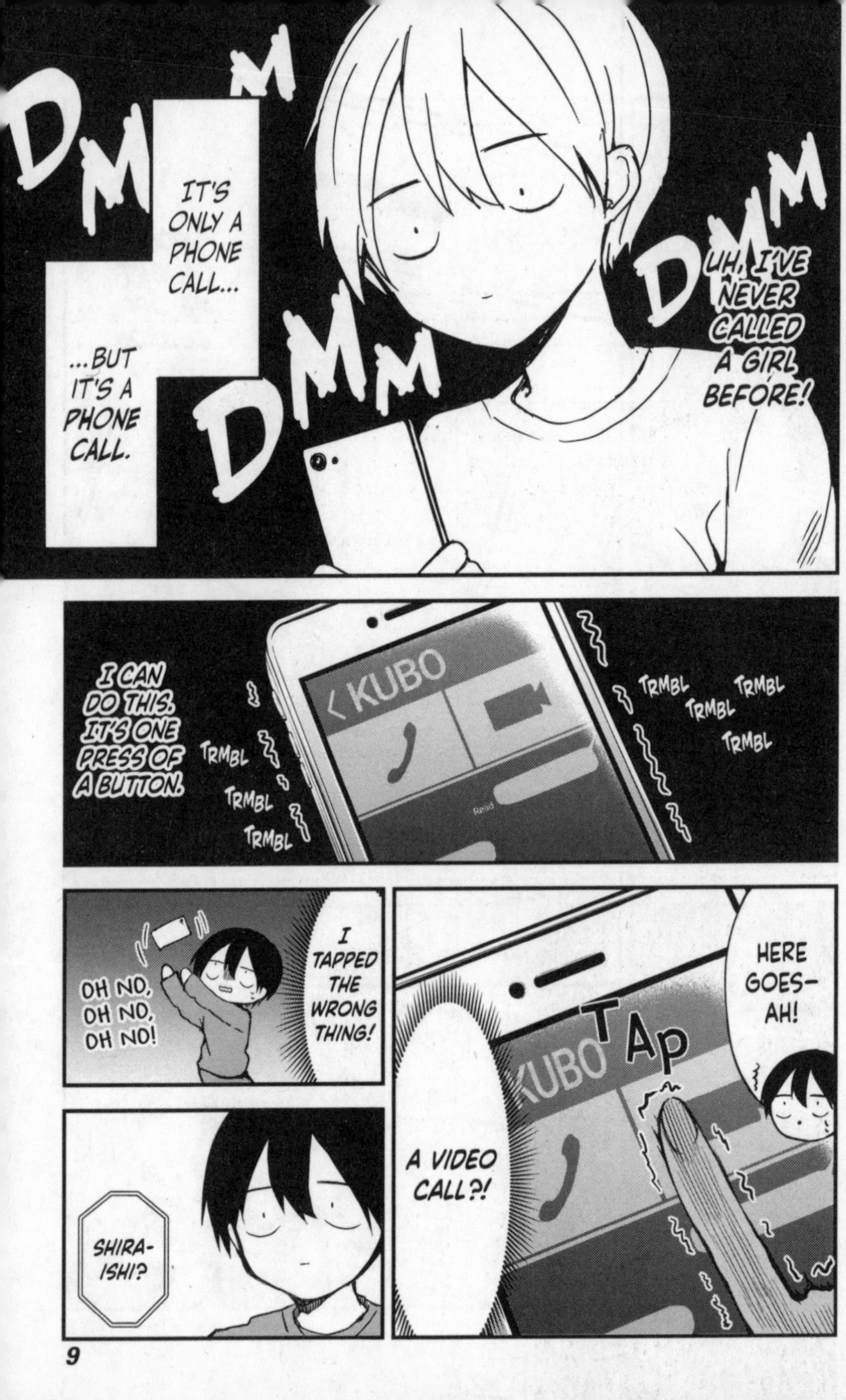
DMM
DMMM
UH, I'VE NEVER CALLED A GIRL BEFORE!
DMM
IT'S ONLY A PHONE CALL...
...BUT IT'S A PHONE CALL.
TRMBL
TRMBL
TRMBL
TRMBL
KUBO
Read
I CAN DO THIS. IT'S ONE PRESS OF A BUTTON.
TRMBL
TRMBL
TRMBL
HERE GOES—AH!
TAP
KUBO
A VIDEO CALL?!
I TAPPED THE WRONG THING!
OH NO, OH NO, OH NO!
SHIRA-ISHI?

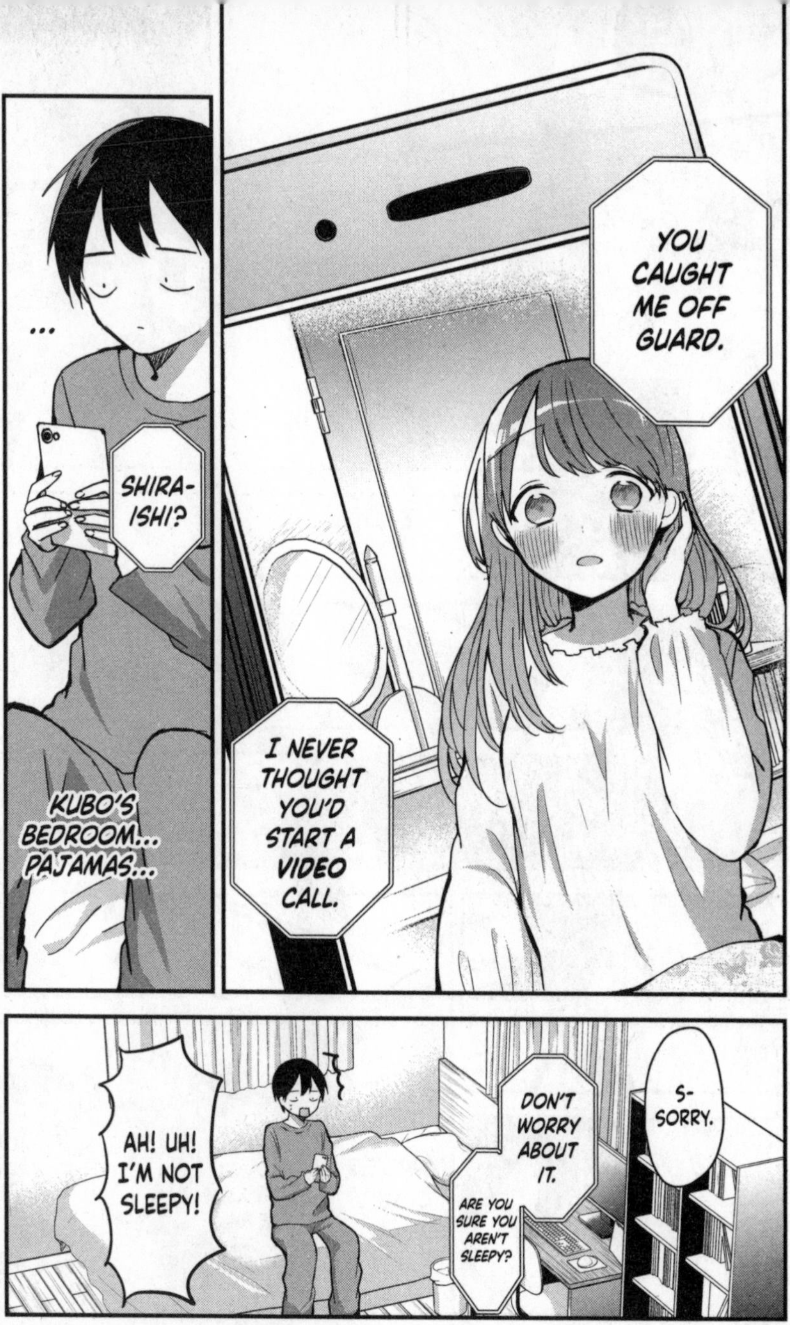
YOU CAUGHT ME OFF GUARD.
I NEVER THOUGHT YOU'D START A VIDEO CALL.
...
SHIRA-ISHI?
KUBO'S BEDROOM... PAJAMAS...
S-SORRY.
DON'T WORRY ABOUT IT.
ARE YOU SURE YOU AREN'T SLEEPY?
AH! UH! I'M NOT SLEEPY!

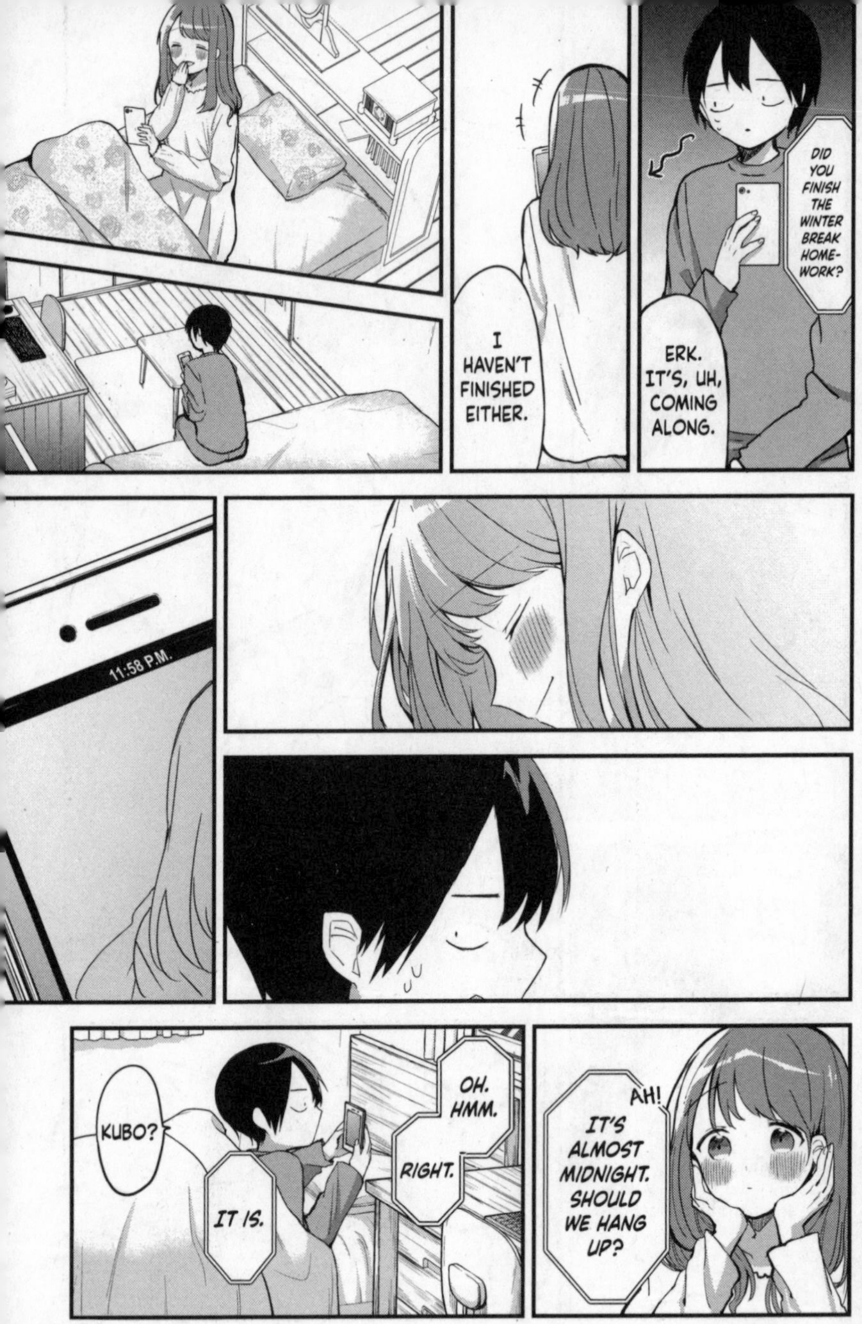
DID YOU FINISH THE WINTER BREAK HOME-WORK?
ERK. IT'S, UH, COMING ALONG.
I HAVEN'T FINISHED EITHER.
11:58 P.M.
AH! IT'S ALMOST MIDNIGHT. SHOULD WE HANG UP?
OH. HMM.
RIGHT.
KUBO?
IT IS.

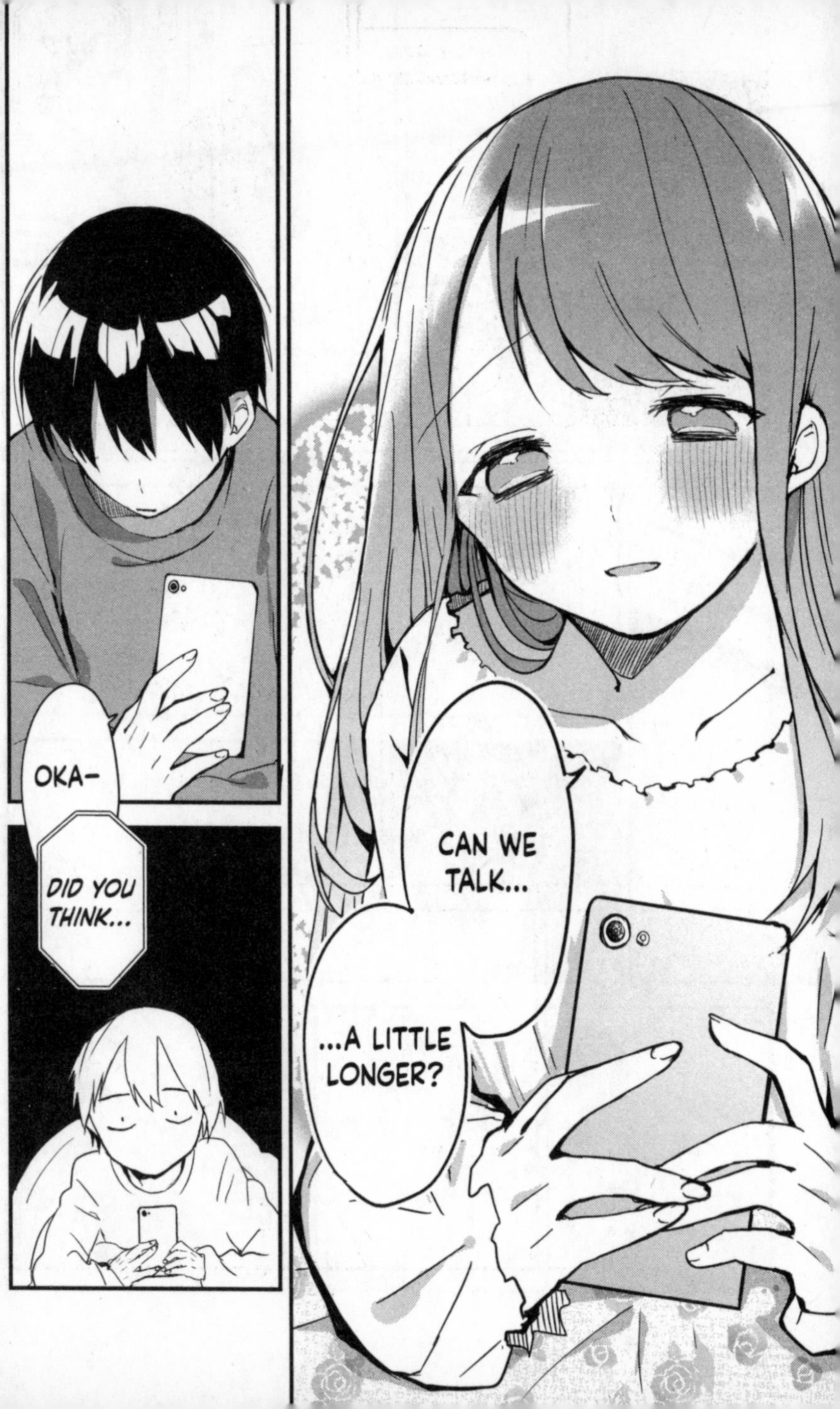
CAN WE TALK...
...A LITTLE LONGER?
OKA-
DID YOU THINK...

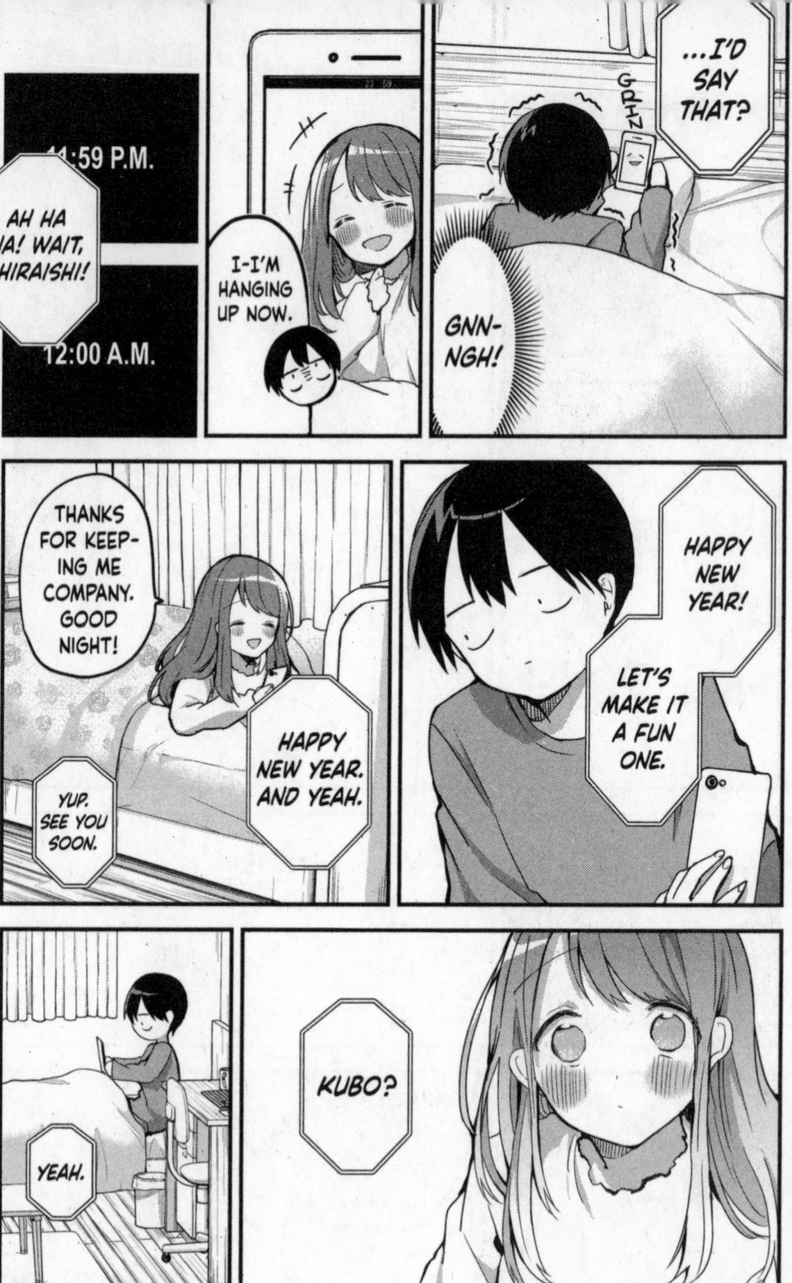
...I'D SAY THAT?
GRIN
GNN-NGH!
I-I'M HANGING UP NOW.
11:59 P.M.
AH HA HA! WAIT, SHIRAISHI!
12:00 A.M.
HAPPY NEW YEAR!
LET'S MAKE IT A FUN ONE.
THANKS FOR KEEP-ING ME COMPANY. GOOD NIGHT!
HAPPY NEW YEAR. AND YEAH.
YUP. SEE YOU SOON.
KUBO?
YEAH.

ACK.

KUBO, WAI—

Blp

ALL DONE!

SEE YOU SOON.

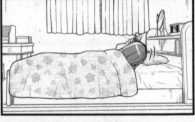

"SOON," HE SAYS...

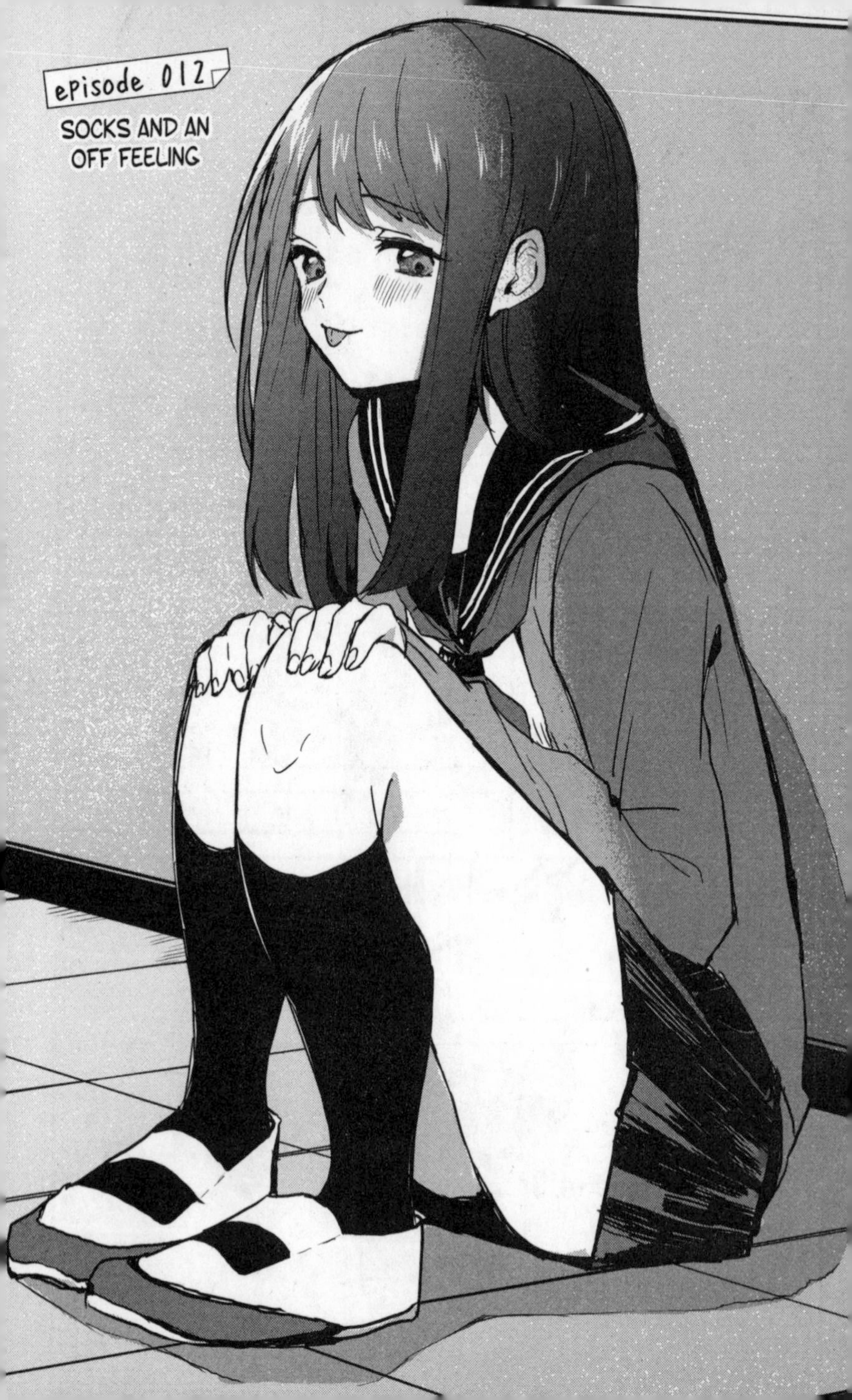
episode 012
SOCKS AND AN OFF FEELING

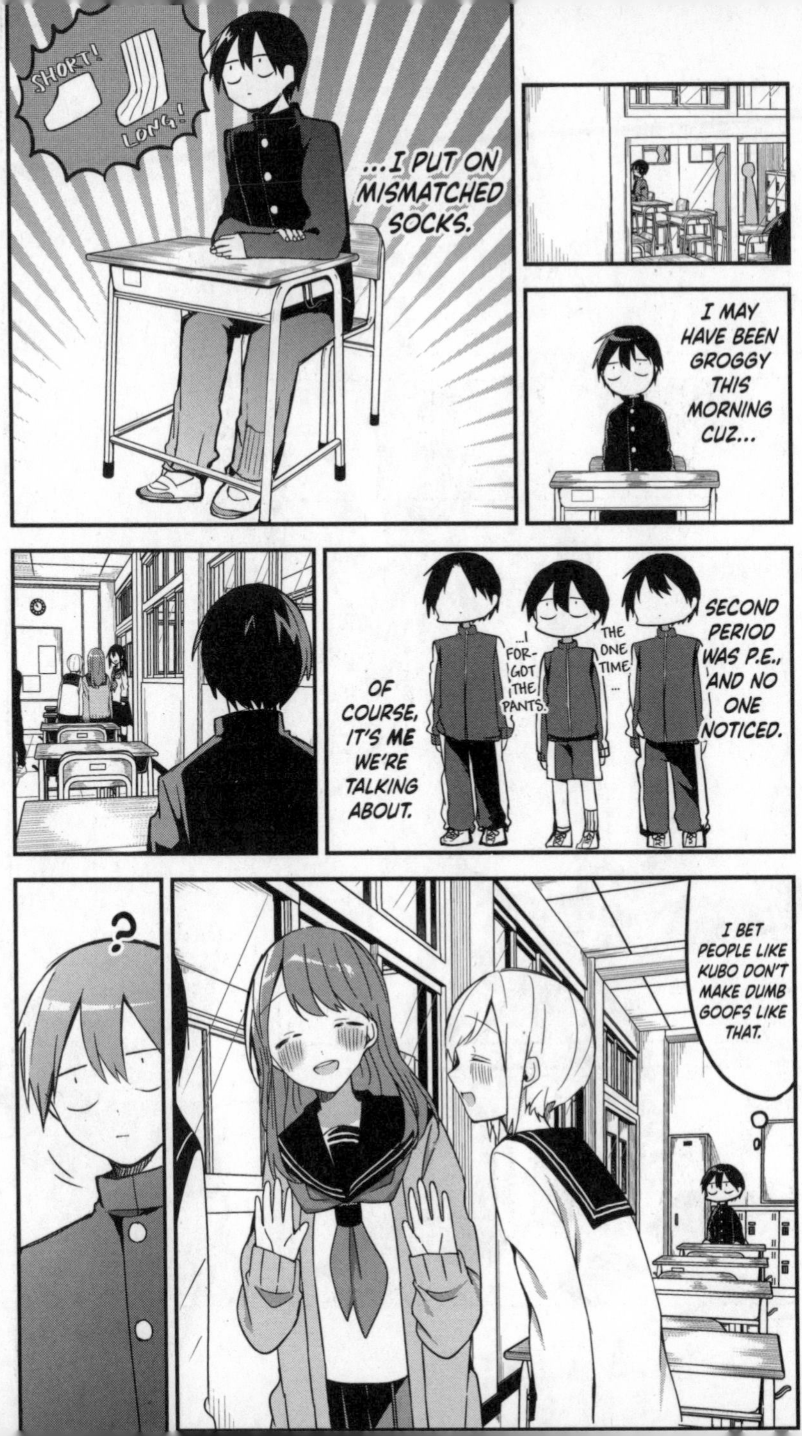

I MAY HAVE BEEN GROGGY THIS MORNING CUZ...
SHORT!
LONG!
...I PUT ON MISMATCHED SOCKS.
SECOND PERIOD WAS P.E., AND NO ONE NOTICED.
THE ONE TIME...
...I FORGOT THE PANTS.
OF COURSE, IT'S ME WE'RE TALKING ABOUT.
I BET PEOPLE LIKE KUBO DON'T MAKE DUMB GOOFS LIKE THAT.
?

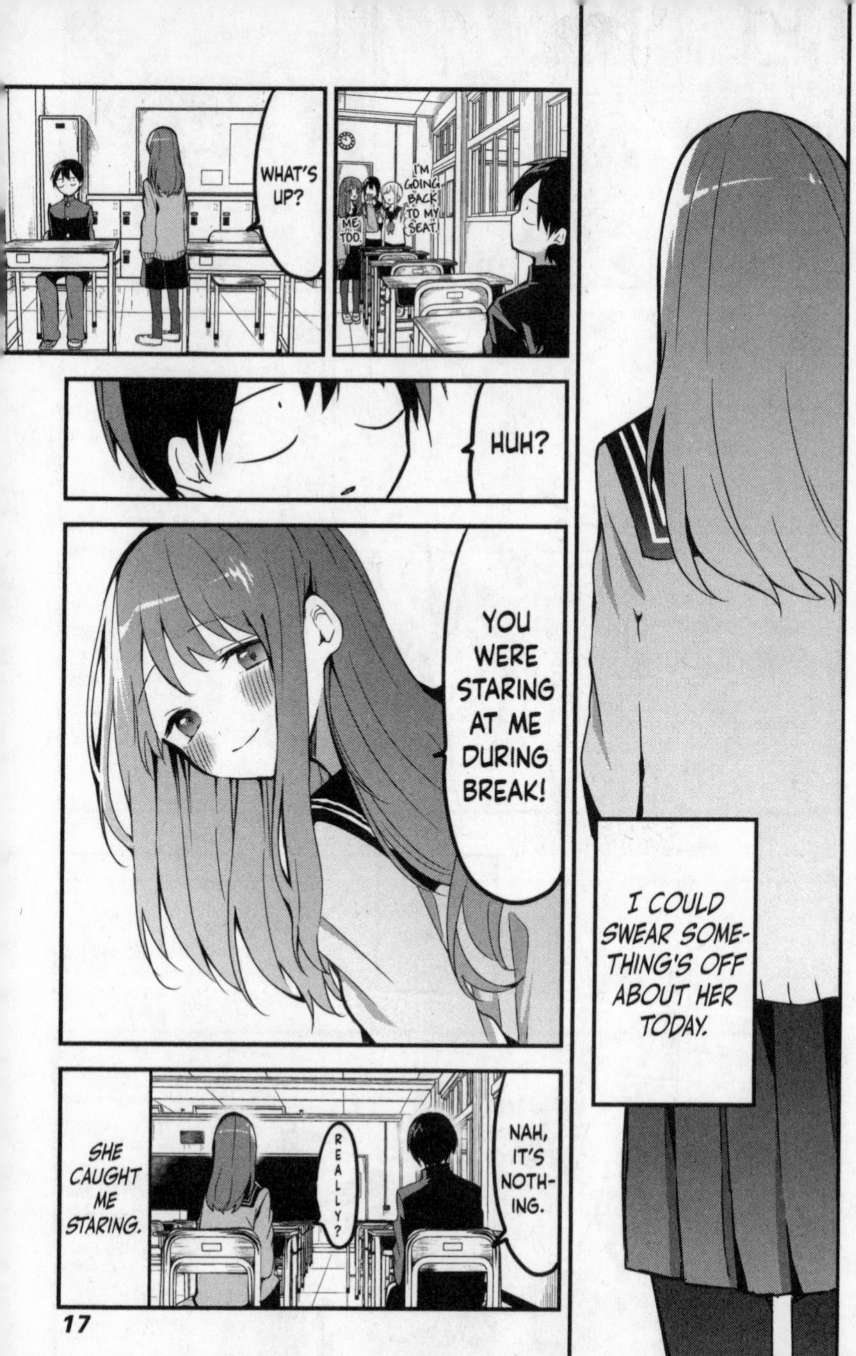
I COULD SWEAR SOME-THING'S OFF ABOUT HER TODAY.
I'M GOING BACK TO MY SEAT!
ME TOO.
WHAT'S UP?
HUH?
YOU WERE STARING AT ME DURING BREAK!
NAH, IT'S NOTH-ING.
REALLY?
SHE CAUGHT ME STARING.

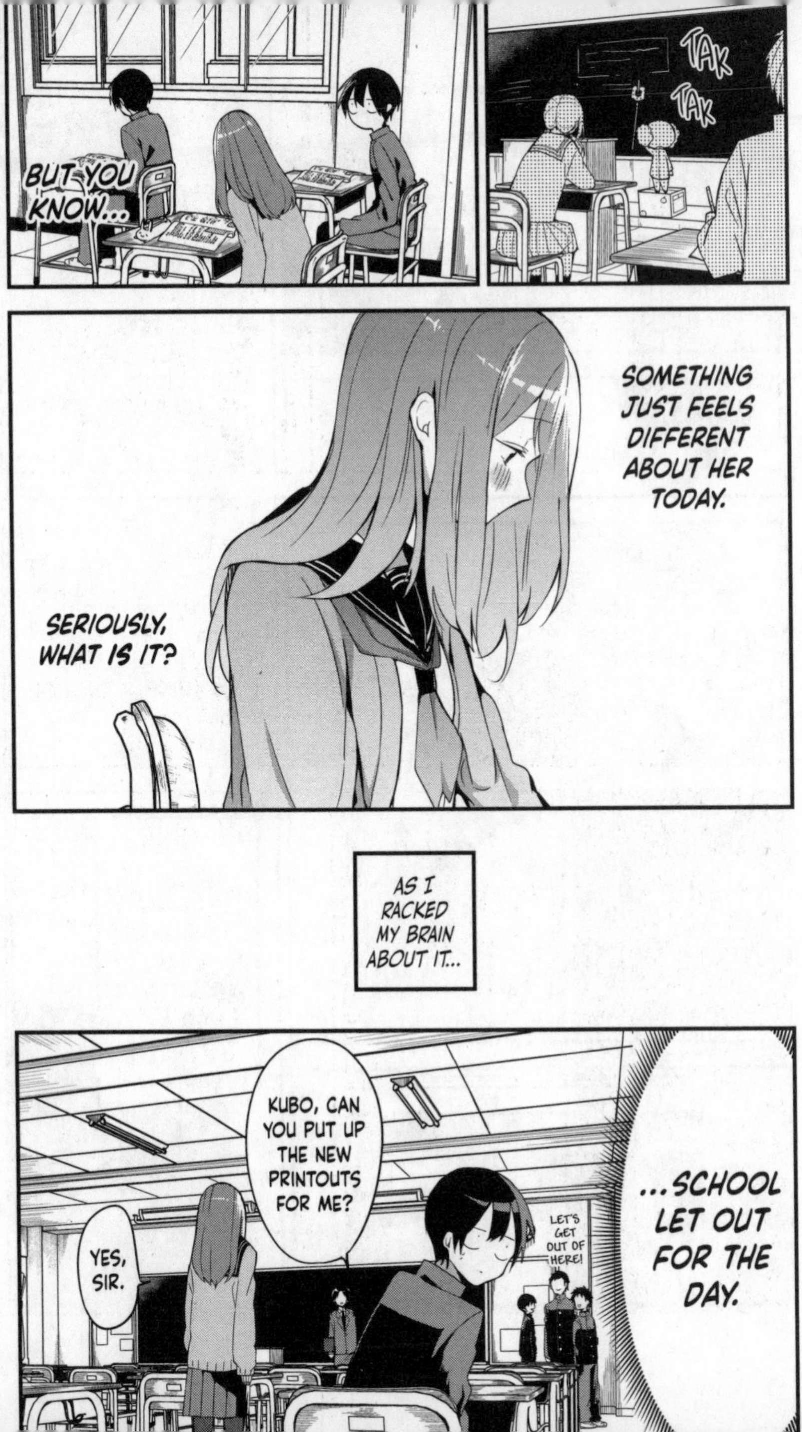
TAK
TAK
BUT YOU KNOW...
SOMETHING JUST FEELS DIFFERENT ABOUT HER TODAY.
SERIOUSLY, WHAT IS IT?
AS I RACKED MY BRAIN ABOUT IT...
...SCHOOL LET OUT FOR THE DAY.
LET'S GET OUT OF HERE!
KUBO, CAN YOU PUT UP THE NEW PRINTOUTS FOR ME?
YES, SIR.

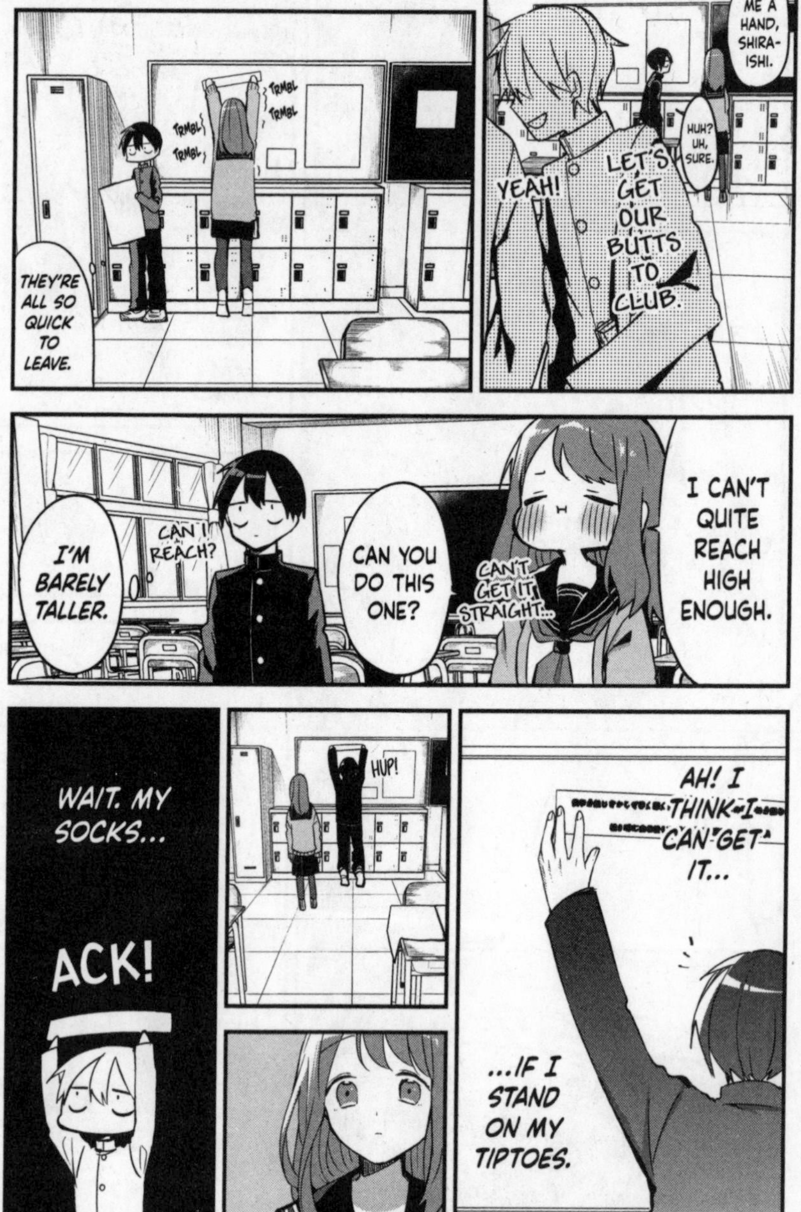
GIVE ME A HAND, SHIRAISHI.
HUH? UH, SURE.
LET'S GET OUR BUTTS TO CLUB.
YEAH!
TRMBL TRMBL
TRMBL TRMBL
THEY'RE ALL SO QUICK TO LEAVE.
I CAN'T QUITE REACH HIGH ENOUGH.
CAN'T GET IT STRAIGHT...
CAN YOU DO THIS ONE?
CAN I REACH?
I'M BARELY TALLER.
AH! I THINK I CAN GET IT...
...IF I STAND ON MY TIPTOES.
HUP!
WAIT. MY SOCKS...
ACK!

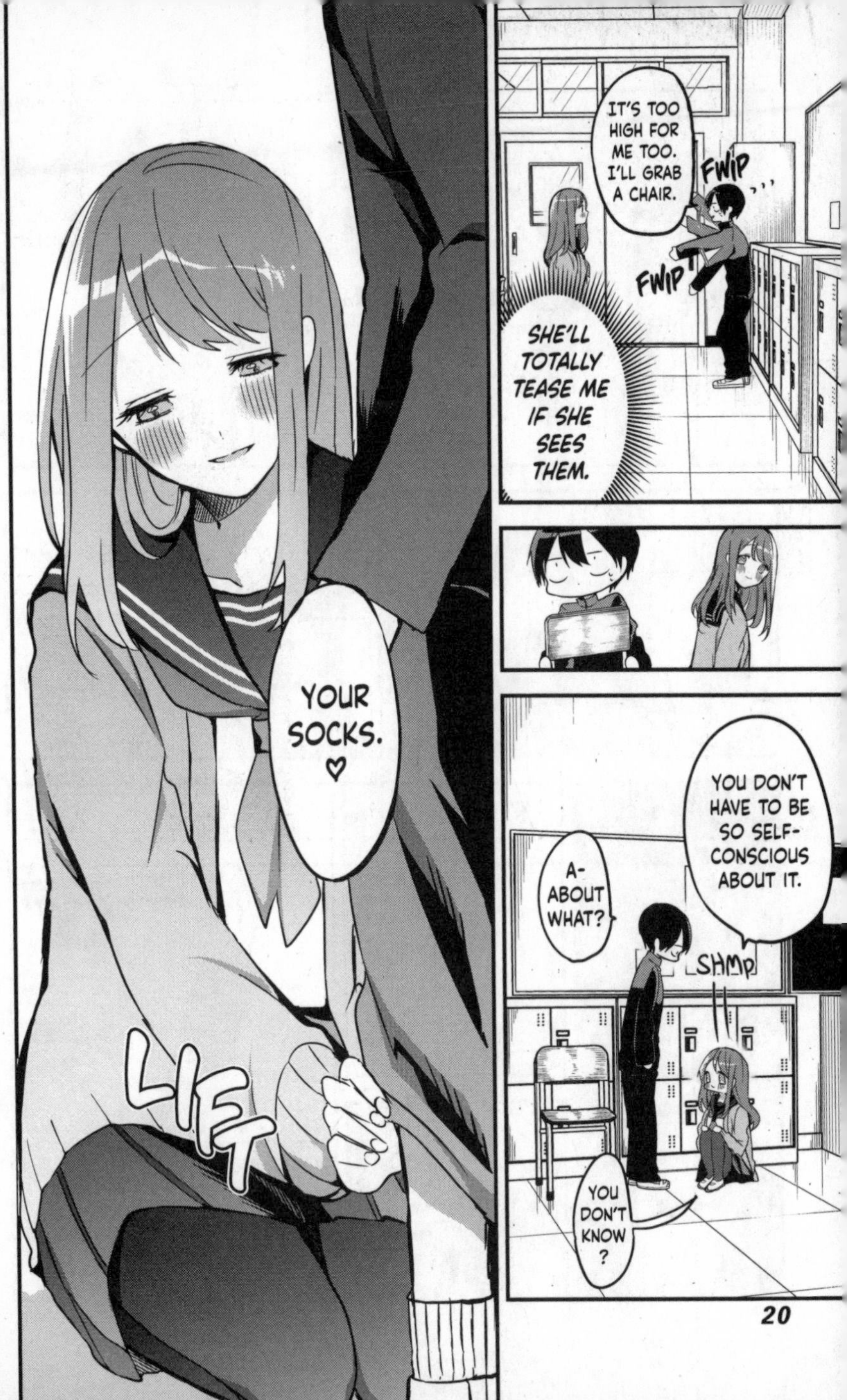
IT'S TOO HIGH FOR ME TOO. I'LL GRAB A CHAIR.
FWIP
FWIP
SHE'LL TOTALLY TEASE ME IF SHE SEES THEM.
YOU DON'T HAVE TO BE SO SELF-CONSCIOUS ABOUT IT.
SHMP
A- ABOUT WHAT?
YOU DON'T KNOW?
YOUR SOCKS. ♡
LIFT

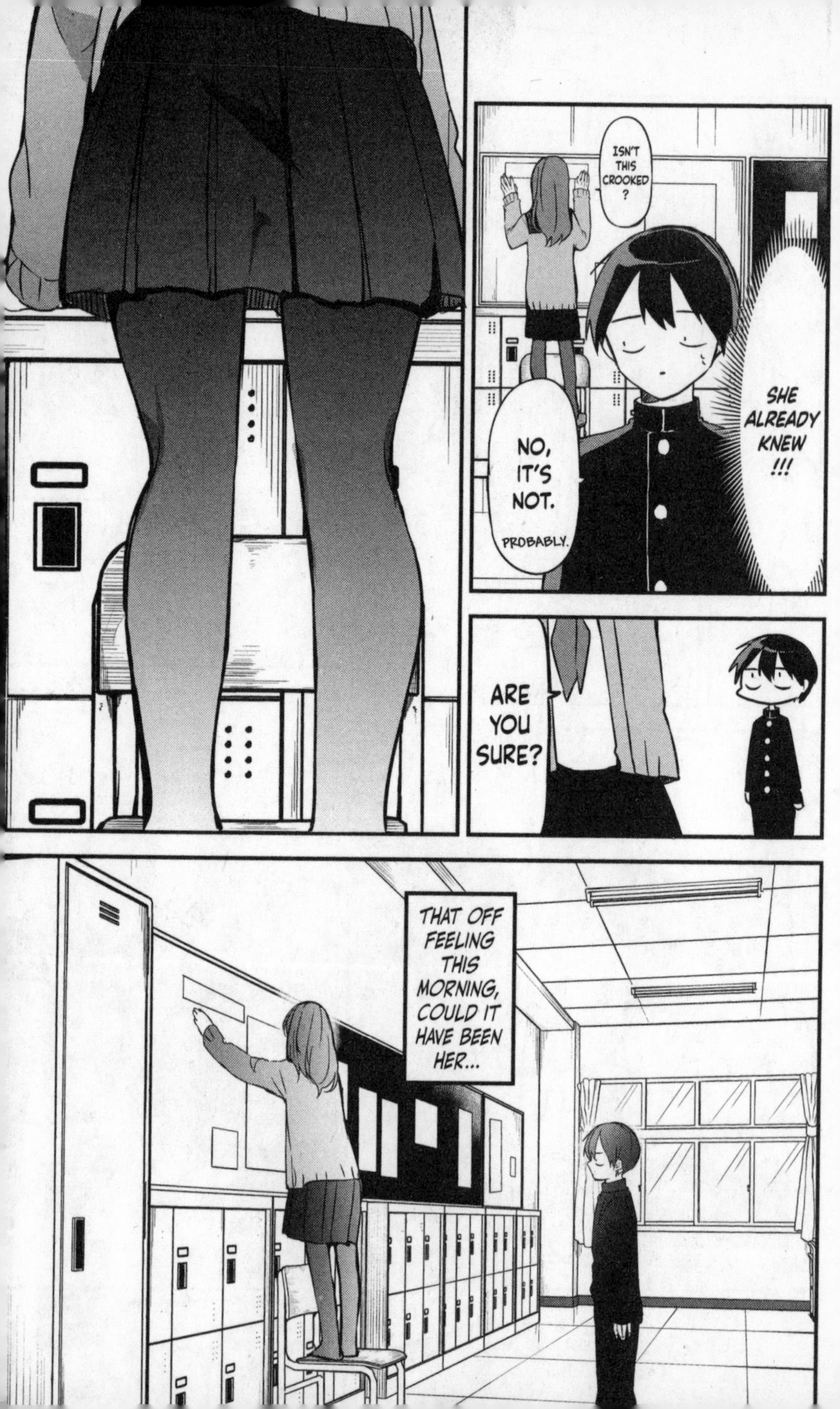
ISN'T THIS CROOKED?
NO, IT'S NOT.
PROBABLY.
SHE ALREADY KNEW!!!
ARE YOU SURE?
THAT OFF FEELING THIS MORNING, COULD IT HAVE BEEN HER...

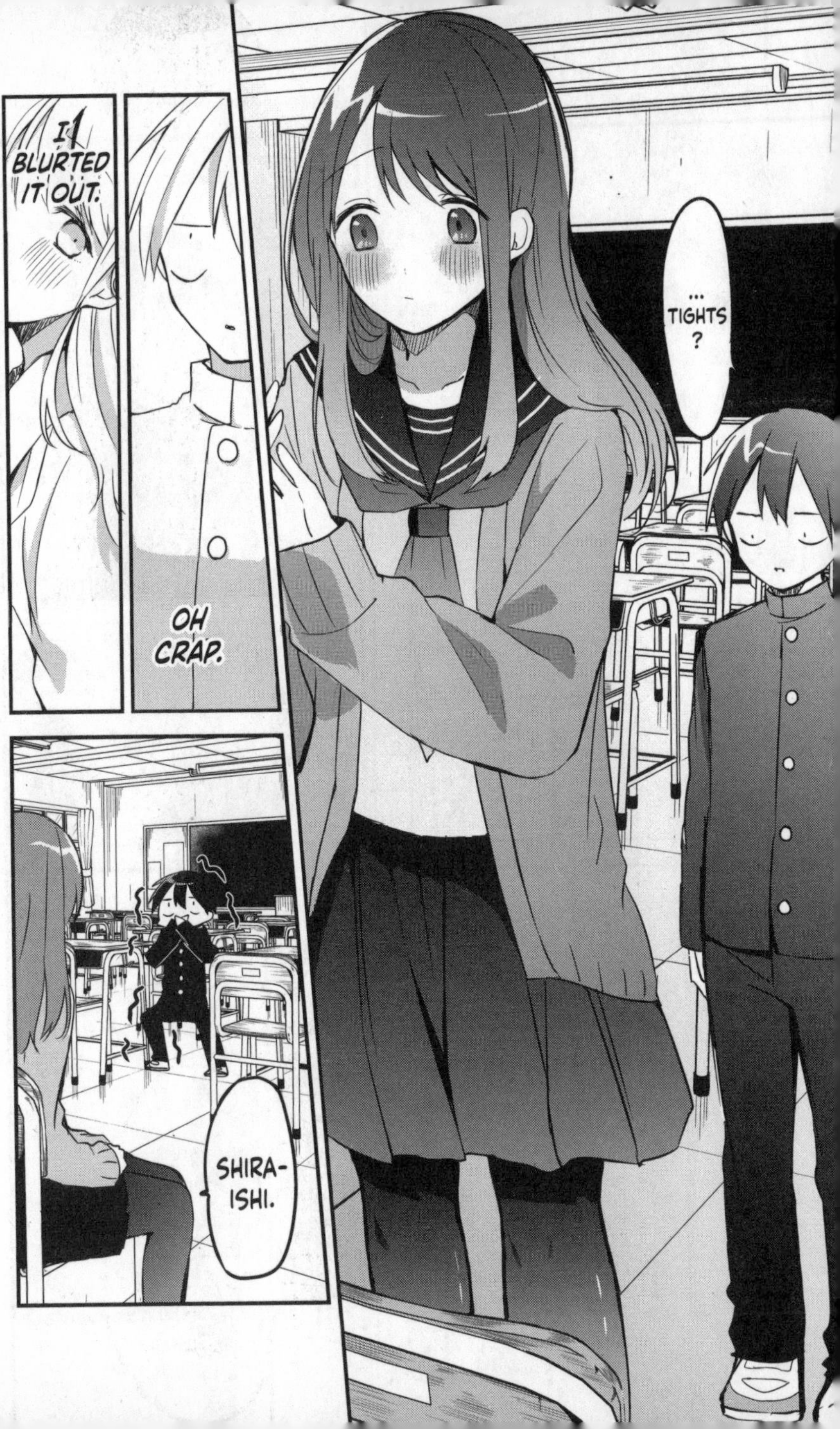
... TIGHTS?
OH CRAP.
I BLURTED IT OUT.
SHIRA-ISHI.

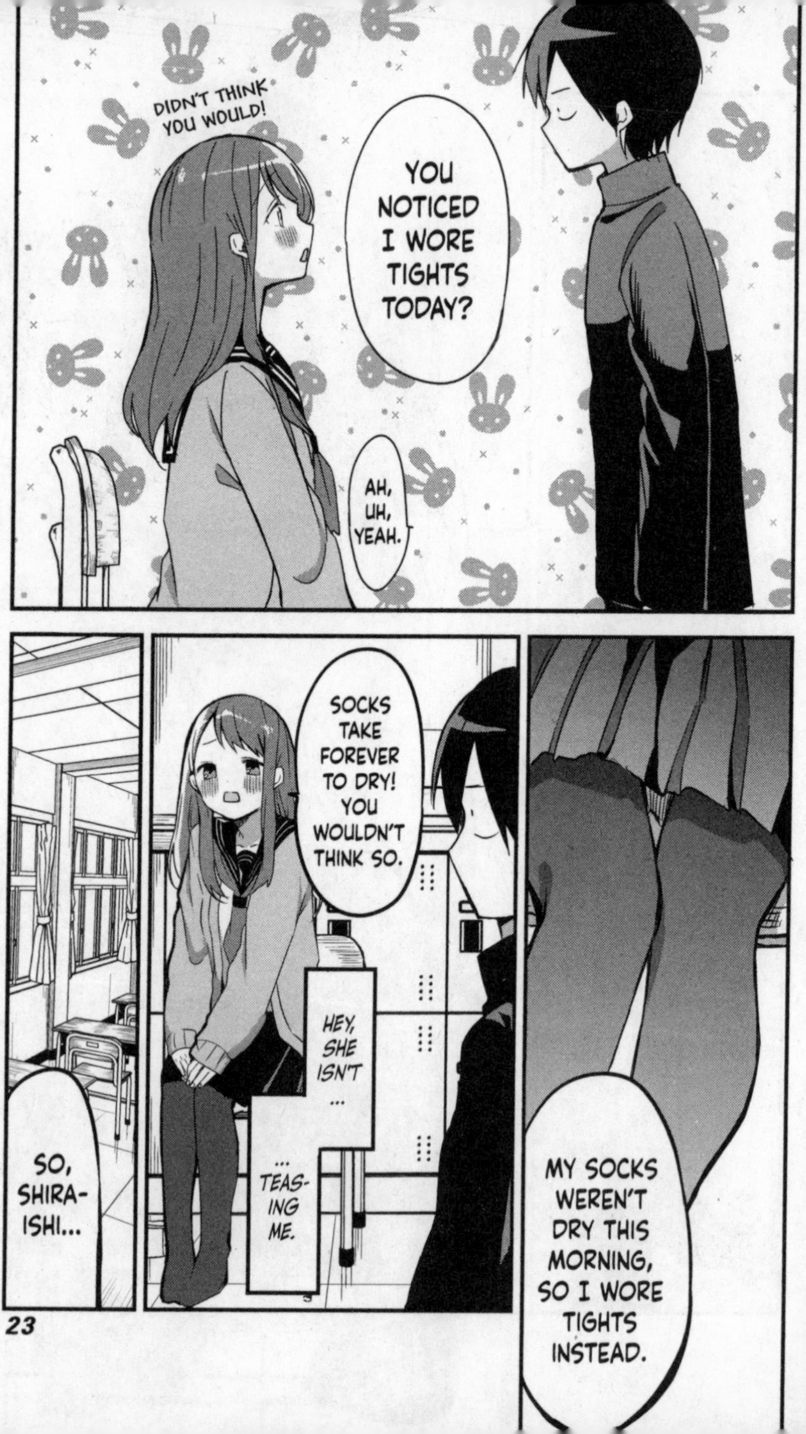

YOU NOTICED I WORE TIGHTS TODAY?
DIDN'T THINK YOU WOULD!
AH, UH, YEAH.
MY SOCKS WEREN'T DRY THIS MORNING, SO I WORE TIGHTS INSTEAD.
SOCKS TAKE FOREVER TO DRY! YOU WOULDN'T THINK SO.
HEY, SHE ISN'T ...
... TEAS-ING ME.
SO, SHIRA-ISHI...

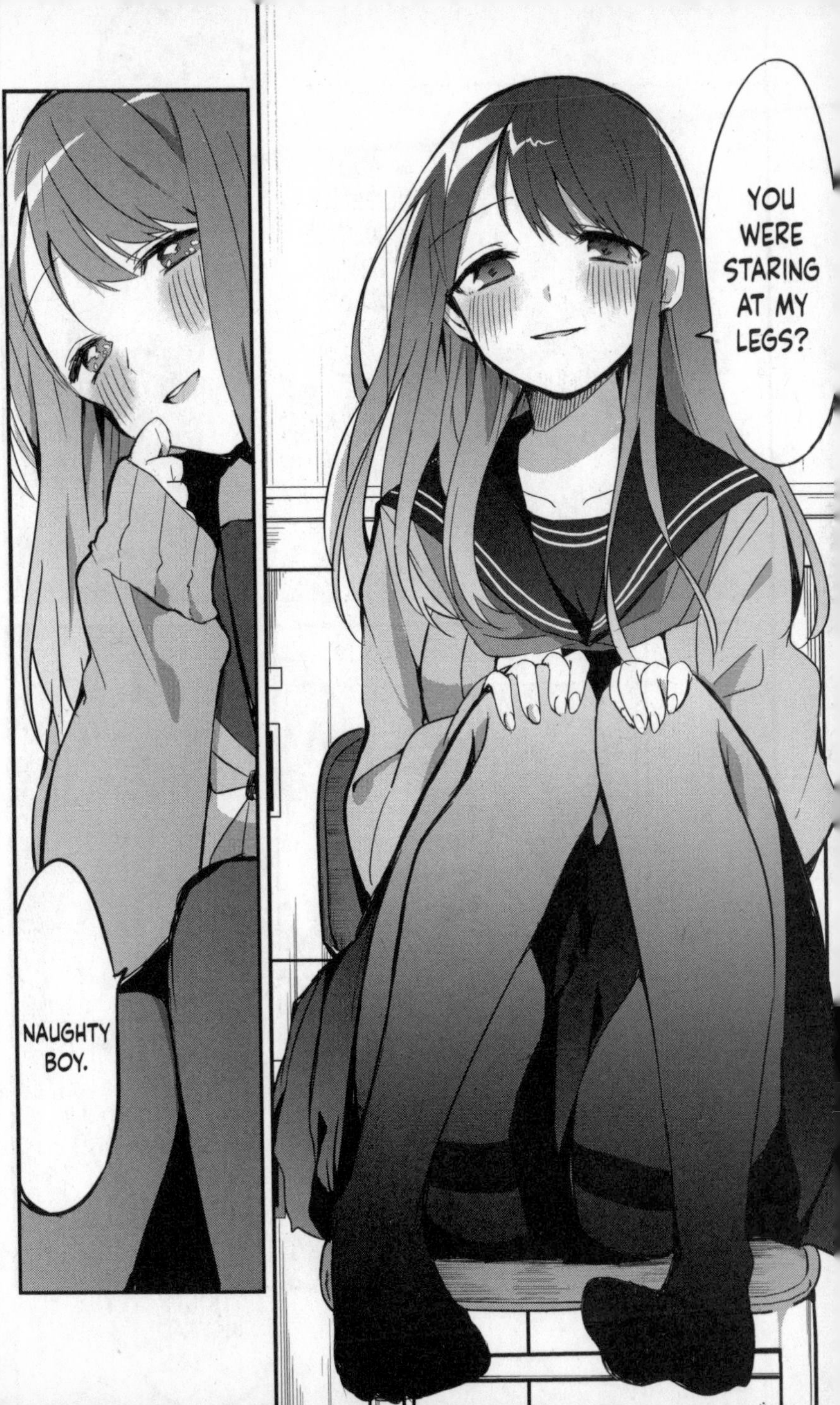
YOU WERE STARING AT MY LEGS?
NAUGHTY BOY.

NO! THAT'S NOT... ER...

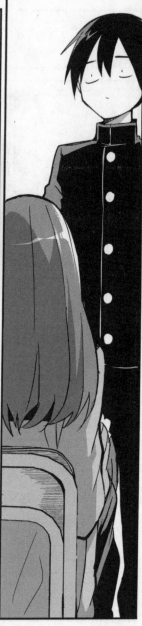

HMM. OKAY.

IT'S NOT THAT I WAS STARING AT THEM JUST NOW—I HAD THIS FEELING SOMETHING WAS DIFFERENT ALL DAY.

25

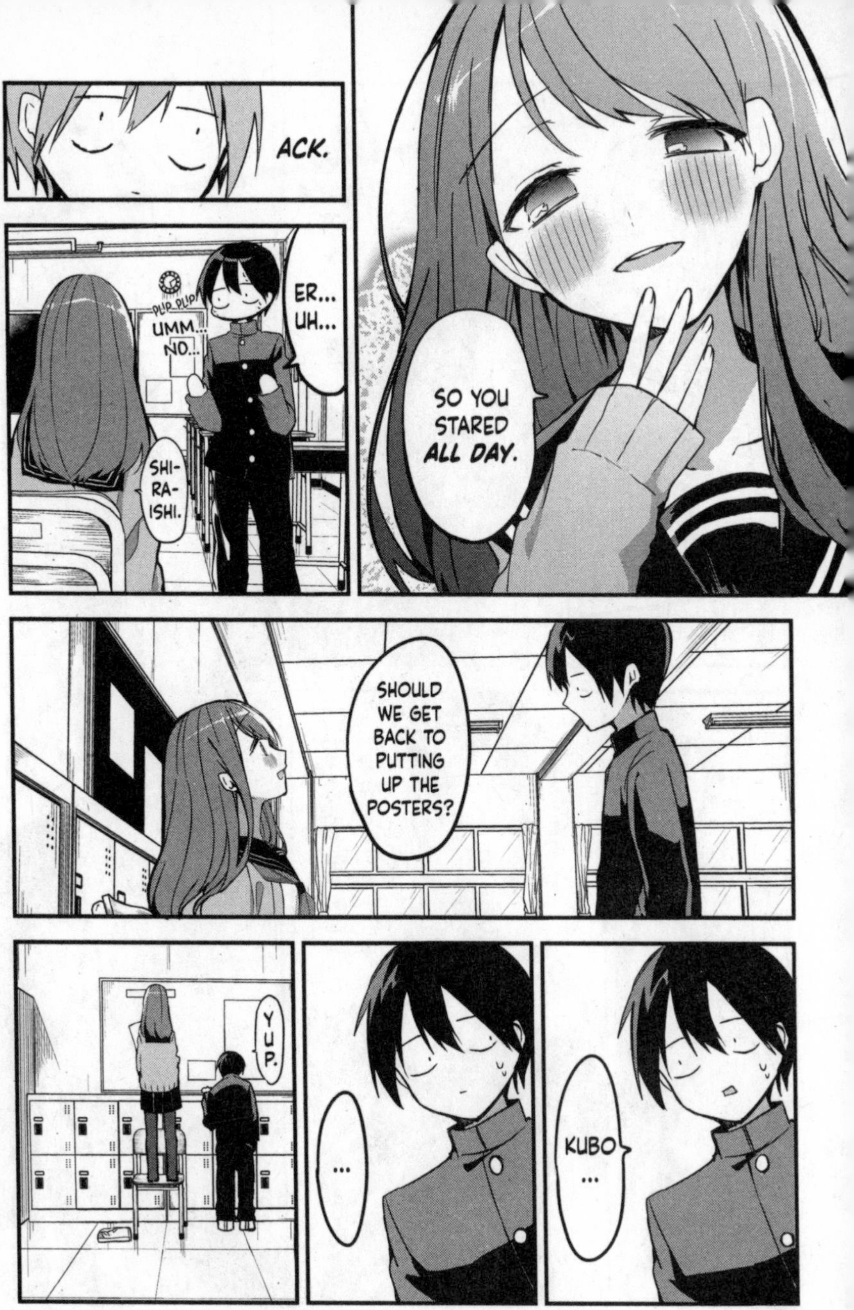
SO YOU STARED ALL DAY.
ACK.
ER... UH...
PLIP PLIP
UMM... NO...
SHI-RA-ISHI.
SHOULD WE GET BACK TO PUTTING UP THE POSTERS?
KUBO...
...
YUP.

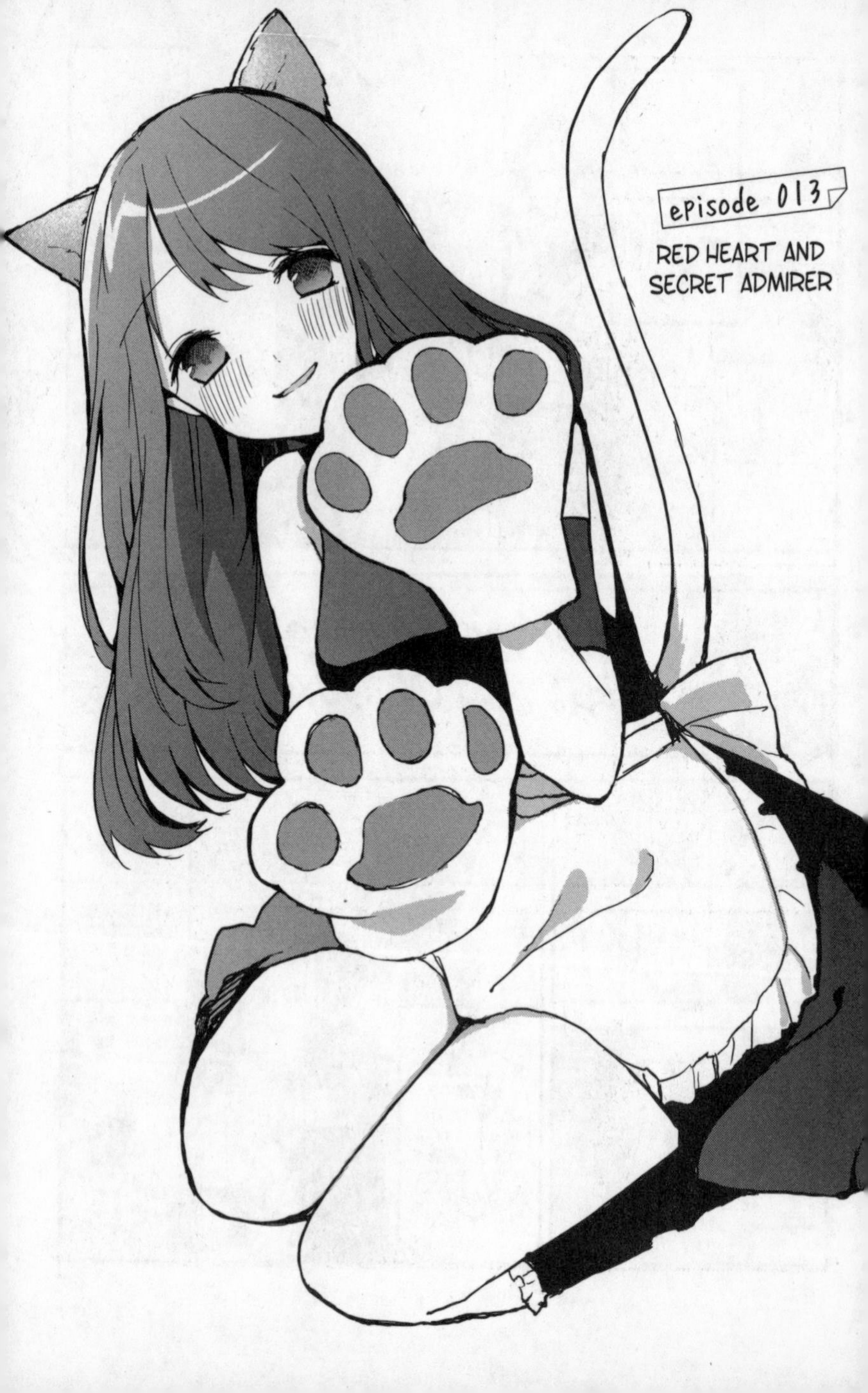
episode 013
RED HEART AND SECRET ADMIRER

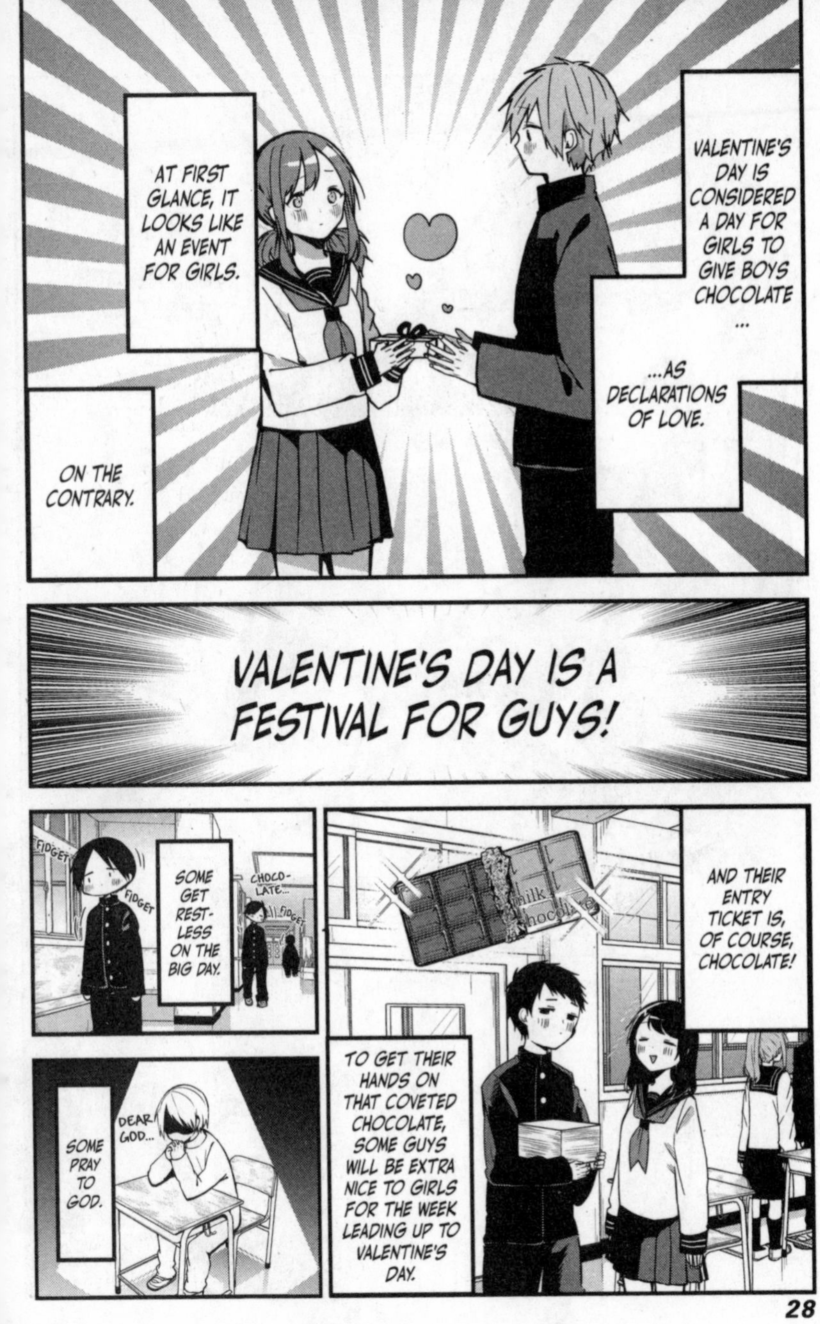
VALENTINE'S DAY IS CONSIDERED A DAY FOR GIRLS TO GIVE BOYS CHOCOLATE ...
...AS DECLARATIONS OF LOVE.
AT FIRST GLANCE, IT LOOKS LIKE AN EVENT FOR GIRLS.
ON THE CONTRARY.
VALENTINE'S DAY IS A FESTIVAL FOR GUYS!
AND THEIR ENTRY TICKET IS, OF COURSE, CHOCOLATE!
milk chocolate
TO GET THEIR HANDS ON THAT COVETED CHOCOLATE, SOME GUYS WILL BE EXTRA NICE TO GIRLS FOR THE WEEK LEADING UP TO VALENTINE'S DAY.
CHOCO-LATE...
FIDGET
SOME GET REST-LESS ON THE BIG DAY.
FIDGET
FIDGET
DEAR GOD...
SOME PRAY TO GOD.

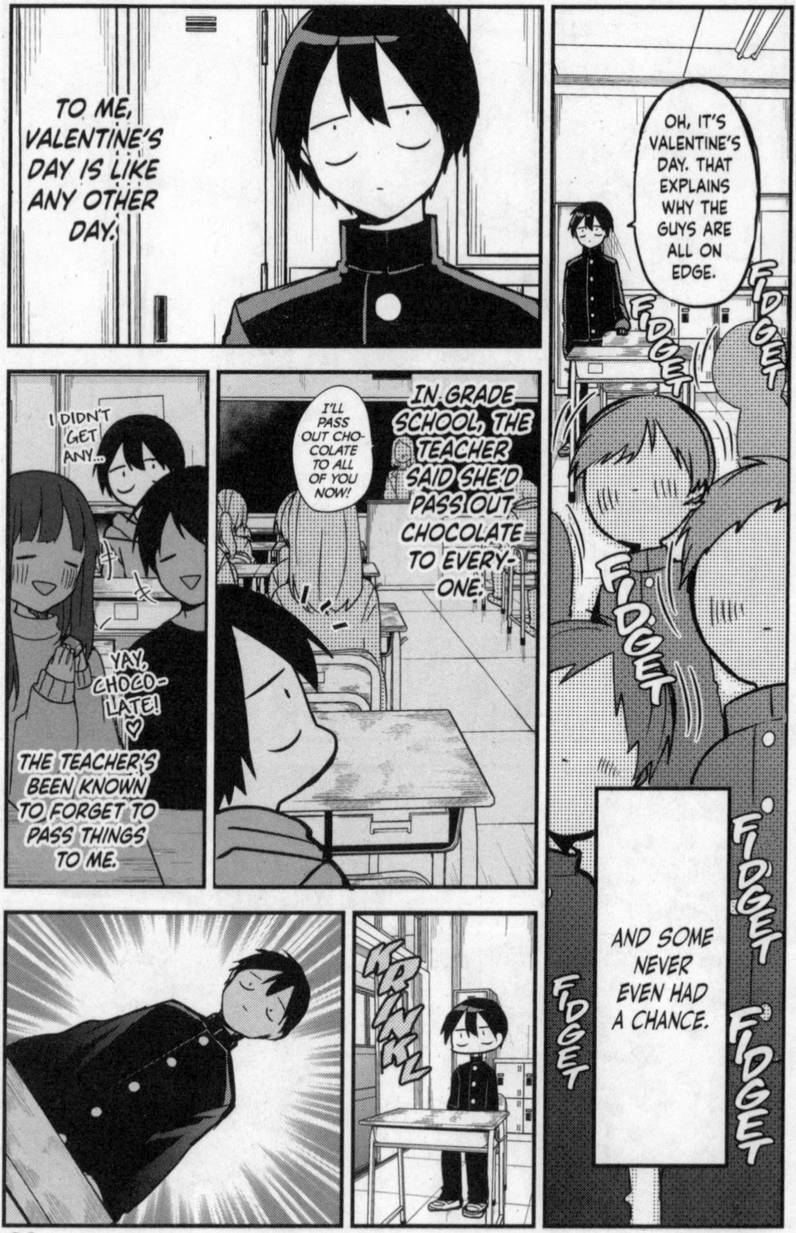
OH, IT'S VALENTINE'S DAY. THAT EXPLAINS WHY THE GUYS ARE ALL ON EDGE.
FIDGET
FIDGET
FIDGET
FIDGET
AND SOME NEVER EVEN HAD A CHANCE.
FIDGET
FIDGET
FIDGET
TO ME, VALENTINE'S DAY IS LIKE ANY OTHER DAY.
IN GRADE SCHOOL, THE TEACHER SAID SHE'D PASS OUT CHOCOLATE TO EVERYONE.
I'LL PASS OUT CHOCOLATE TO ALL OF YOU NOW!
I DIDN'T GET ANY...
YAY, CHOCOLATE! ♡
THE TEACHER'S BEEN KNOWN TO FORGET TO PASS THINGS TO ME.
KRINKL

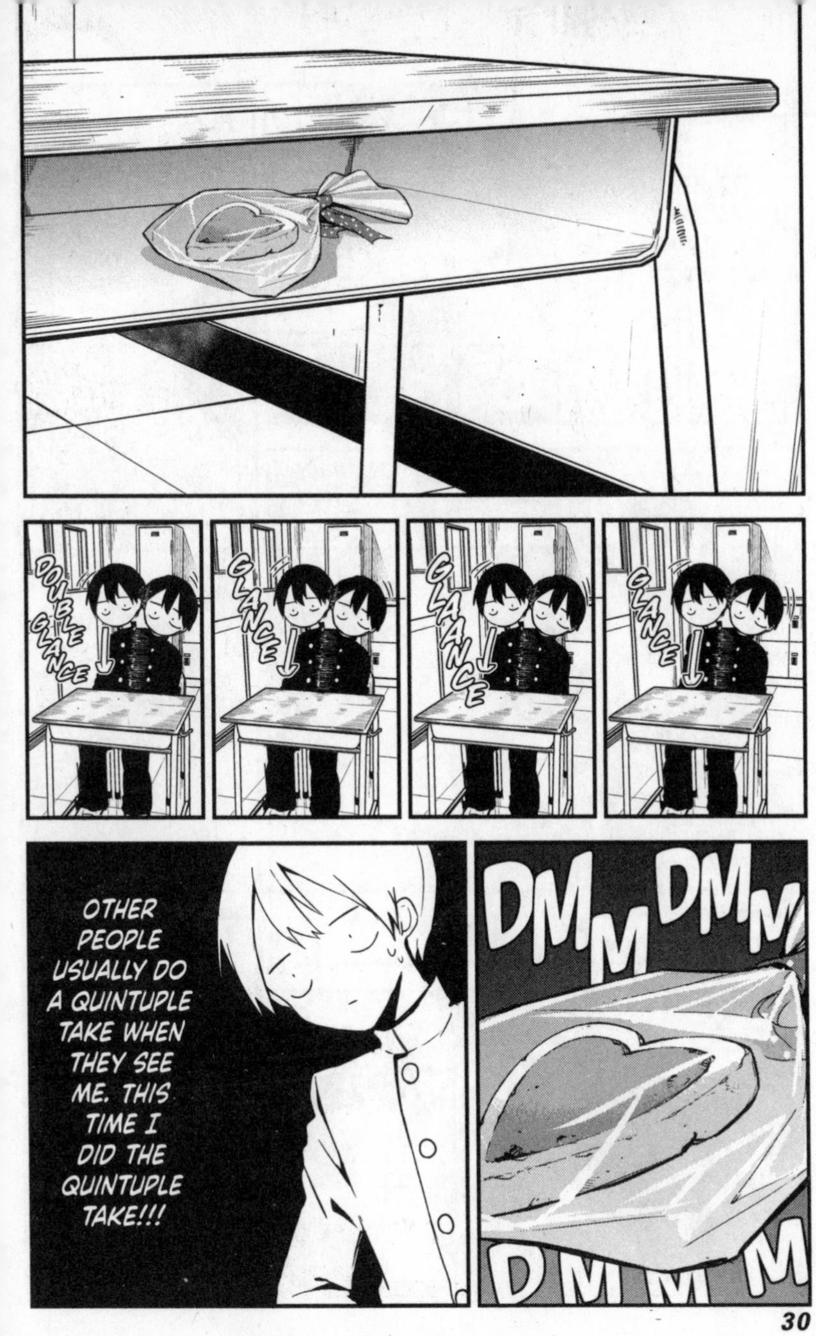
GLANCE
GLANCE
GLANCE
DOUBLE GLANCE
DMM DMM
DMMMM
OTHER PEOPLE USUALLY DO A QUINTUPLE TAKE WHEN THEY SEE ME. THIS TIME I DID THE QUINTUPLE TAKE!!!

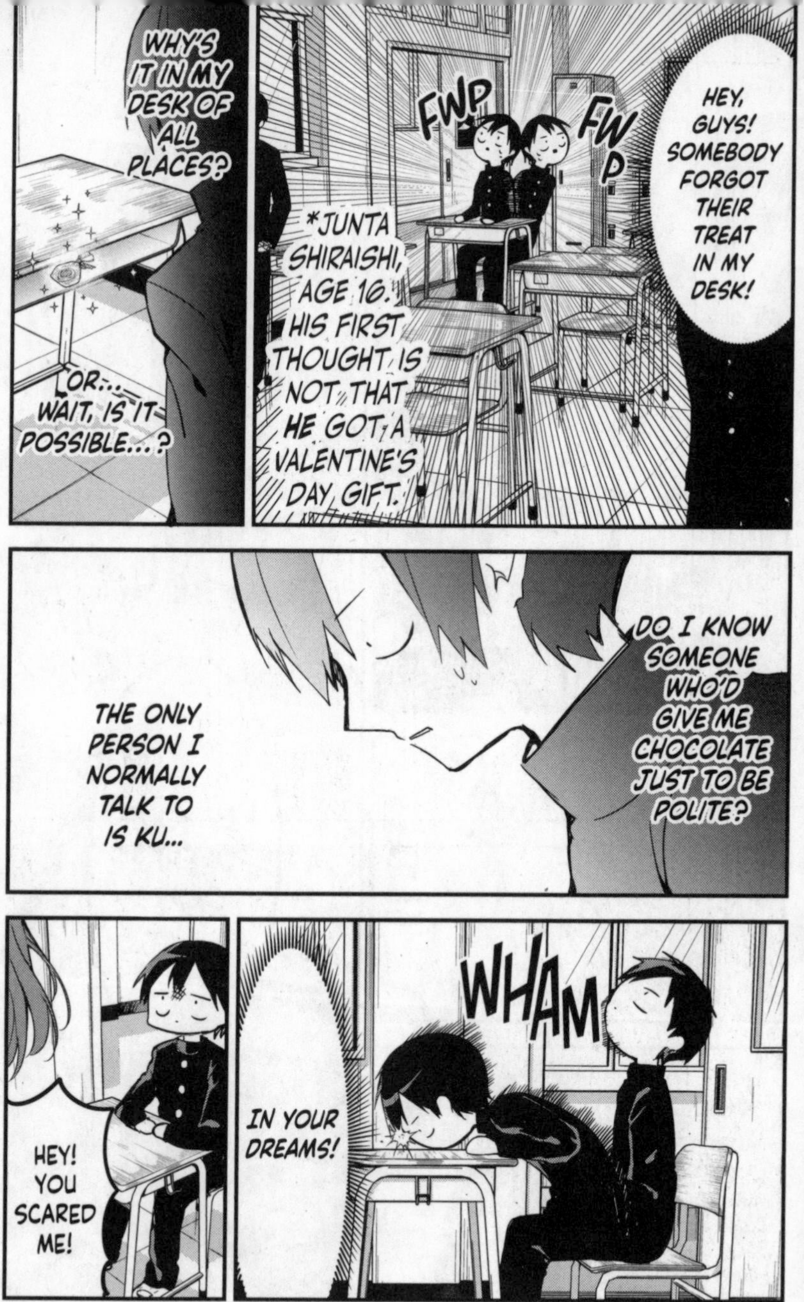
HEY, GUYS! SOMEBODY FORGOT THEIR TREAT IN MY DESK!
FWP
FWP
*JUNTA SHIRAISHI, AGE 16. HIS FIRST THOUGHT IS NOT THAT HE GOT A VALENTINE'S DAY GIFT.
WHY'S IT IN MY DESK OF ALL PLACES?
OR... WAIT, IS IT POSSIBLE...?
DO I KNOW SOMEONE WHO'D GIVE ME CHOCOLATE JUST TO BE POLITE?
THE ONLY PERSON I NORMALLY TALK TO IS KU...
WHAM
IN YOUR DREAMS!
HEY! YOU SCARED ME!

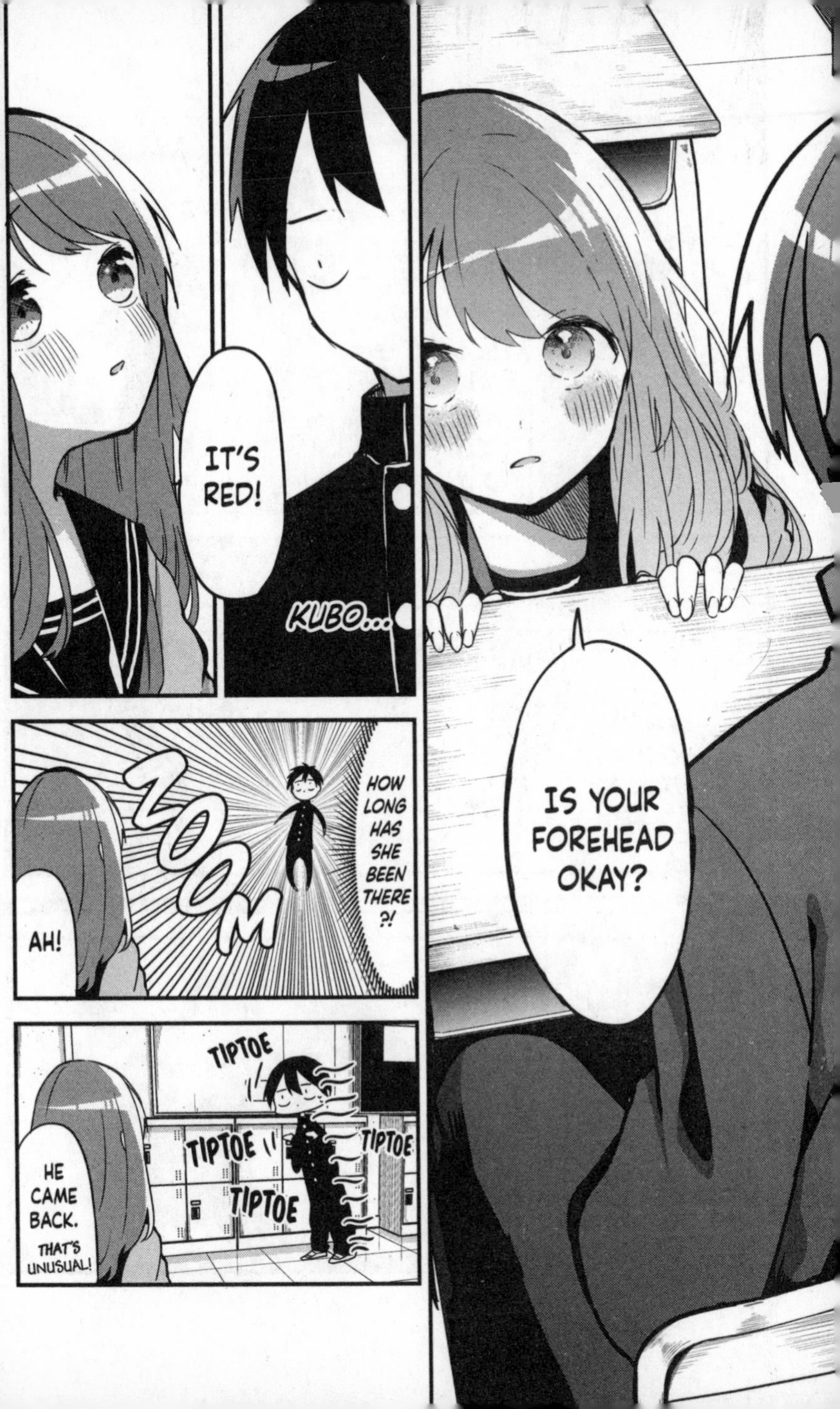
IS YOUR FOREHEAD OKAY?
IT'S RED!
KUBO...
HOW LONG HAS SHE BEEN THERE ?!
ZOOM
AH!
TIPTOE
TIPTOE
TIPTOE
TIPTOE
HE CAME BACK.
THAT'S UNUSUAL!

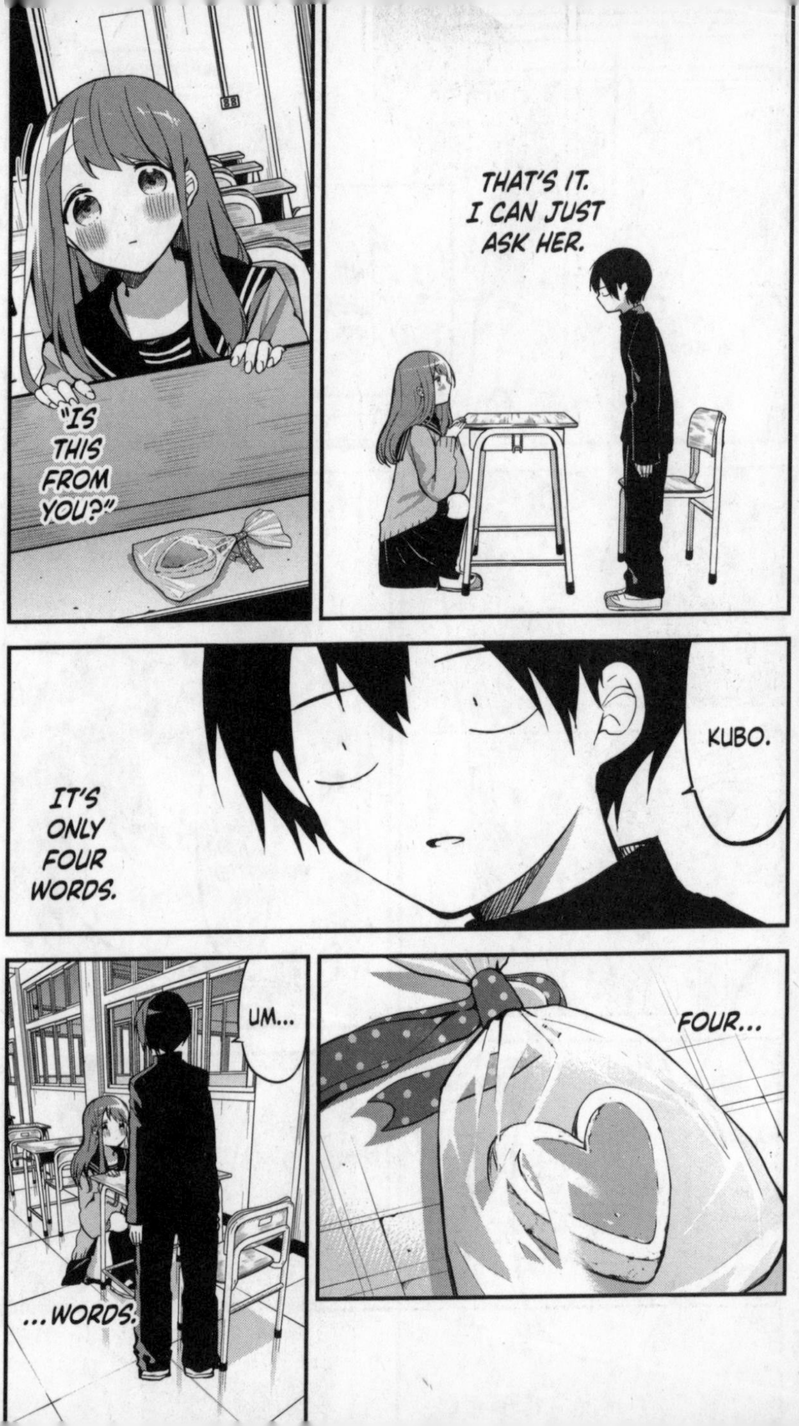
THAT'S IT. I CAN JUST ASK HER.
"IS THIS FROM YOU?"
KUBO.
IT'S ONLY FOUR WORDS.
FOUR...
UM...
...WORDS.

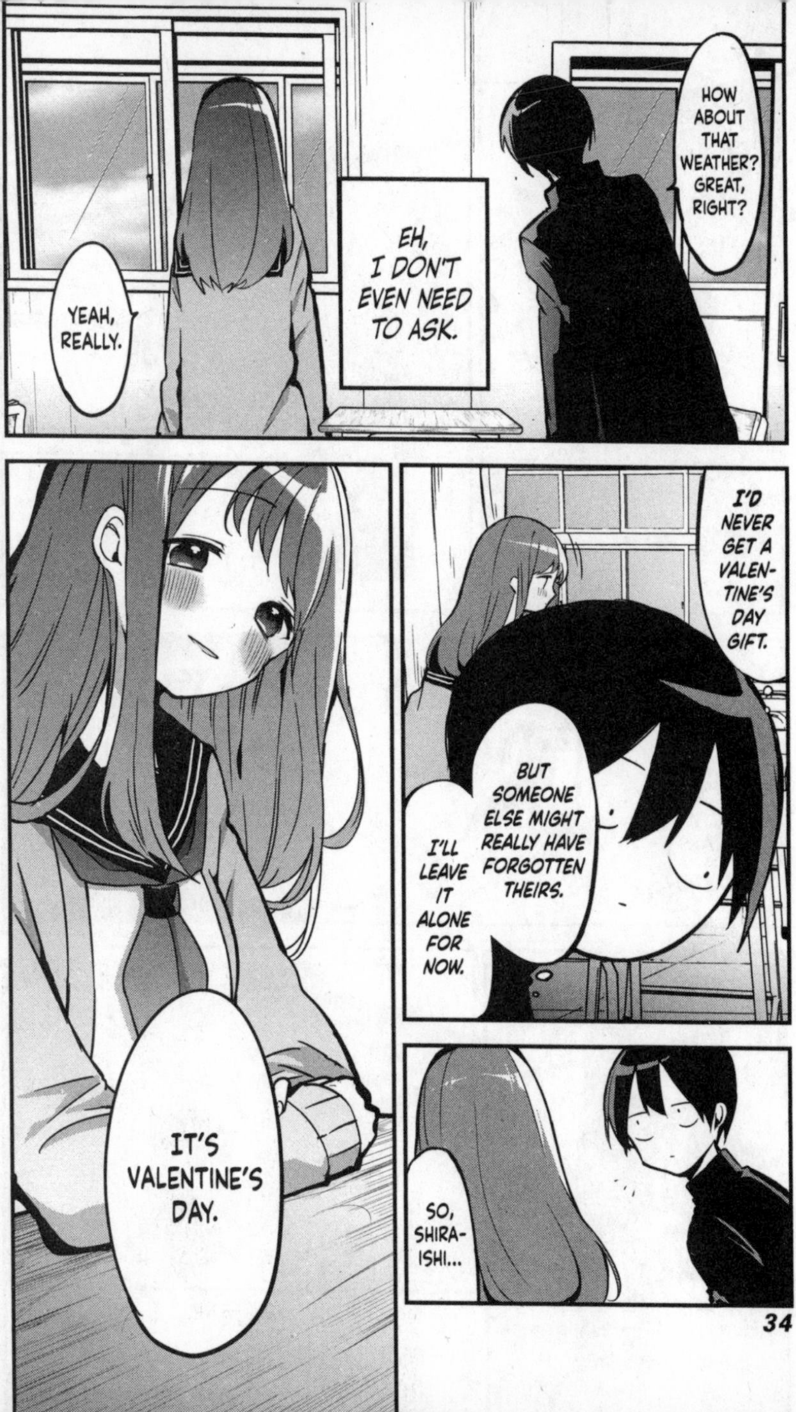
HOW ABOUT THAT WEATHER? GREAT, RIGHT?
EH, I DON'T EVEN NEED TO ASK.
YEAH, REALLY.
I'D NEVER GET A VALEN-TINE'S DAY GIFT.
BUT SOMEONE ELSE MIGHT REALLY HAVE FORGOTTEN THEIRS.
I'LL LEAVE IT ALONE FOR NOW.
SO, SHIRA-ISHI...
IT'S VALENTINE'S DAY.

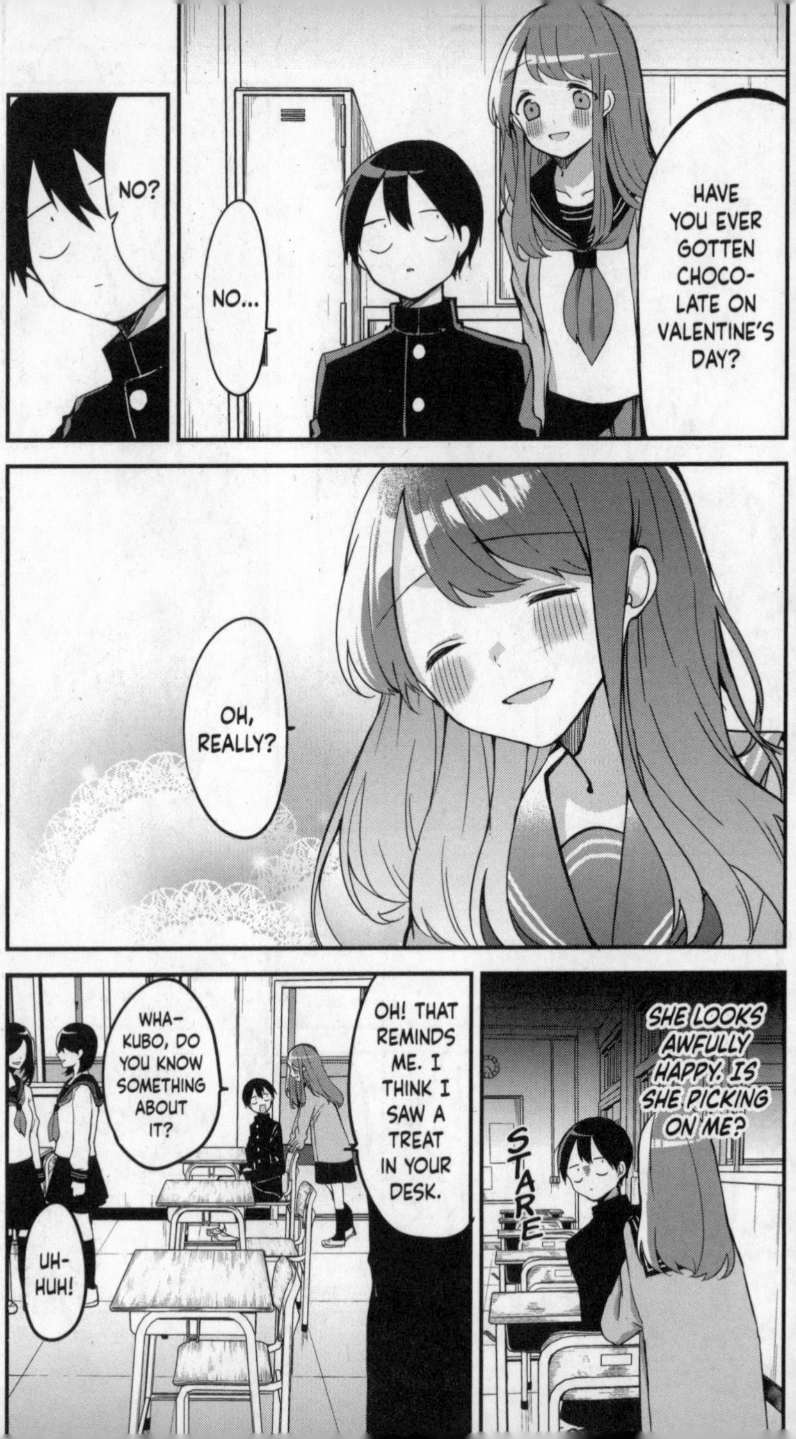
HAVE YOU EVER GOTTEN CHOCOLATE ON VALENTINE'S DAY?
NO...
NO?
OH, REALLY?
SHE LOOKS AWFULLY HAPPY. IS SHE PICKING ON ME?
STARE
OH! THAT REMINDS ME. I THINK I SAW A TREAT IN YOUR DESK.
WHA- KUBO, DO YOU KNOW SOMETHING ABOUT IT?
UH-HUH!

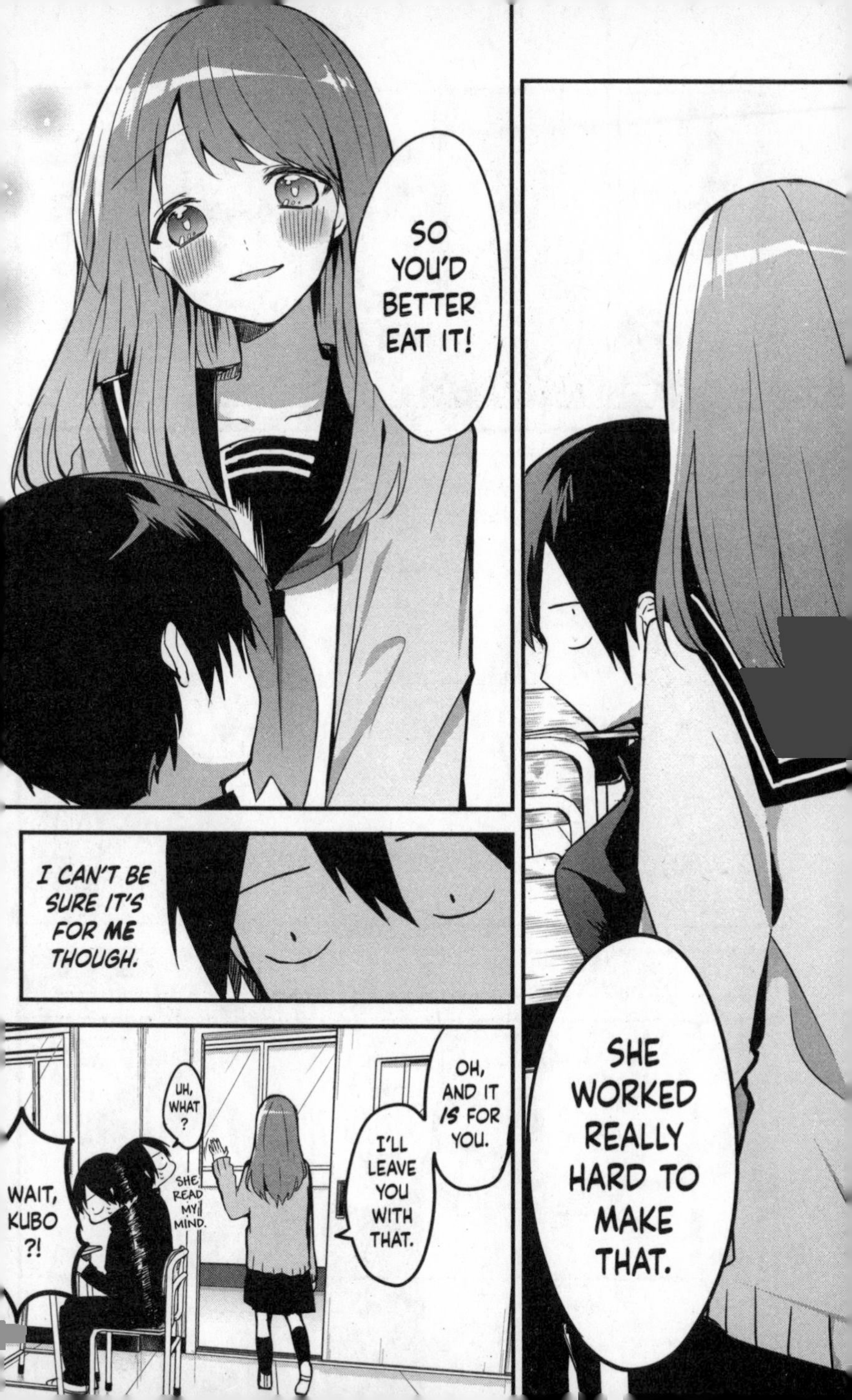
SO YOU'D BETTER EAT IT!
SHE WORKED REALLY HARD TO MAKE THAT.
I CAN'T BE SURE IT'S FOR ME THOUGH.
OH, AND IT IS FOR YOU.
I'LL LEAVE YOU WITH THAT.
UH, WHAT?
SHE READ MY MIND.
WAIT, KUBO?!

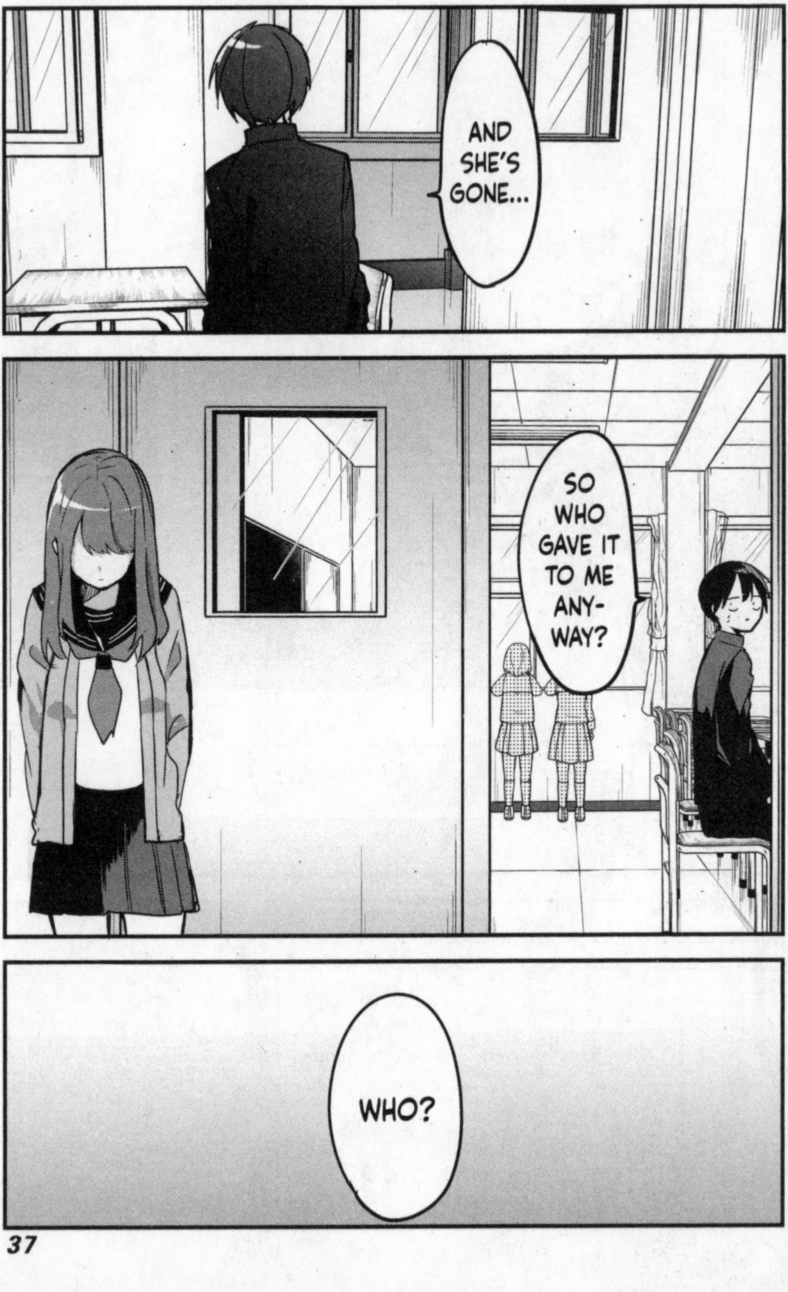
AND SHE'S GONE...
SO WHO GAVE IT TO ME ANY-WAY?
WHO?

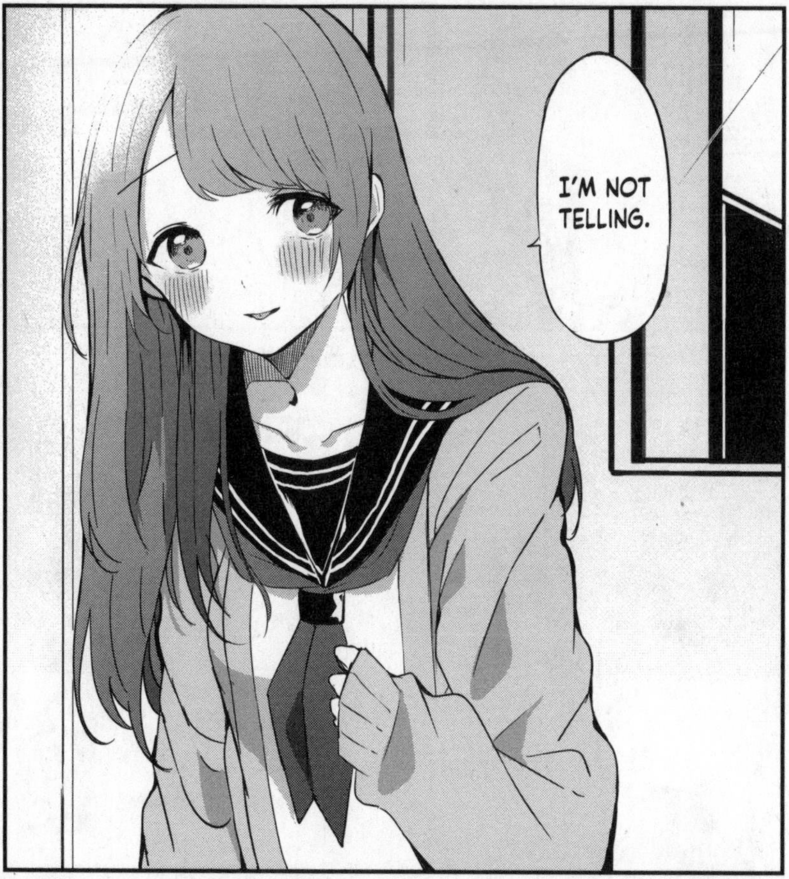
I'M NOT TELLING.
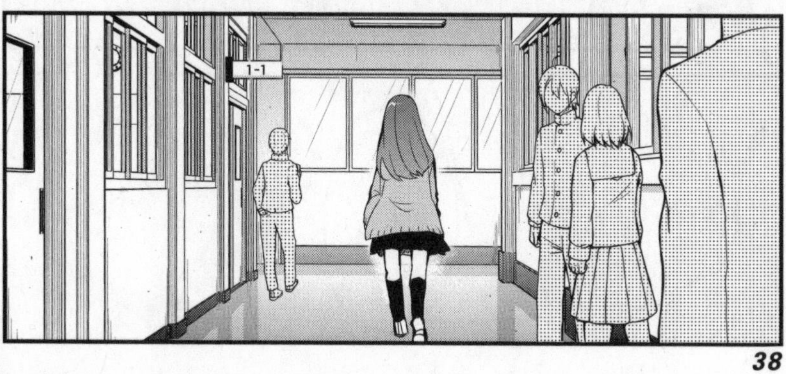
1-1

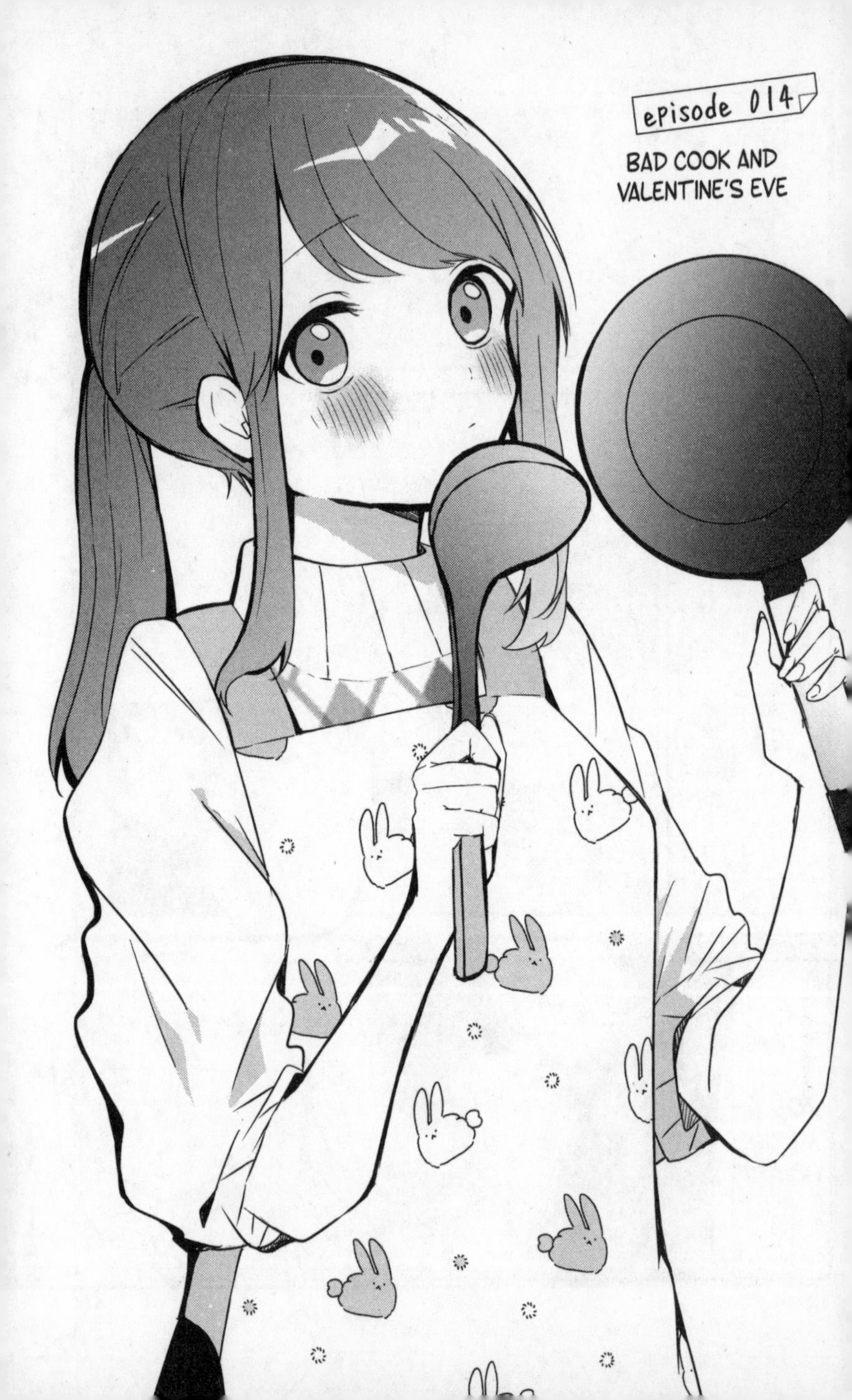
episode 014
BAD COOK AND VALENTINE'S EVE

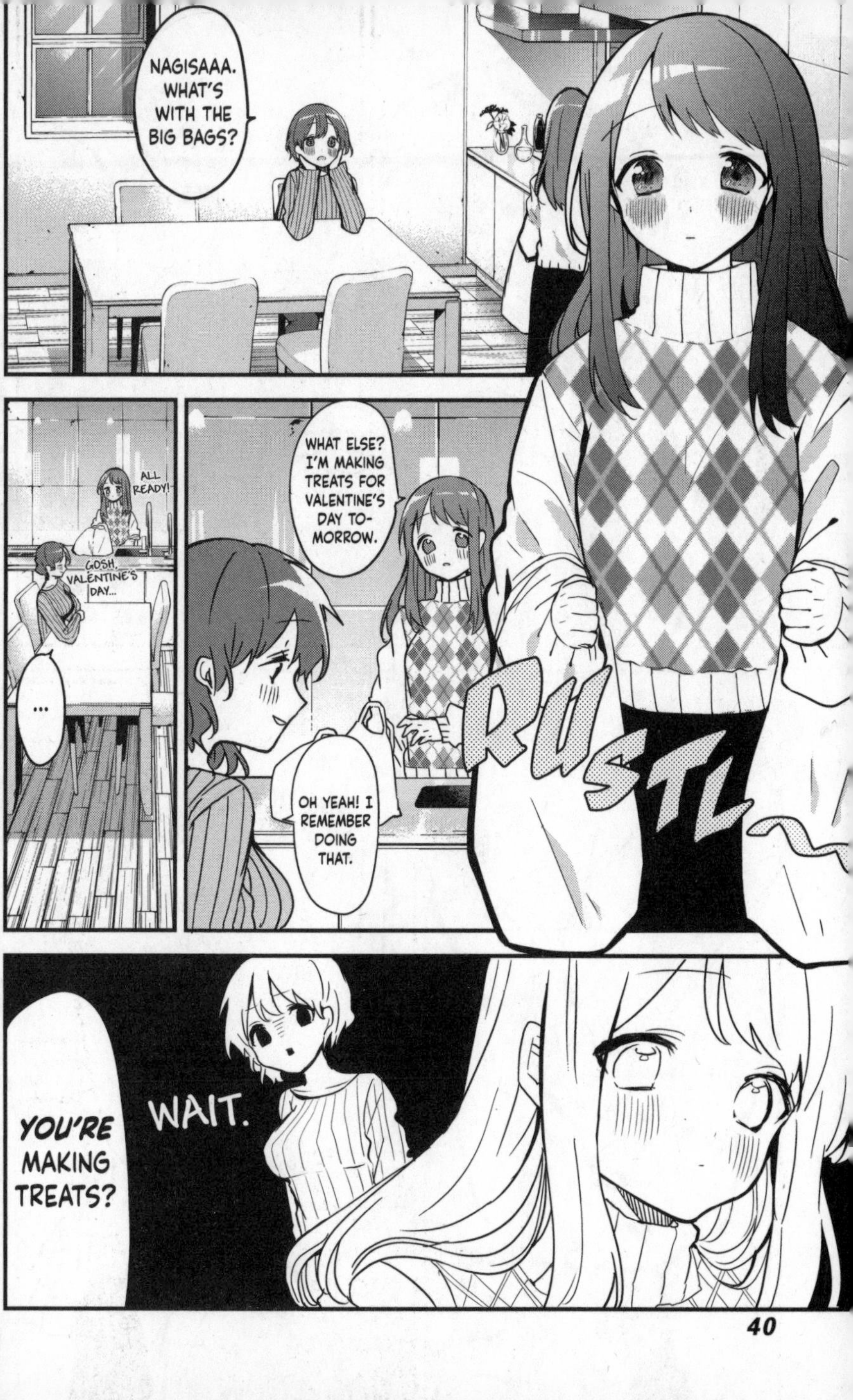
RUSTL~
NAGISAAA. WHAT'S WITH THE BIG BAGS?
WHAT ELSE? I'M MAKING TREATS FOR VALENTINE'S DAY TO-MORROW.
OH YEAH! I REMEMBER DOING THAT.
ALL READY!
GOSH, VALENTINE'S DAY...
...
WAIT.
YOU'RE MAKING TREATS?

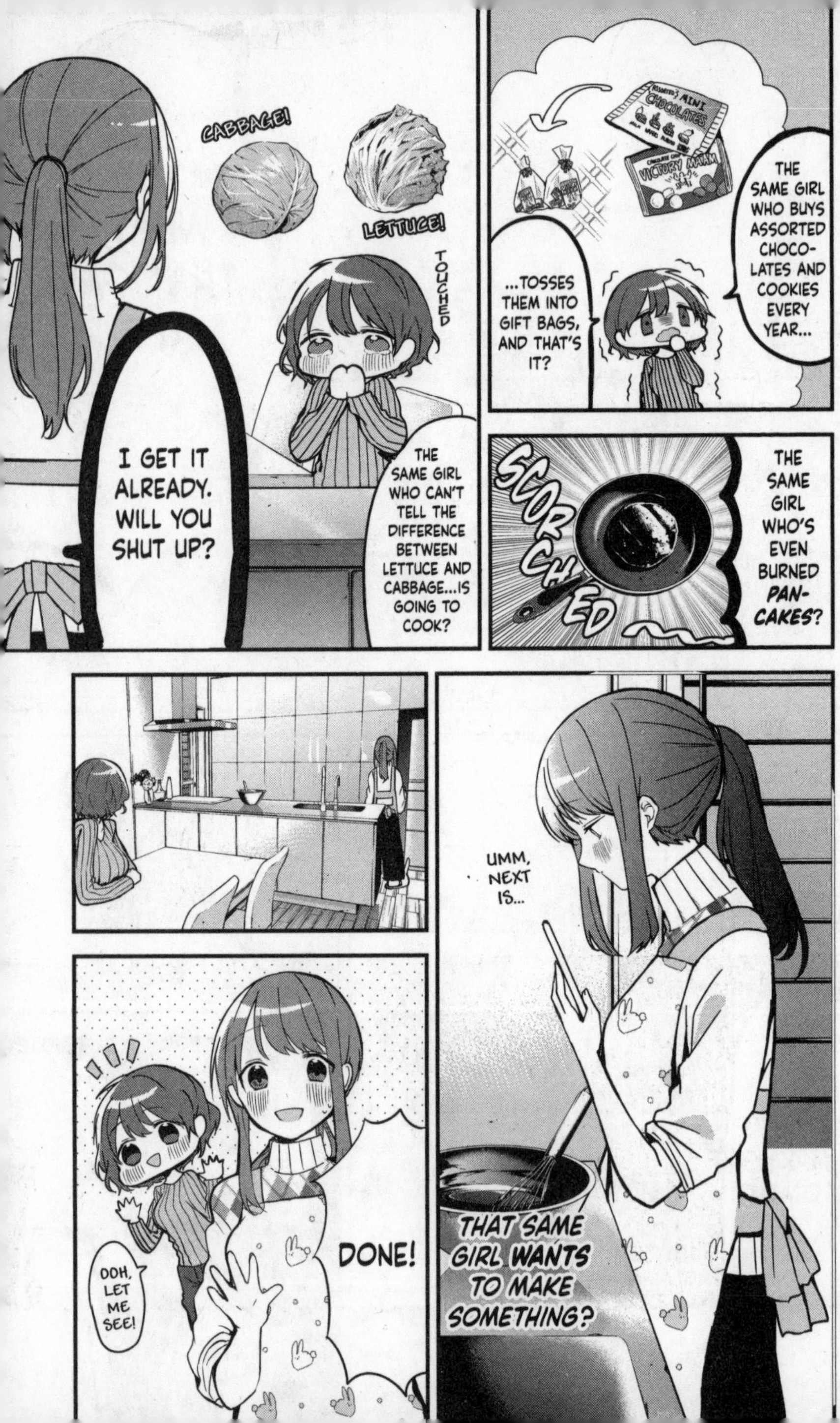
THE SAME GIRL WHO BUYS ASSORTED CHOCOLATES AND COOKIES EVERY YEAR...
...TOSSES THEM INTO GIFT BAGS, AND THAT'S IT?
THE SAME GIRL WHO'S EVEN BURNED PANCAKES?
SCORCHED
CABBAGE!
LETTUCE!
TOUCHED
THE SAME GIRL WHO CAN'T TELL THE DIFFERENCE BETWEEN LETTUCE AND CABBAGE...IS GOING TO COOK?
I GET IT ALREADY. WILL YOU SHUT UP?
UMM, NEXT IS...
THAT SAME GIRL WANTS TO MAKE SOMETHING?
DONE!
OOH, LET ME SEE!

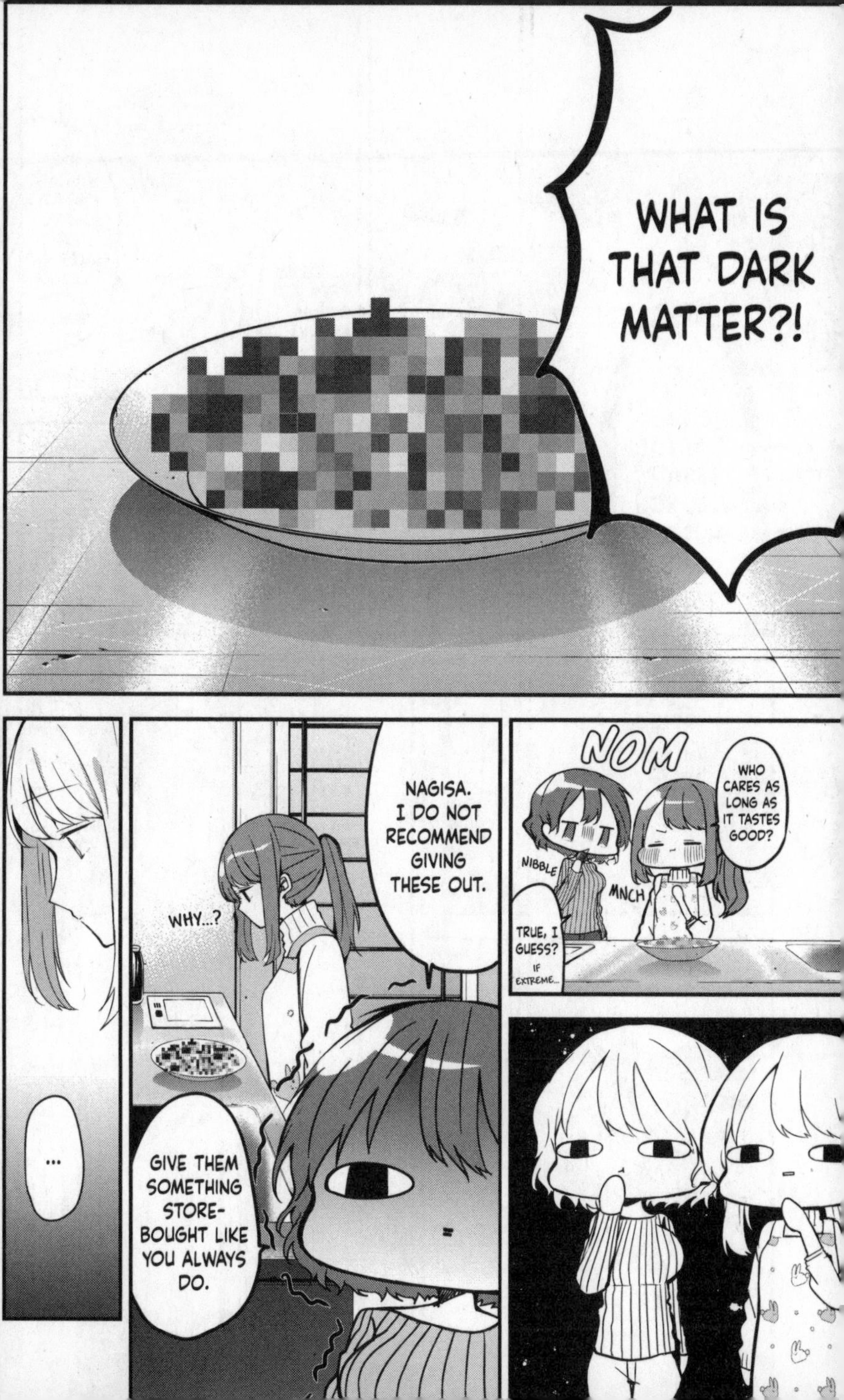
WHAT IS THAT DARK MATTER?!
NOM
WHO CARES AS LONG AS IT TASTES GOOD?
NIBBLE
MNCH
TRUE, I GUESS?
IF EXTREME...
NAGISA. I DO NOT RECOMMEND GIVING THESE OUT.
WHY...?
GIVE THEM SOMETHING STORE-BOUGHT LIKE YOU ALWAYS DO.
...

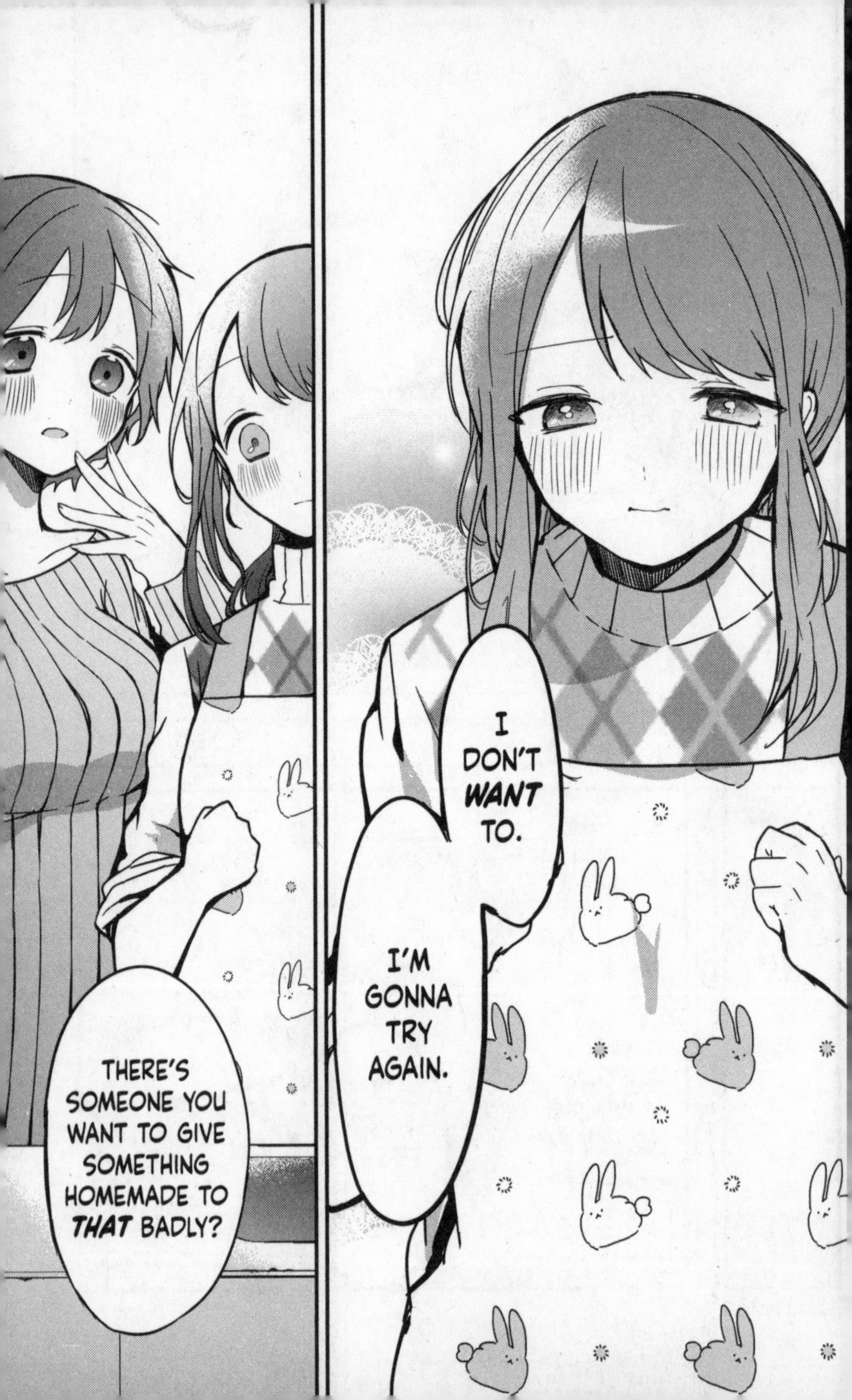
I DON'T *WANT* TO.
I'M GONNA TRY AGAIN.
THERE'S SOMEONE YOU WANT TO GIVE SOMETHING HOMEMADE TO *THAT* BADLY?

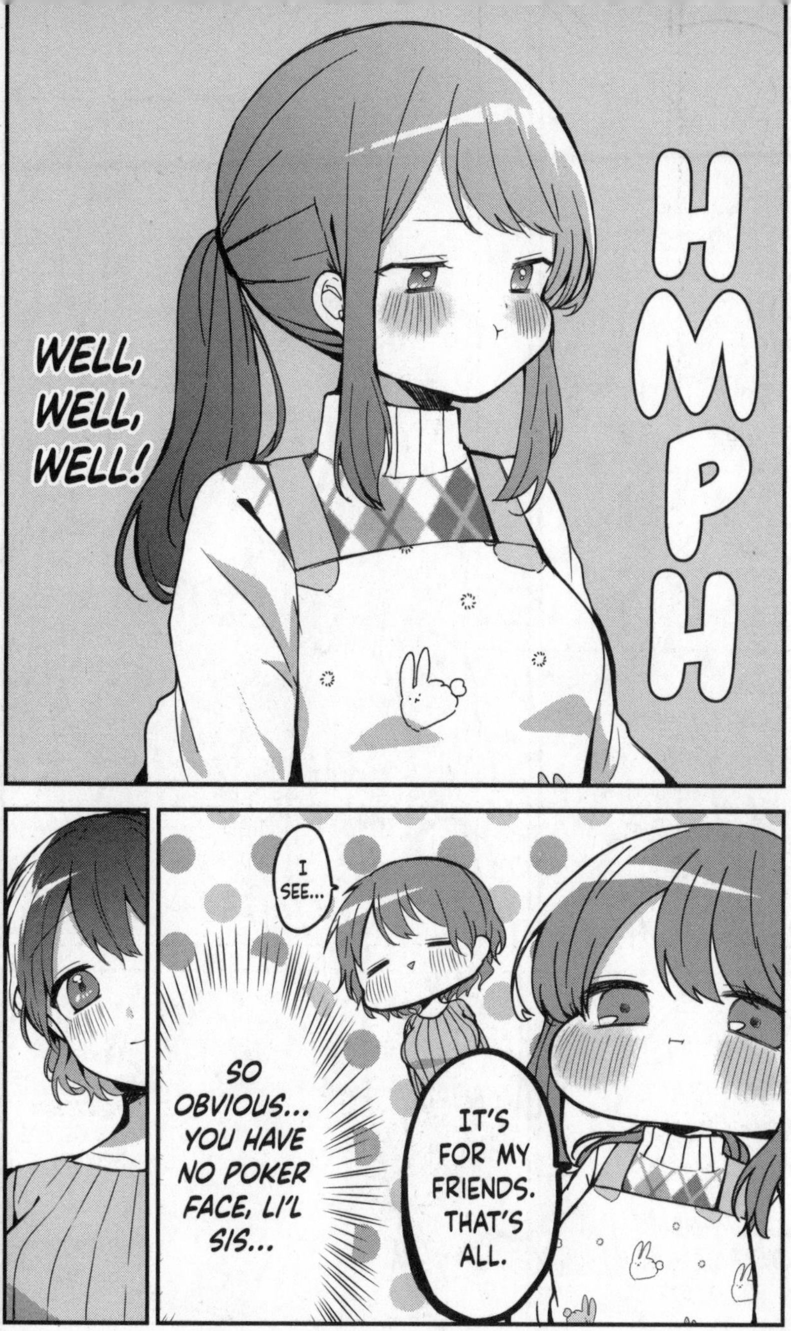
HMPH
WELL, WELL, WELL!
IT'S FOR MY FRIENDS. THAT'S ALL.
I SEE...
SO OBVIOUS... YOU HAVE NO POKER FACE, LI'L SIS...

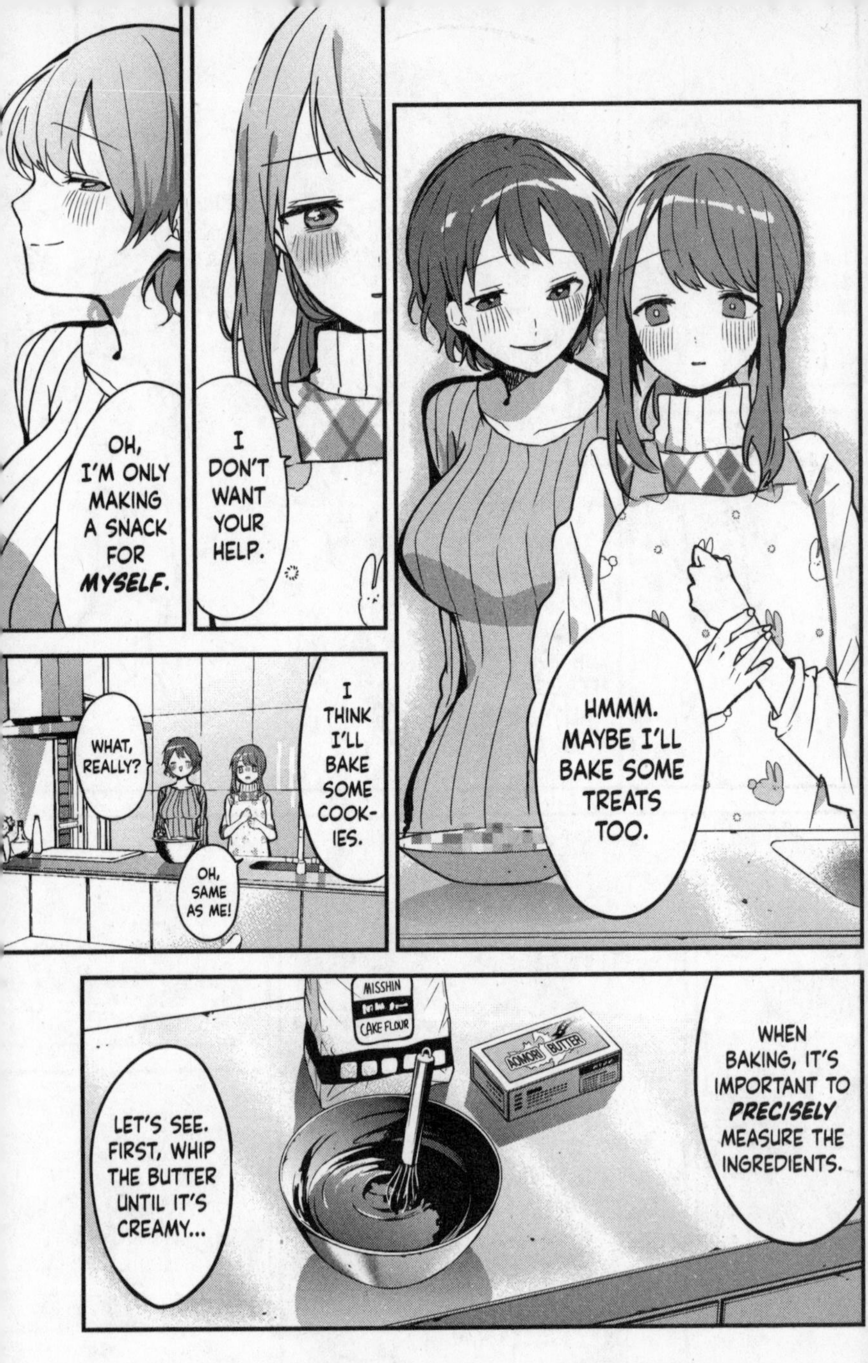
HMMM. MAYBE I'LL BAKE SOME TREATS TOO.
I DON'T WANT YOUR HELP.
OH, I'M ONLY MAKING A SNACK FOR *MYSELF*.
I THINK I'LL BAKE SOME COOK-IES.
WHAT, REALLY?
OH, SAME AS ME!
WHEN BAKING, IT'S IMPORTANT TO *PRECISELY* MEASURE THE INGREDIENTS.
MISSHIN
CAKE FLOUR
AOMORI BUTTER
LET'S SEE. FIRST, WHIP THE BUTTER UNTIL IT'S CREAMY...

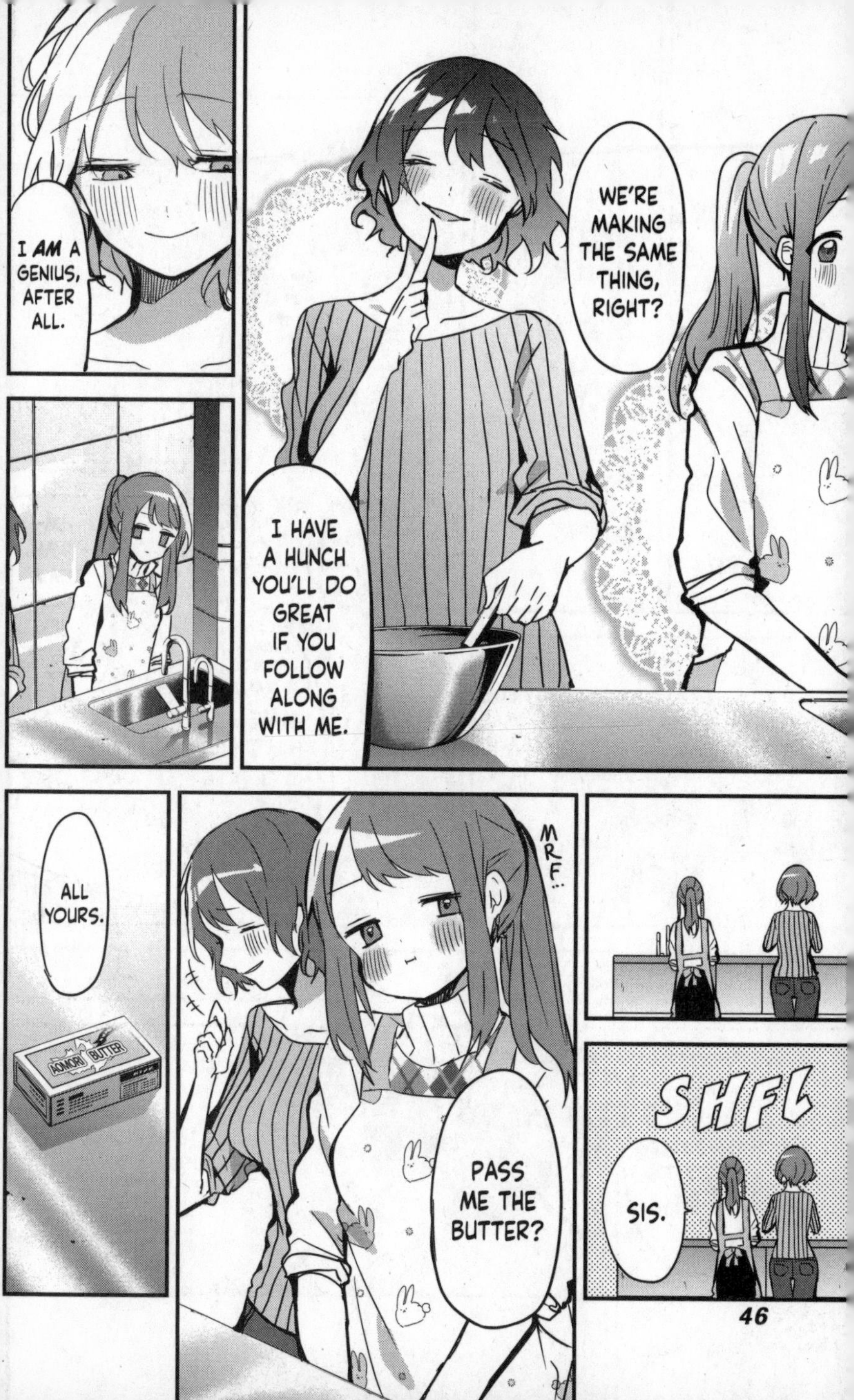
WE'RE MAKING THE SAME THING, RIGHT?
I HAVE A HUNCH YOU'LL DO GREAT IF YOU FOLLOW ALONG WITH ME.
I *AM* A GENIUS, AFTER ALL.
SHFL
SIS.
MRF...
PASS ME THE BUTTER?
ALL YOURS.
AOMORI BUTTER

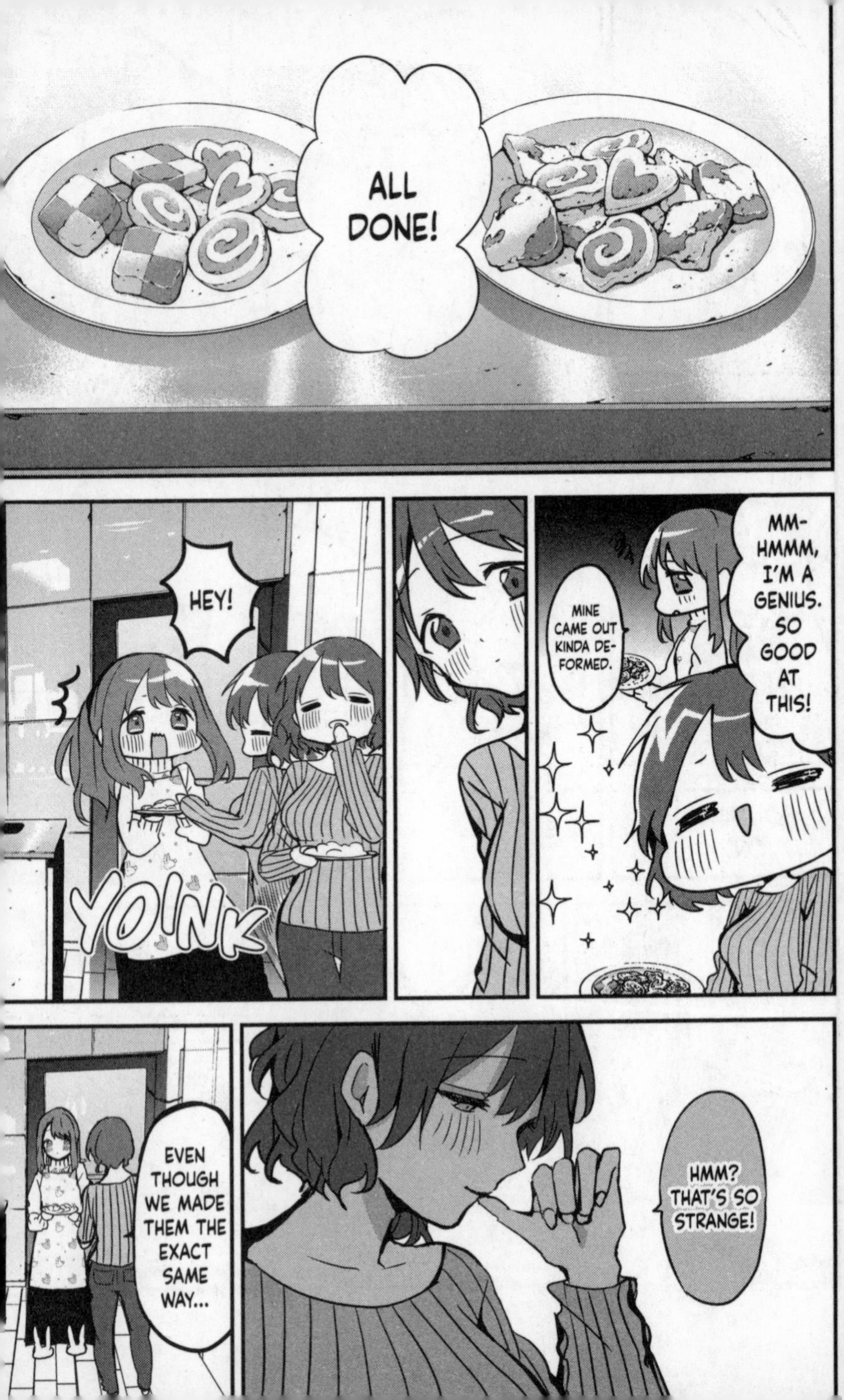
ALL DONE!
MM-HMMM, I'M A GENIUS. SO GOOD AT THIS!
MINE CAME OUT KINDA DE-FORMED.
HEY!
YOINK
HMM? THAT'S SO STRANGE!
EVEN THOUGH WE MADE THEM THE EXACT SAME WAY...

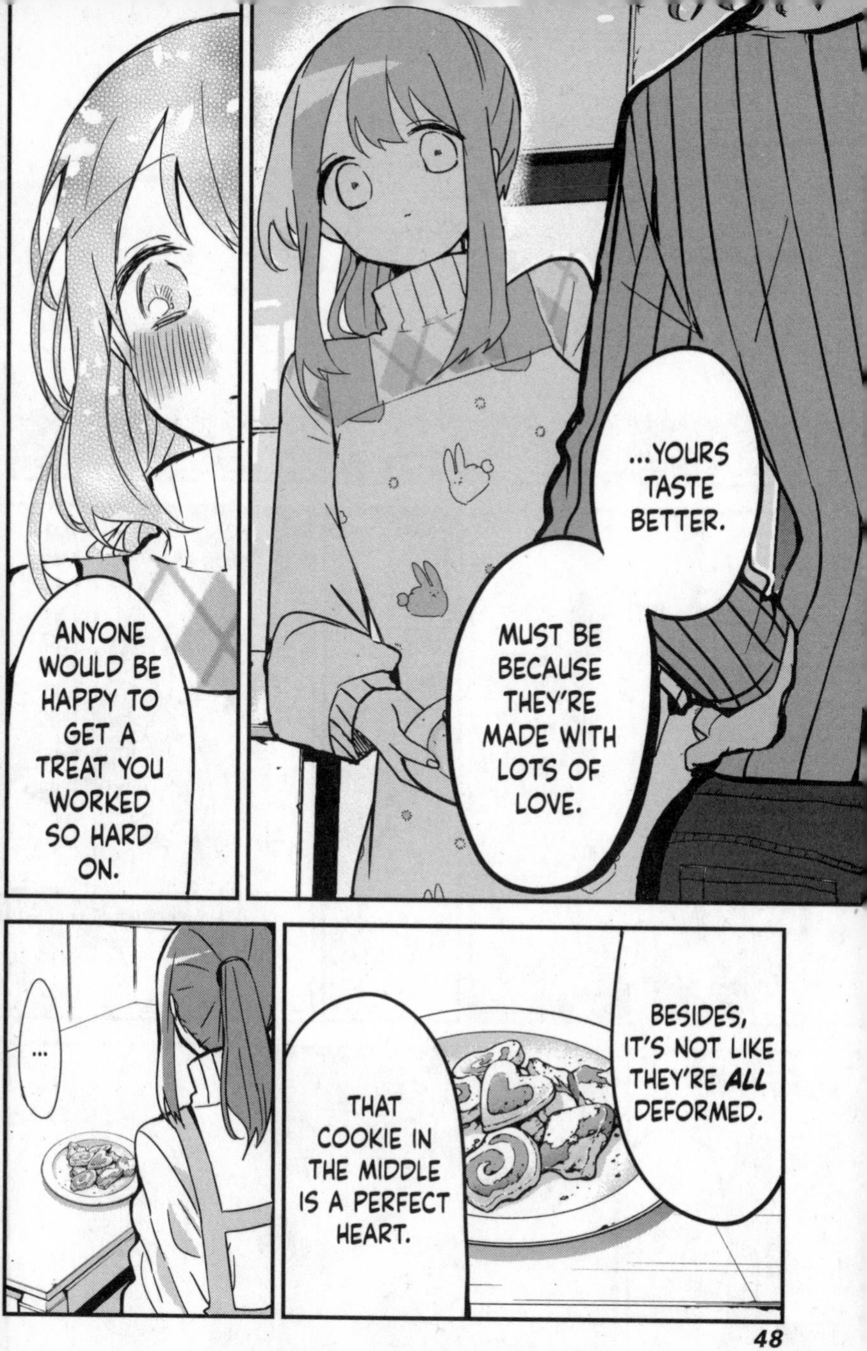
...YOURS TASTE BETTER.
MUST BE BECAUSE THEY'RE MADE WITH LOTS OF LOVE.
ANYONE WOULD BE HAPPY TO GET A TREAT YOU WORKED SO HARD ON.
BESIDES, IT'S NOT LIKE THEY'RE *ALL* DEFORMED.
THAT COOKIE IN THE MIDDLE IS A PERFECT HEART.
...

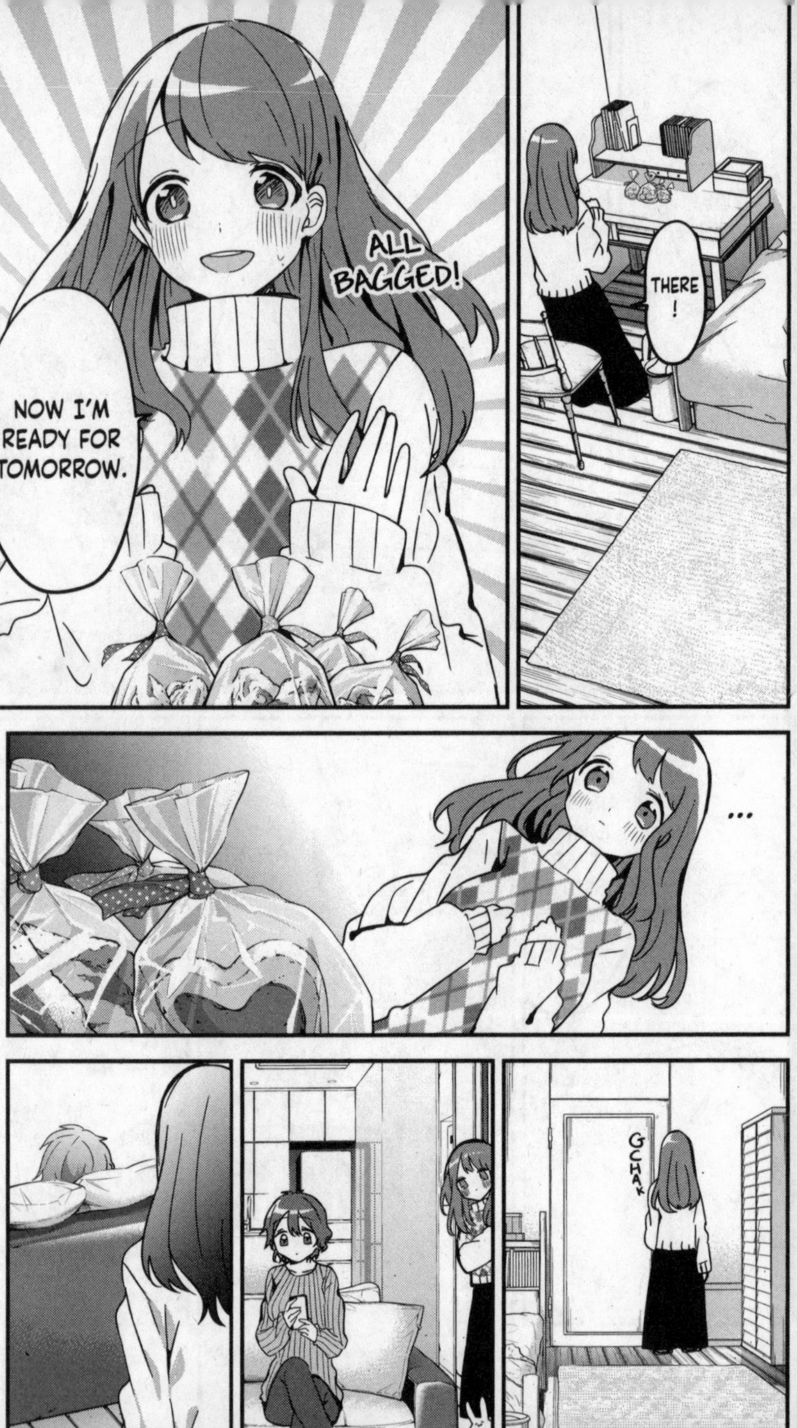
THERE!
ALL BAGGED!
NOW I'M READY FOR TOMORROW.
...
GCHAK

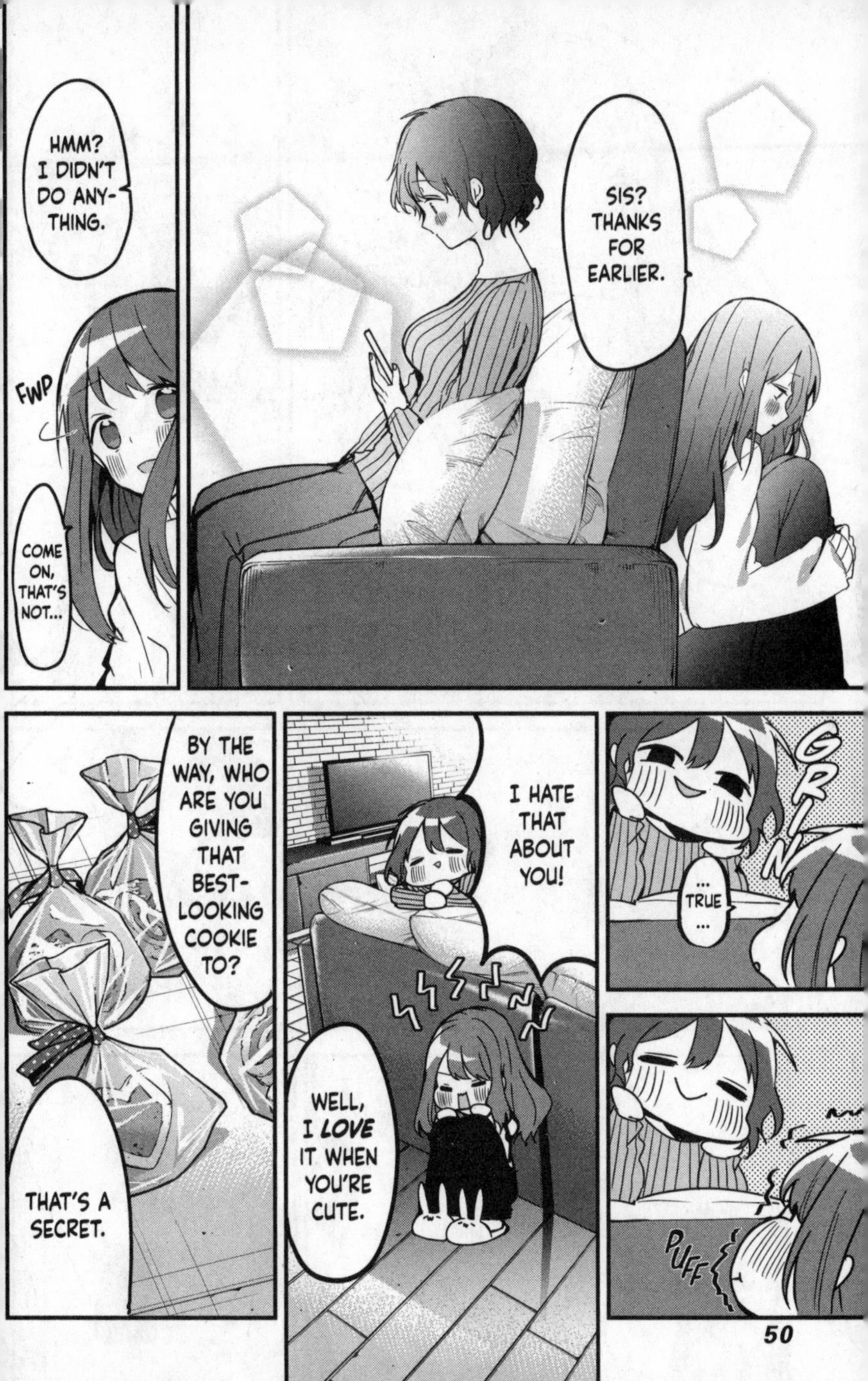
SIS? THANKS FOR EARLIER.
HMM? I DIDN'T DO ANYTHING.
FWP
COME ON, THAT'S NOT...
GRIN
... TRUE ...
PUFF
I HATE THAT ABOUT YOU!
WELL, I *LOVE* IT WHEN YOU'RE CUTE.
BY THE WAY, WHO ARE YOU GIVING THAT BEST-LOOKING COOKIE TO?
THAT'S A SECRET.

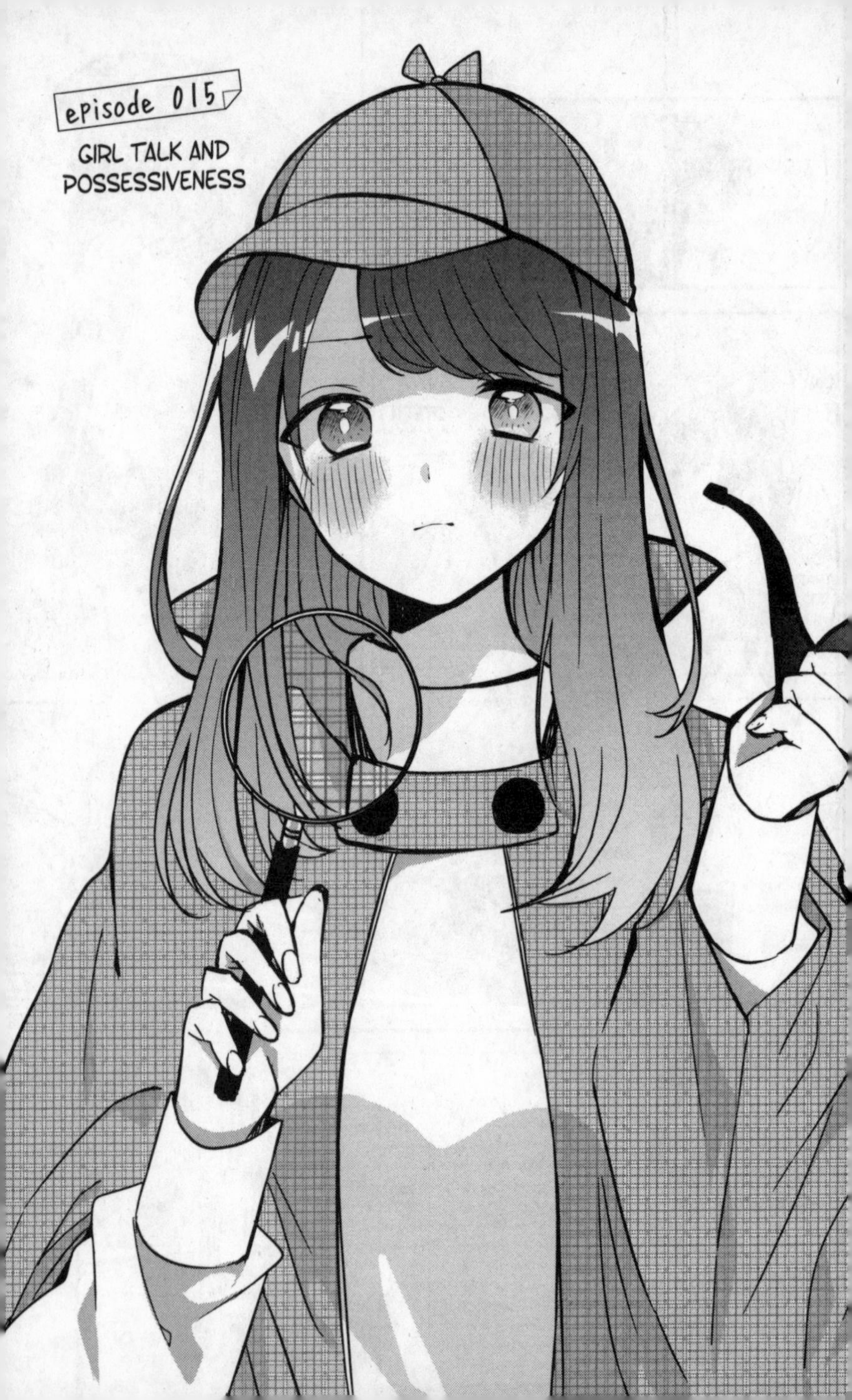
episode 015
GIRL TALK AND POSSESSIVENESS

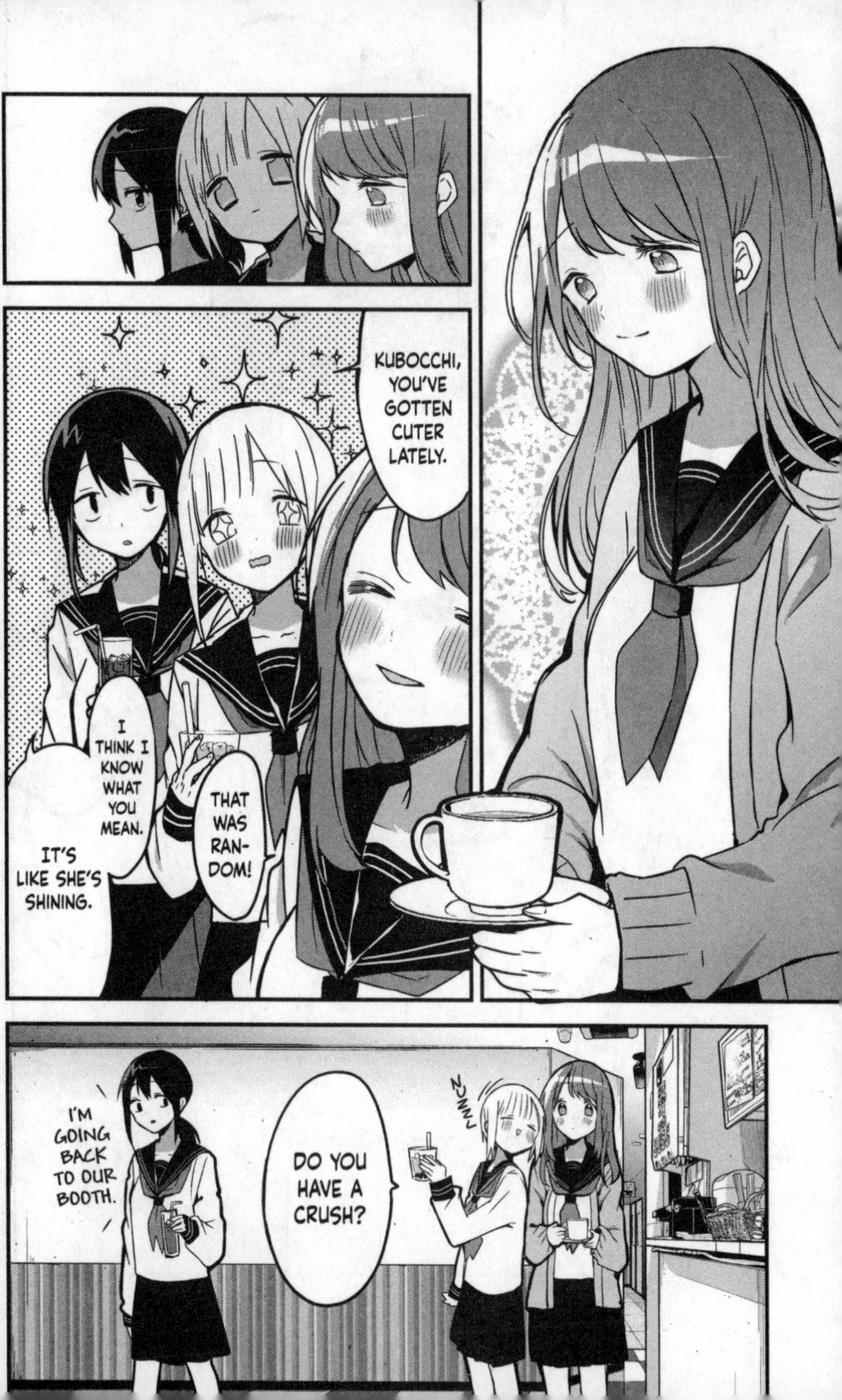
KUBOCCHI, YOU'VE GOTTEN CUTER LATELY.
THAT WAS RAN-DOM!
I THINK I KNOW WHAT YOU MEAN.
IT'S LIKE SHE'S SHINING.
NUZZ
DO YOU HAVE A CRUSH?
I'M GOING BACK TO OUR BOOTH.

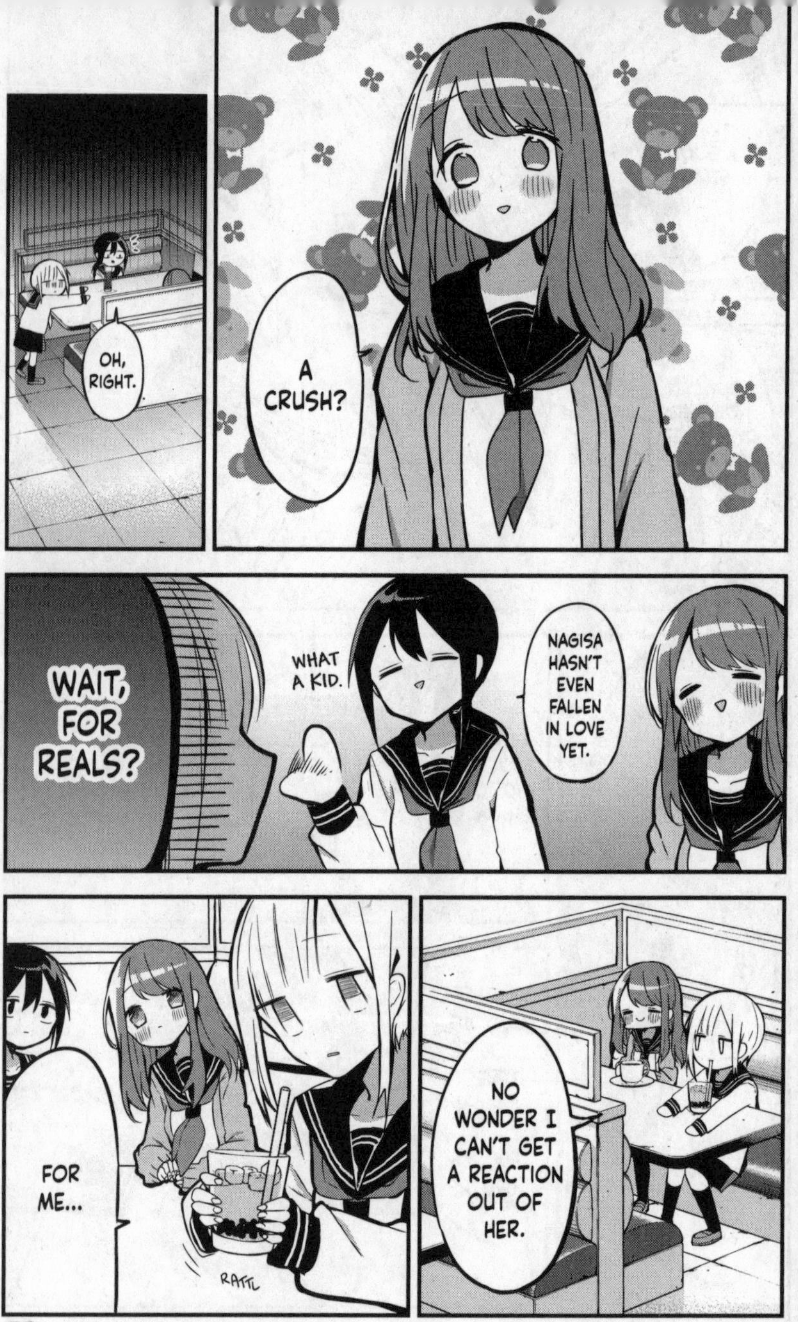
A CRUSH?
OH, RIGHT.
NAGISA HASN'T EVEN FALLEN IN LOVE YET.
WHAT A KID.
WAIT, FOR REALS?
NO WONDER I CAN'T GET A REACTION OUT OF HER.
FOR ME...
RATTL

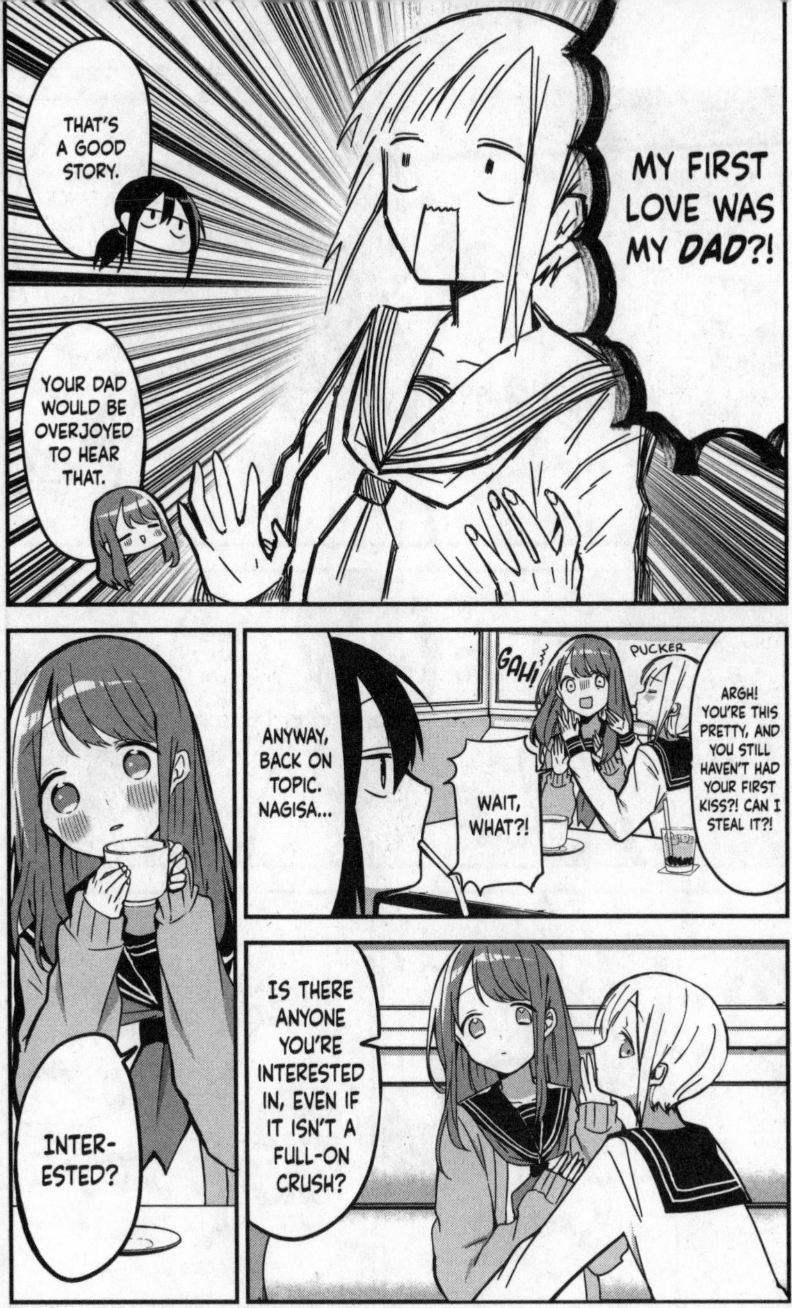
MY FIRST LOVE WAS MY DAD?!
THAT'S A GOOD STORY.
YOUR DAD WOULD BE OVERJOYED TO HEAR THAT.
ARGH! YOU'RE THIS PRETTY, AND YOU STILL HAVEN'T HAD YOUR FIRST KISS?! CAN I STEAL IT?!
PUCKER
GAH!
WAIT, WHAT?!
ANYWAY, BACK ON TOPIC. NAGISA...
IS THERE ANYONE YOU'RE INTERESTED IN, EVEN IF IT ISN'T A FULL-ON CRUSH?
INTER-ESTED?

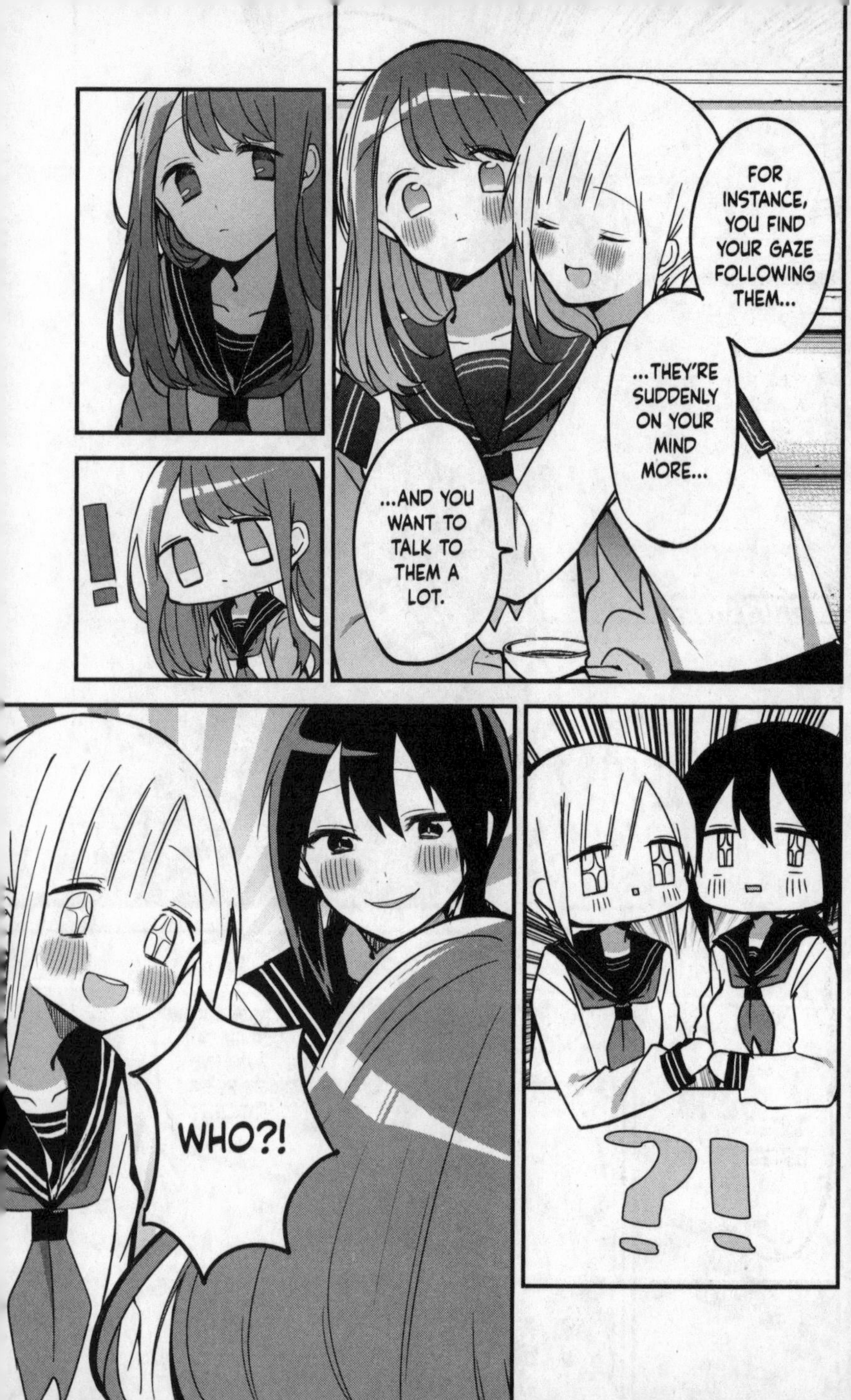
FOR INSTANCE, YOU FIND YOUR GAZE FOLLOWING THEM...
...THEY'RE SUDDENLY ON YOUR MIND MORE...
...AND YOU WANT TO TALK TO THEM A LOT.
!
?!
WHO?!

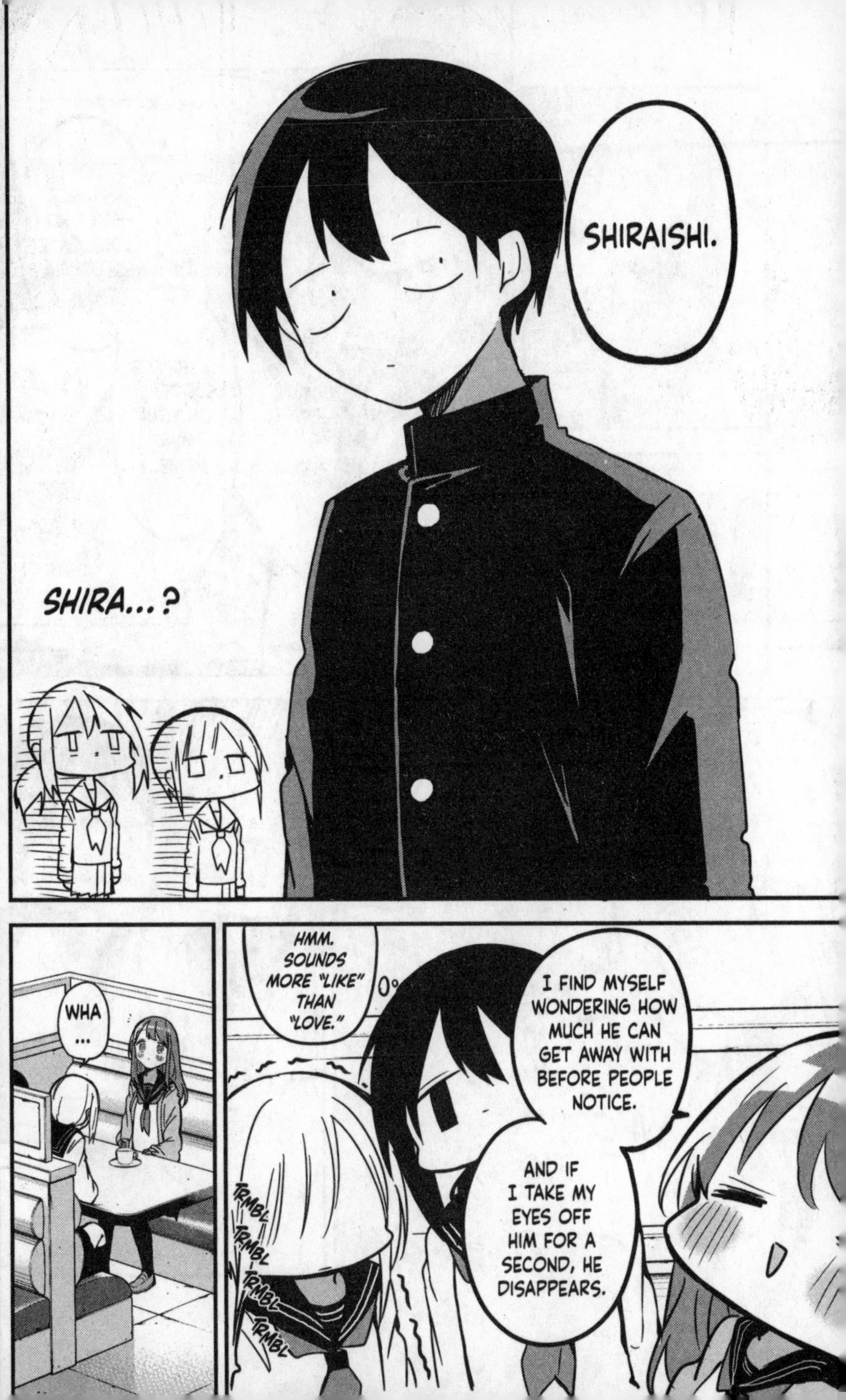
SHIRAISHI.
SHIRA...?
I FIND MYSELF WONDERING HOW MUCH HE CAN GET AWAY WITH BEFORE PEOPLE NOTICE.
AND IF I TAKE MY EYES OFF HIM FOR A SECOND, HE DISAPPEARS.
HMM. SOUNDS MORE "LIKE" THAN "LOVE."
TRMBL TRMBL TRMBL TRMBL
WHA ...

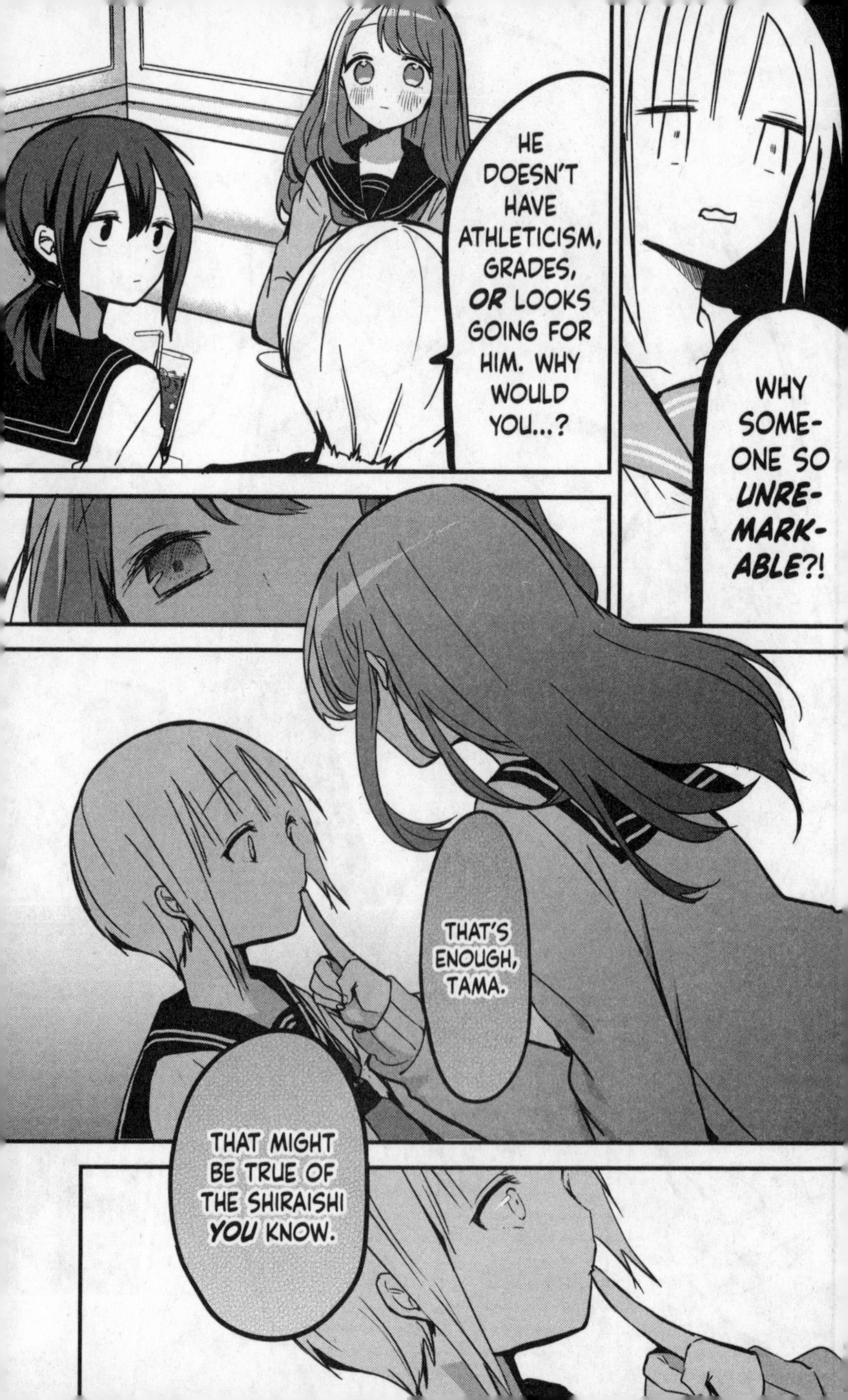
WHY SOME-ONE SO *UNRE-MARK-ABLE*?!
HE DOESN'T HAVE ATHLETICISM, GRADES, *OR* LOOKS GOING FOR HIM. WHY WOULD YOU...?
THAT'S ENOUGH, TAMA.
THAT MIGHT BE TRUE OF THE SHIRAISHI *YOU* KNOW.

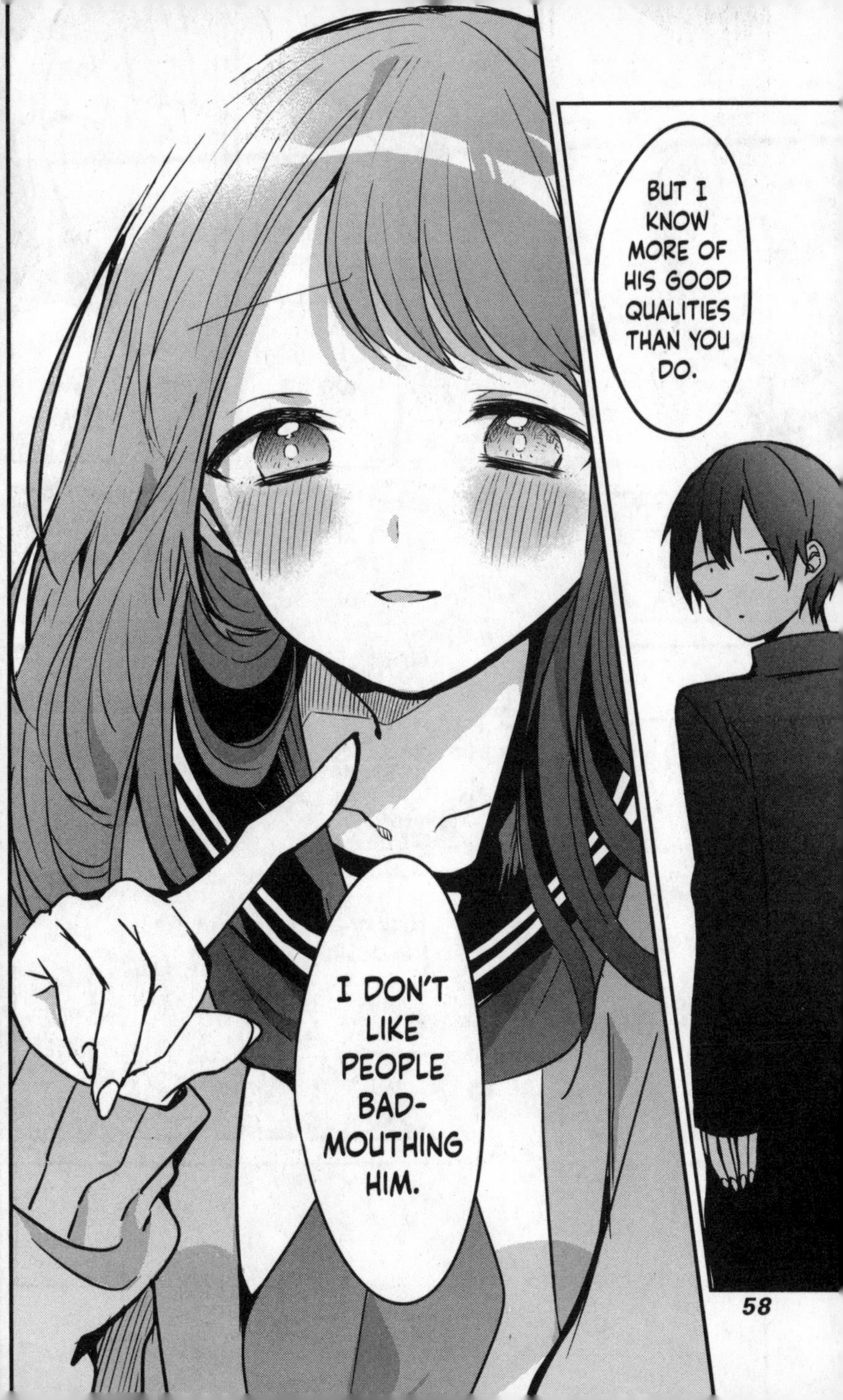
BUT I KNOW MORE OF HIS GOOD QUALITIES THAN YOU DO.
I DON'T LIKE PEOPLE BAD-MOUTHING HIM.

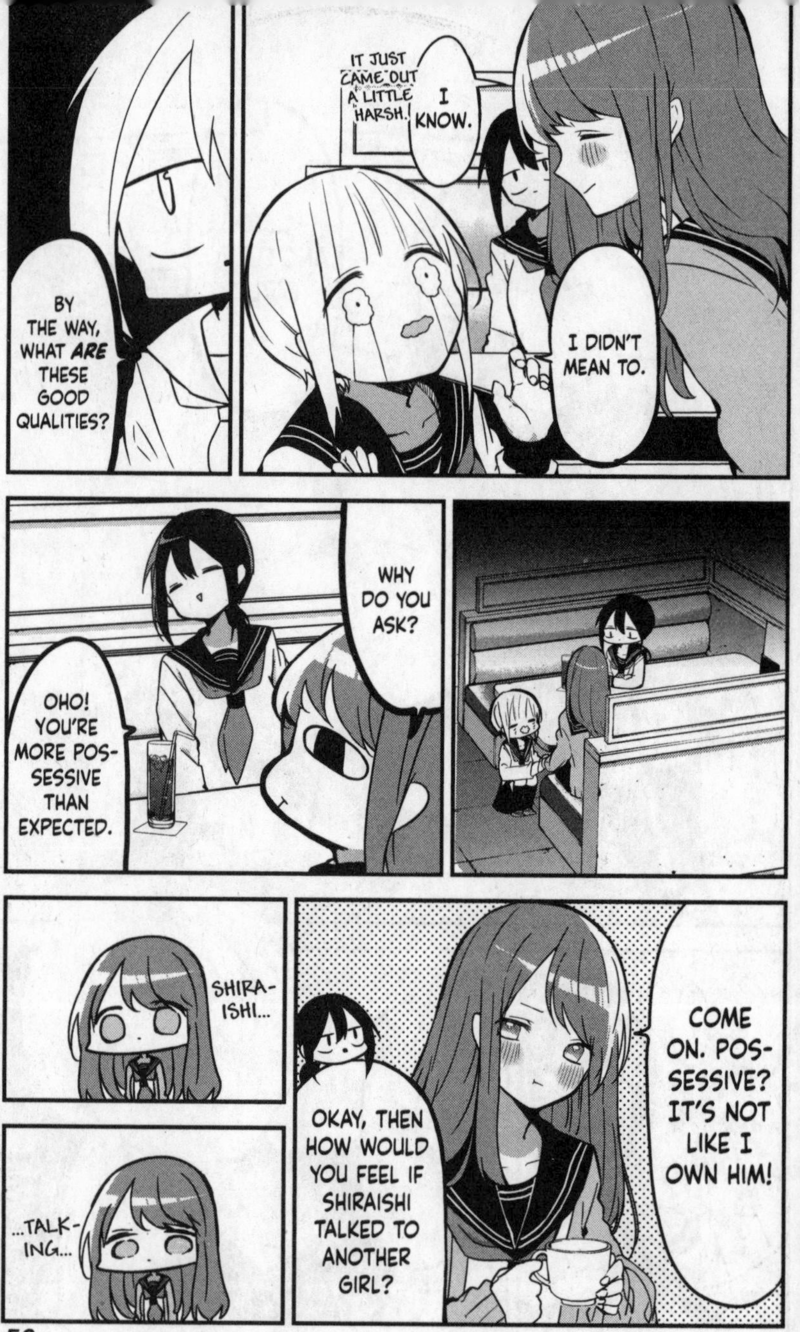
I DIDN'T MEAN TO.
I KNOW.
IT JUST CAME OUT A LITTLE HARSH.
BY THE WAY, WHAT ***ARE*** THESE GOOD QUALITIES?
WHY DO YOU ASK?
OHO! YOU'RE MORE POSSESSIVE THAN EXPECTED.
COME ON. POSSESSIVE? IT'S NOT LIKE I OWN HIM!
OKAY, THEN HOW WOULD YOU FEEL IF SHIRAISHI TALKED TO ANOTHER GIRL?
SHIRAISHI...
...TALKING...

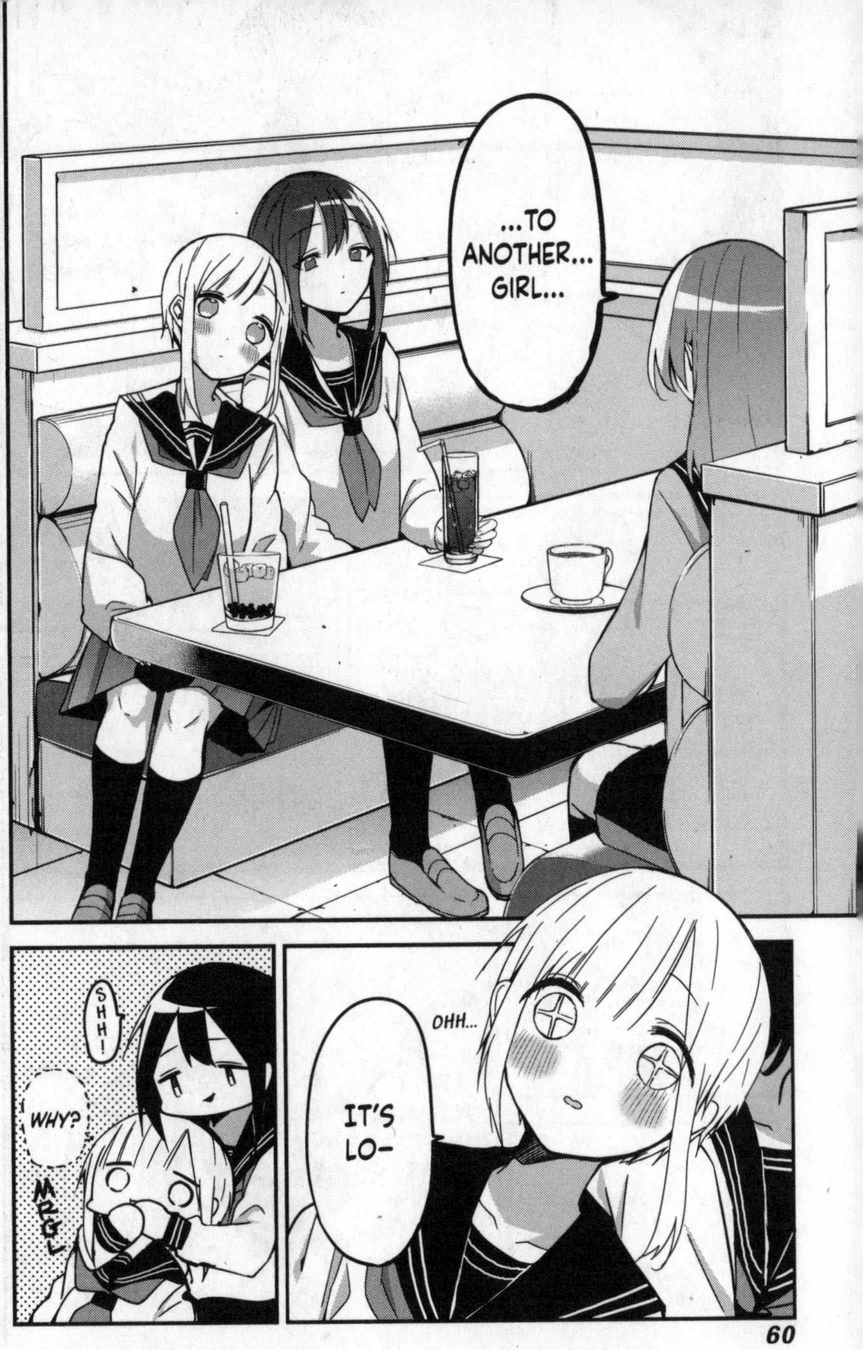
...TO ANOTHER... GIRL...
OHH...
IT'S LO-
SHH!
WHY?
MRGL

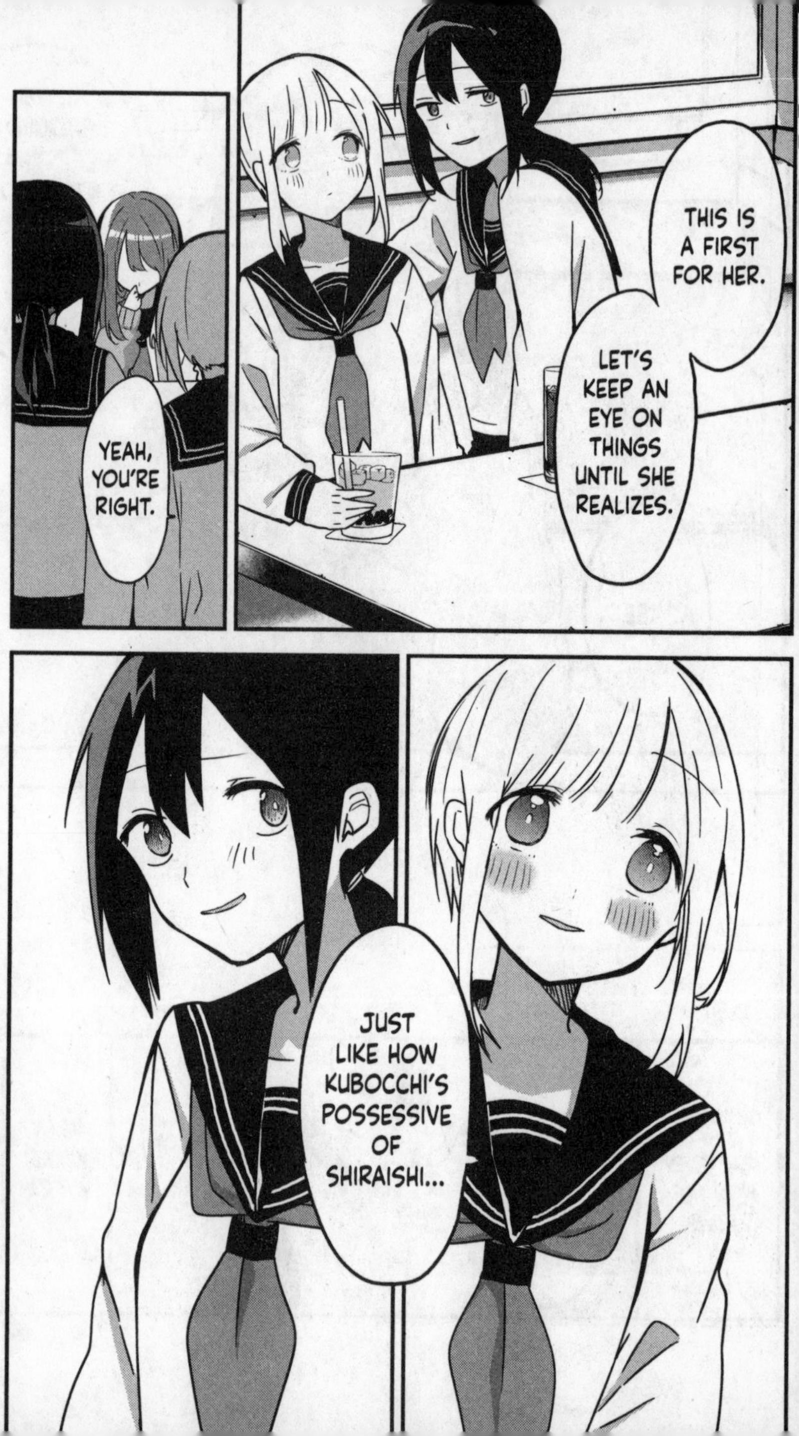
THIS IS A FIRST FOR HER.
LET'S KEEP AN EYE ON THINGS UNTIL SHE REALIZES.
YEAH, YOU'RE RIGHT.
JUST LIKE HOW KUBOCCHI'S POSSESSIVE OF SHIRAISHI...

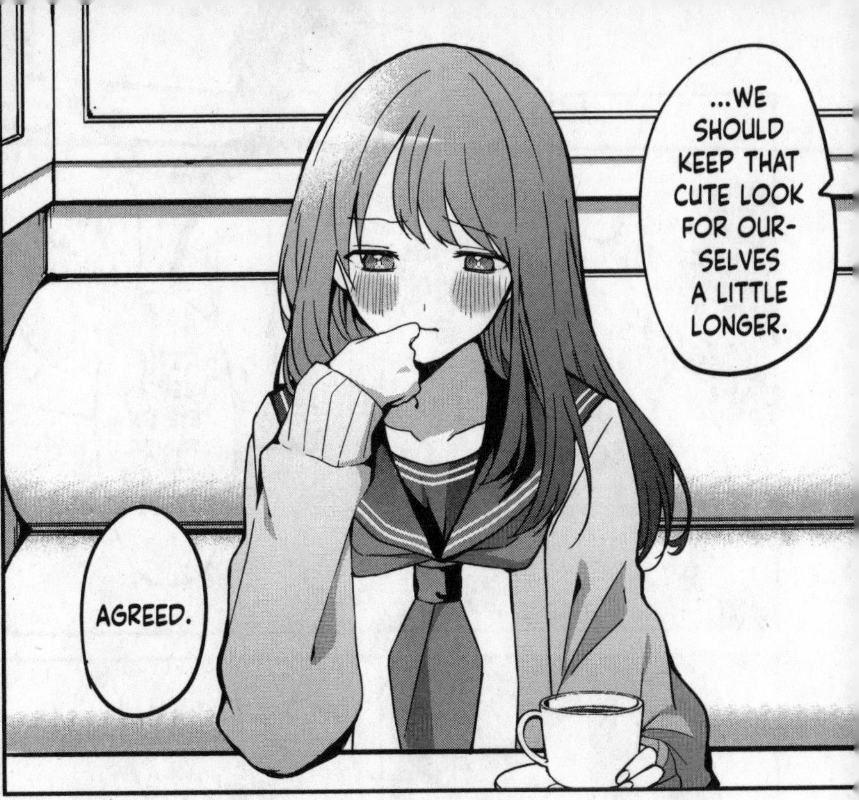
...WE SHOULD KEEP THAT CUTE LOOK FOR OURSELVES A LITTLE LONGER.
AGREED.

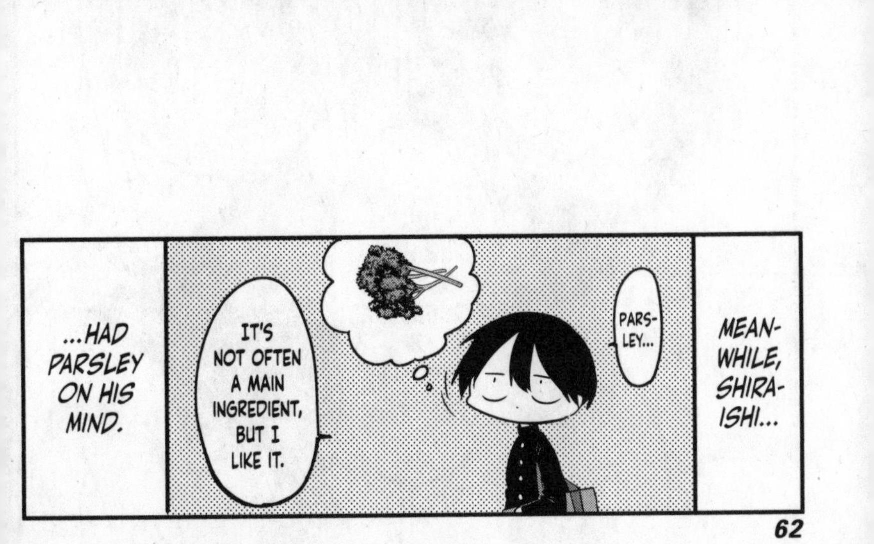
MEANWHILE, SHIRAISHI...
PARSLEY...
IT'S NOT OFTEN A MAIN INGREDIENT, BUT I LIKE IT.
...HAD PARSLEY ON HIS MIND.

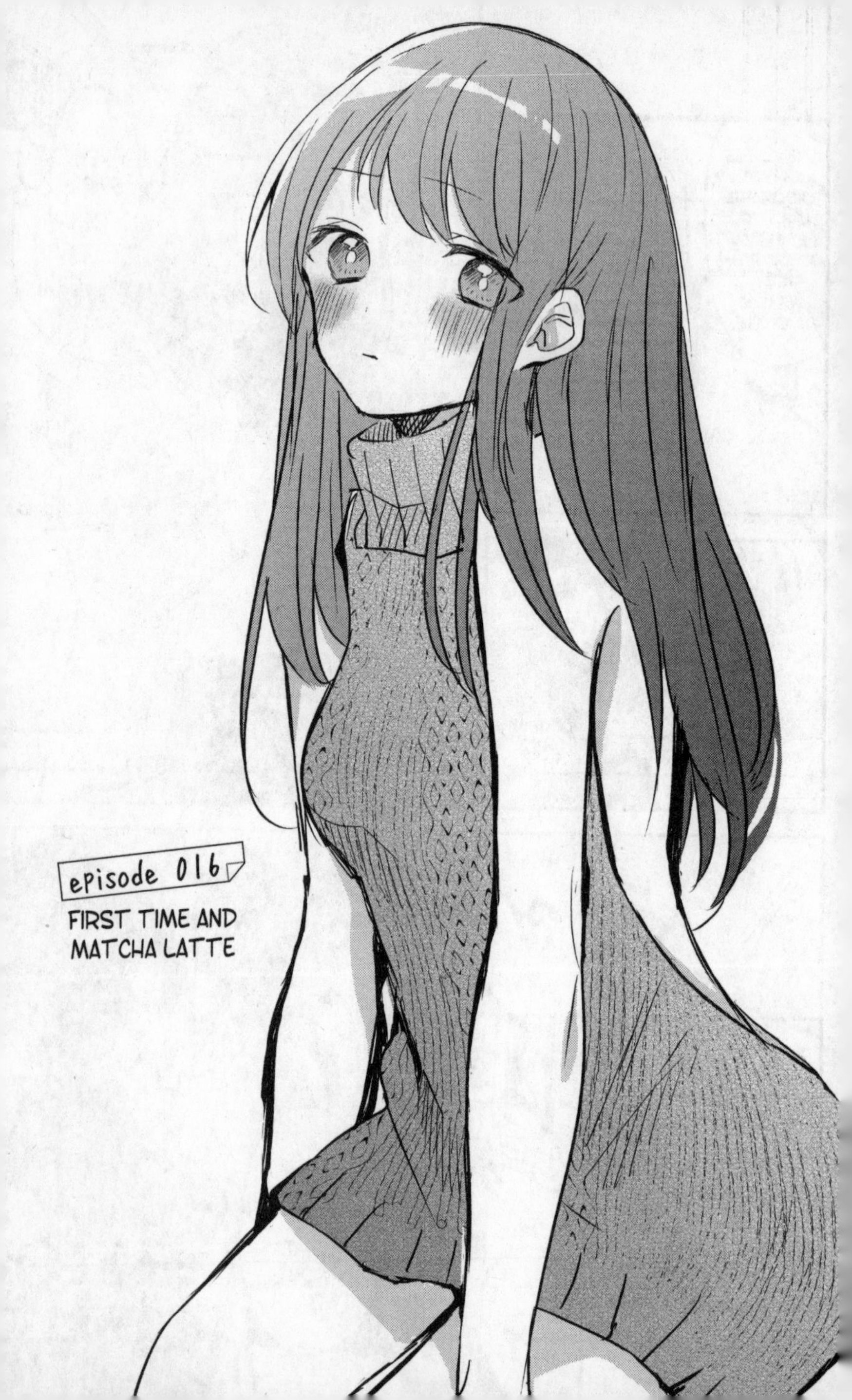
episode 016
FIRST TIME AND
MATCHA LATTE

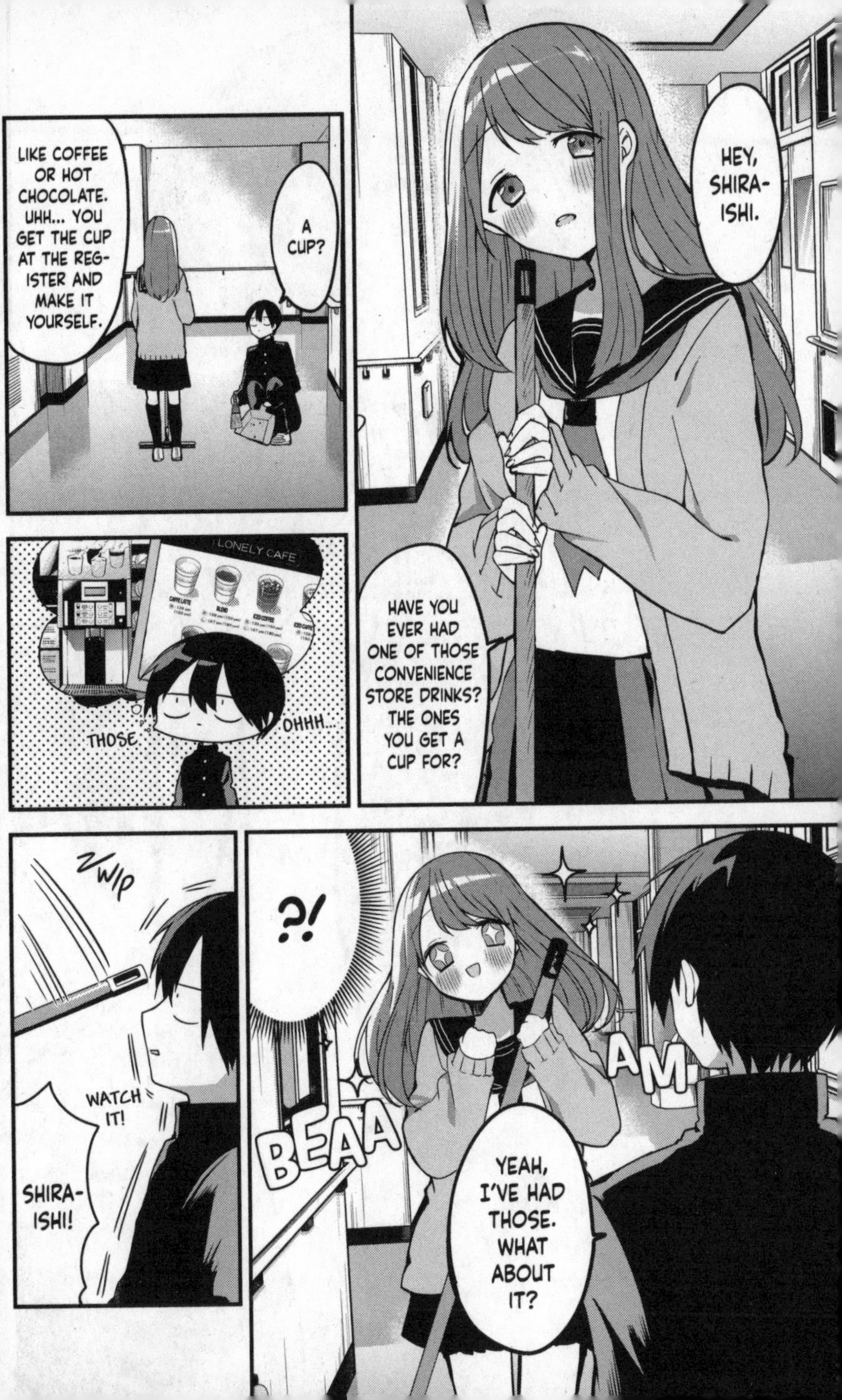
HEY, SHIRA-ISHI.
HAVE YOU EVER HAD ONE OF THOSE CONVENIENCE STORE DRINKS? THE ONES YOU GET A CUP FOR?
A CUP?
LIKE COFFEE OR HOT CHOCOLATE. UHH... YOU GET THE CUP AT THE REGISTER AND MAKE IT YOURSELF.
LONELY CAFE
CAFFE LATTE
BLEND
ICED COFFEE
OHHH...
THOSE
?!
AM
BEAA
YEAH, I'VE HAD THOSE. WHAT ABOUT IT?
ZWIP
WATCH IT!
SHIRA-ISHI!

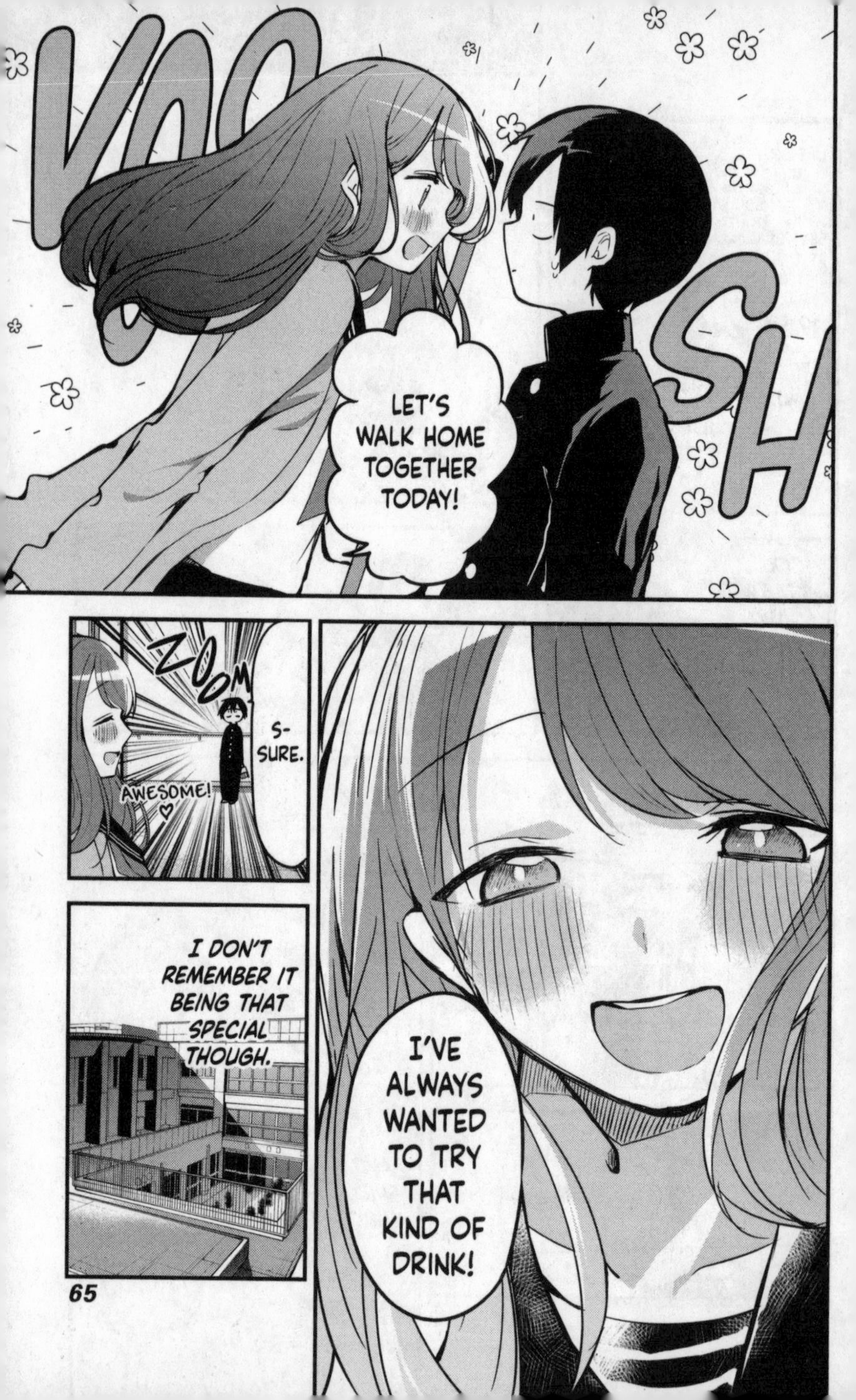
VOO
SH
LET'S WALK HOME TOGETHER TODAY!
I'VE ALWAYS WANTED TO TRY THAT KIND OF DRINK!
ZOOM
S-SURE.
AWESOME! ♡
I DON'T REMEMBER IT BEING THAT SPECIAL THOUGH.

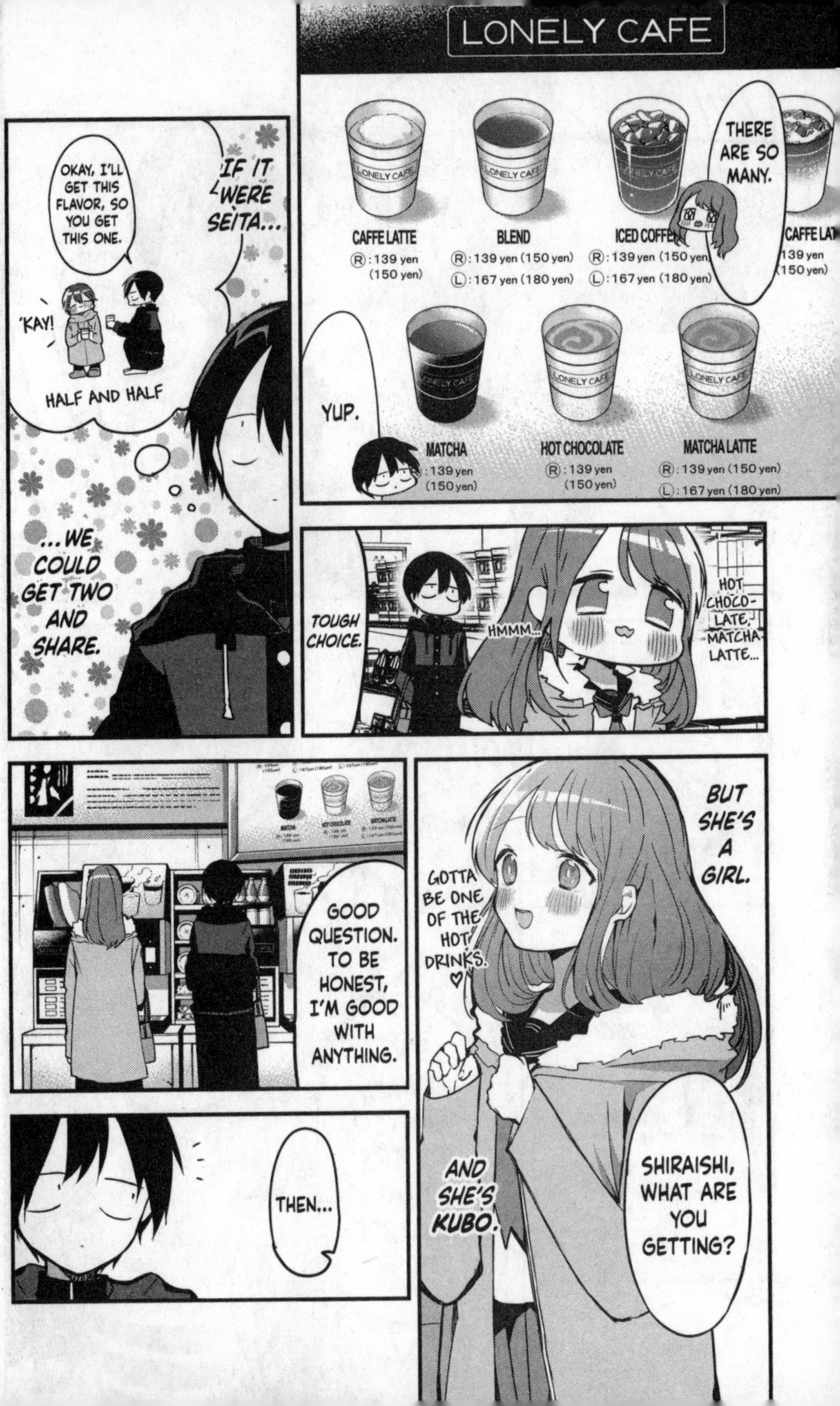
LONELY CAFE
CAFFE LATTE
R: 139 yen (150 yen)
BLEND
R: 139 yen (150 yen)
L: 167 yen (180 yen)
ICED COFFE
R: 139 yen (150 yen)
L: 167 yen (180 yen)
CAFFE LA
139 yen (150 yen)
THERE ARE SO MANY.
YUP.
MATCHA
139 yen (150 yen)
HOT CHOCOLATE
R: 139 yen (150 yen)
MATCHA LATTE
R: 139 yen (150 yen)
L: 167 yen (180 yen)
HOT CHOCO-LATE, MATCHA LATTE...
HMMM...
TOUGH CHOICE.
IF IT WERE SEITA...
OKAY, I'LL GET THIS FLAVOR, SO YOU GET THIS ONE.
'KAY!
HALF AND HALF
...WE COULD GET TWO AND SHARE.
BUT SHE'S A GIRL.
GOTTA BE ONE OF THE HOT DRINKS. ♡
SHIRAISHI, WHAT ARE YOU GETTING?
AND SHE'S KUBO.
GOOD QUESTION. TO BE HONEST, I'M GOOD WITH ANYTHING.
THEN...

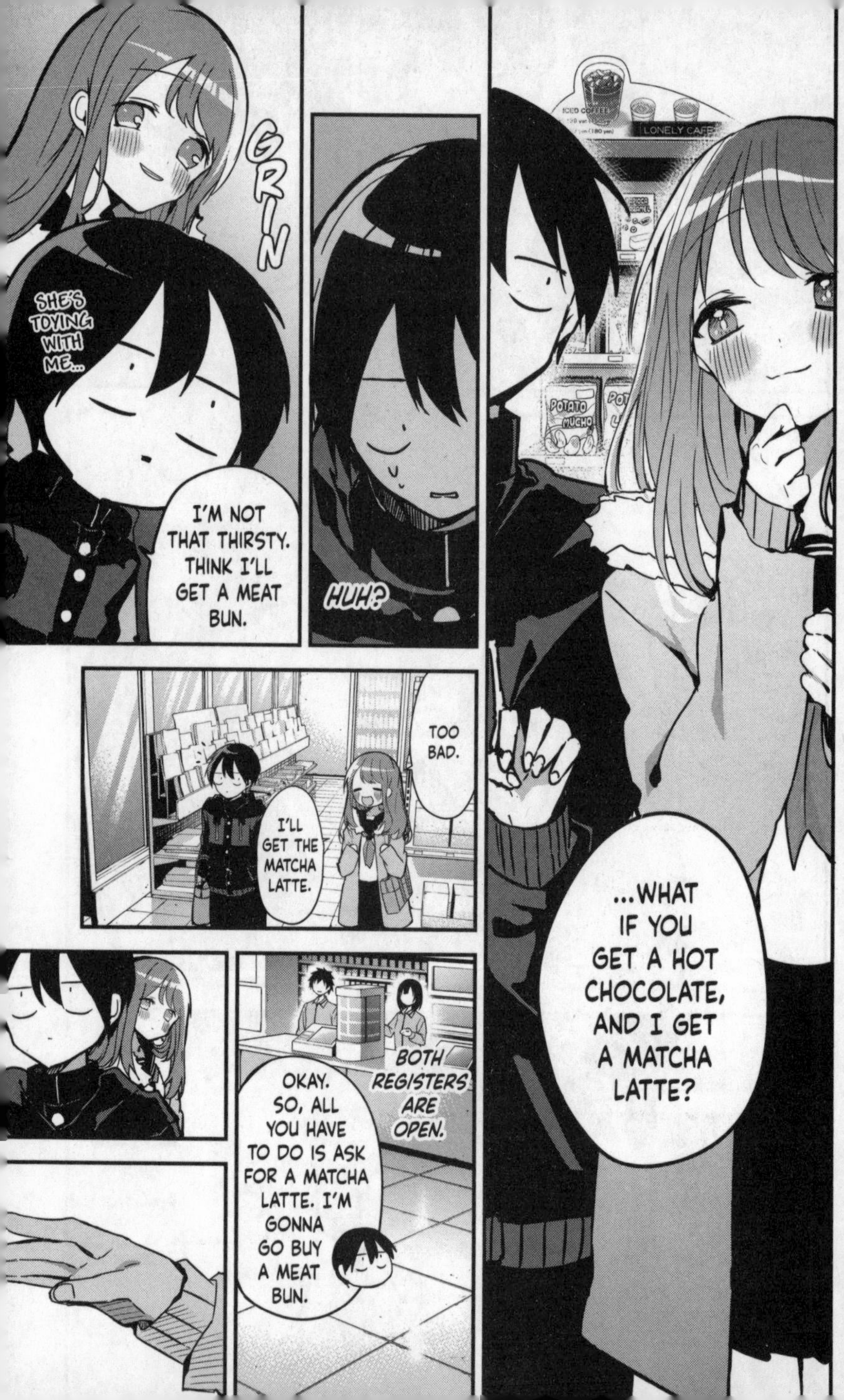
ICED COFFEE
LONELY CAFE
POTATO MUCHO
...WHAT IF YOU GET A HOT CHOCOLATE, AND I GET A MATCHA LATTE?
HUH?
GRIN
SHE'S TOYING WITH ME...
I'M NOT THAT THIRSTY. THINK I'LL GET A MEAT BUN.
TOO BAD.
I'LL GET THE MATCHA LATTE.
BOTH REGISTERS ARE OPEN.
OKAY. SO, ALL YOU HAVE TO DO IS ASK FOR A MATCHA LATTE. I'M GONNA GO BUY A MEAT BUN.

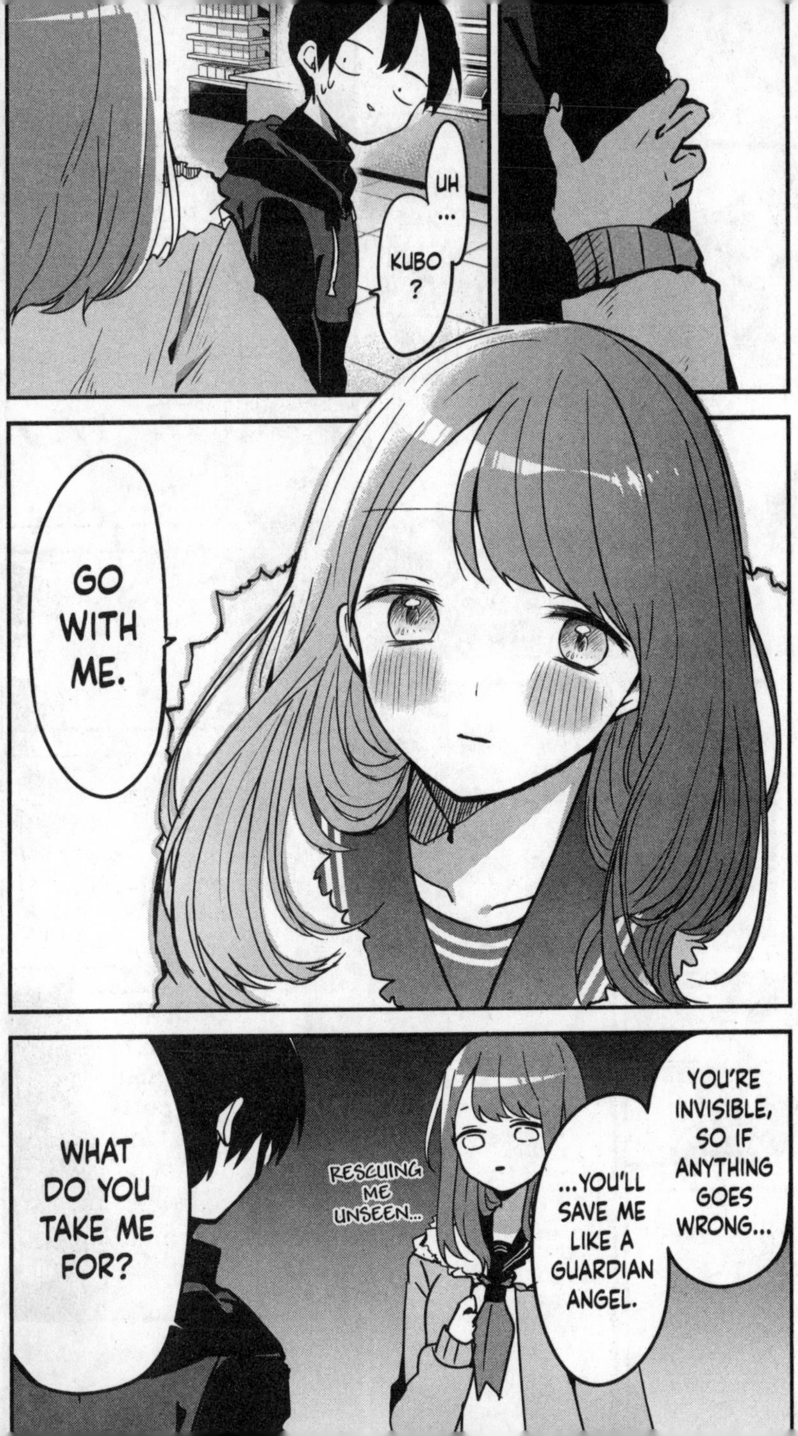
UH ... KUBO ?
GO WITH ME.
YOU'RE INVISIBLE, SO IF ANYTHING GOES WRONG...
...YOU'LL SAVE ME LIKE A GUARDIAN ANGEL.
RESCUING ME UNSEEN...
WHAT DO YOU TAKE ME FOR?

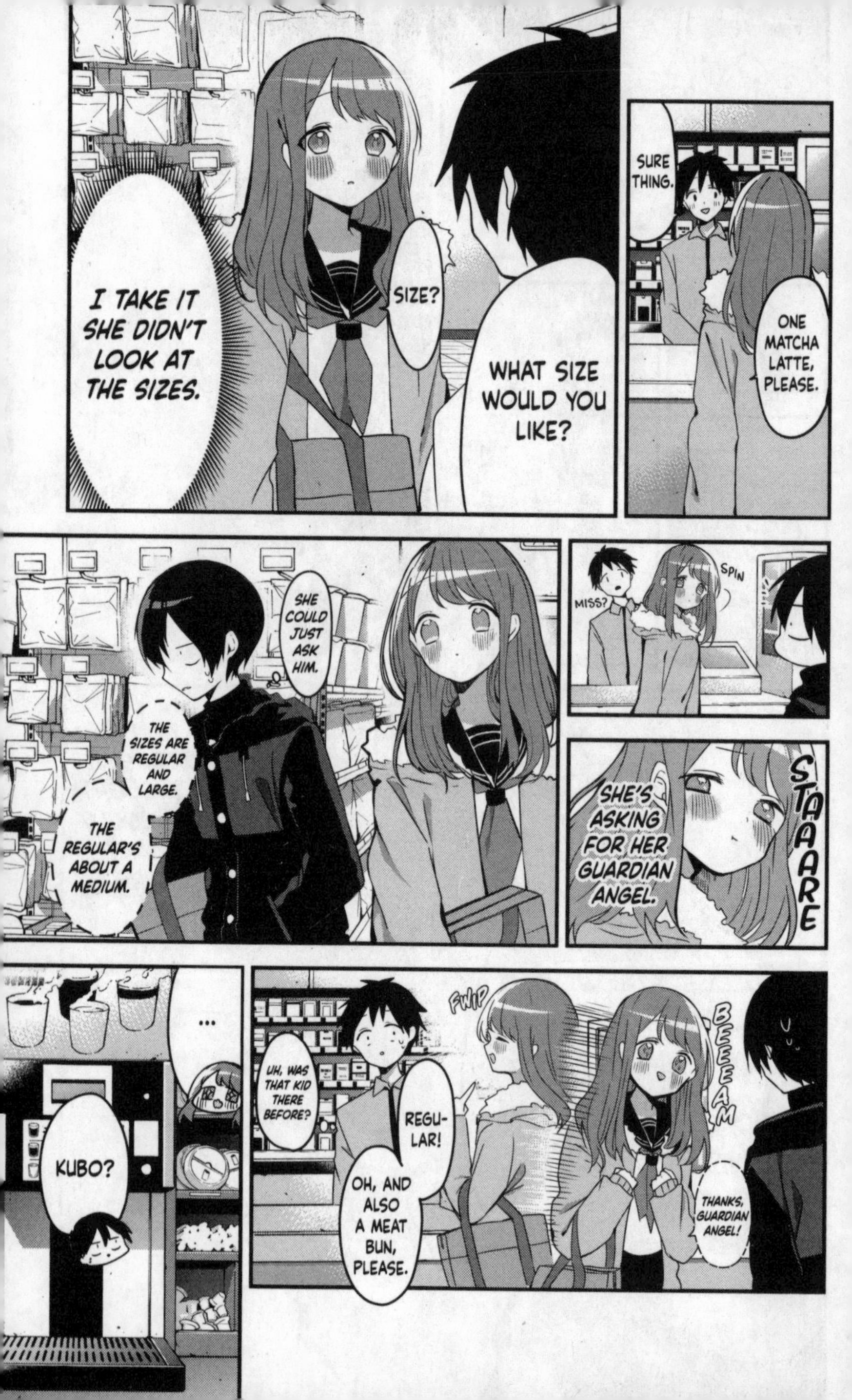
ONE MATCHA LATTE, PLEASE.
SURE THING.
WHAT SIZE WOULD YOU LIKE?
SIZE?
I TAKE IT SHE DIDN'T LOOK AT THE SIZES.
SPIN
MISS?
STAAARE
SHE'S ASKING FOR HER GUARDIAN ANGEL.
SHE COULD JUST ASK HIM.
THE SIZES ARE REGULAR AND LARGE.
THE REGULAR'S ABOUT A MEDIUM.
BEEEEAM
THANKS, GUARDIAN ANGEL!
FWIP
REGU-LAR!
UH, WAS THAT KID THERE BEFORE?
OH, AND ALSO A MEAT BUN, PLEASE.
...
KUBO?

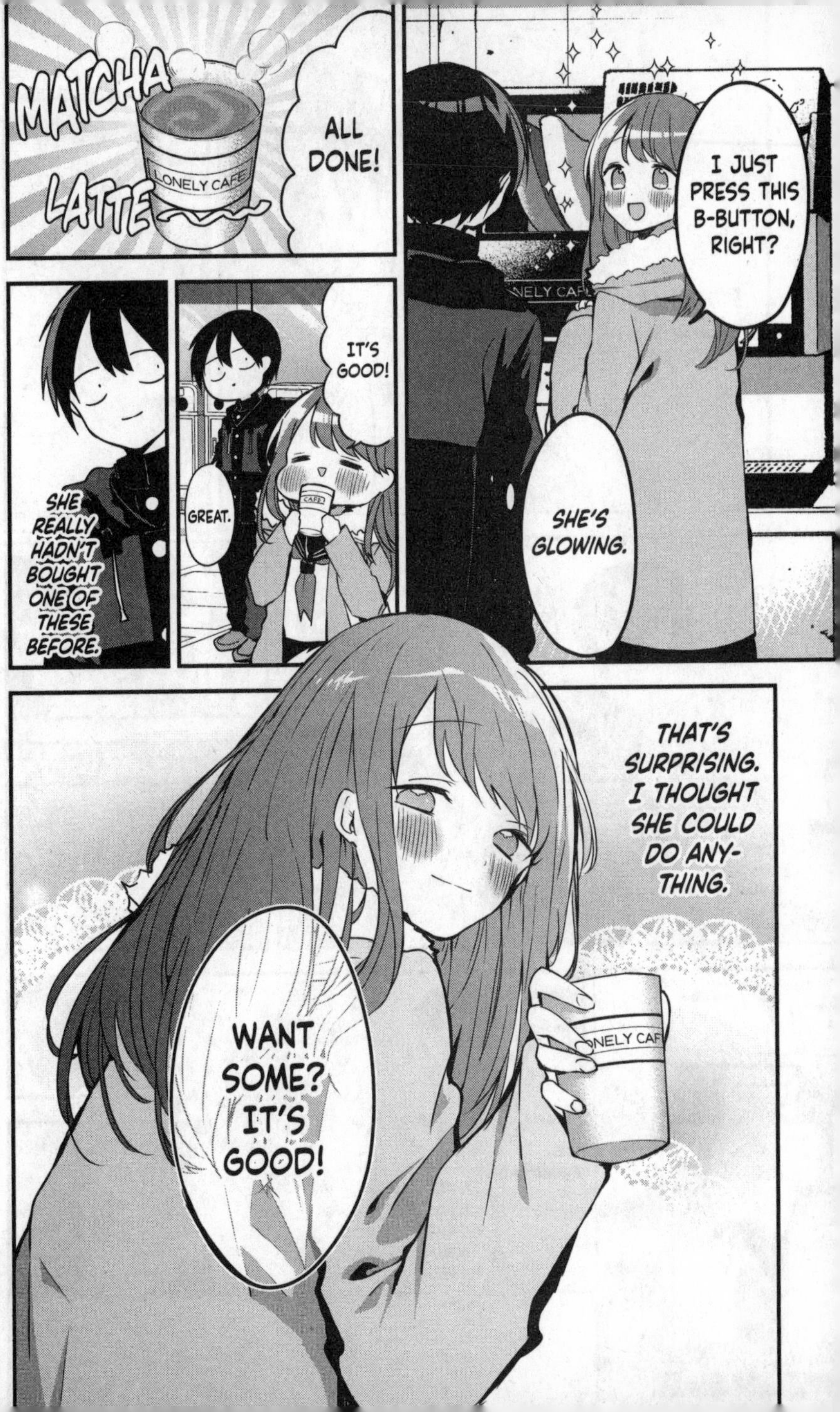
I JUST PRESS THIS B-BUTTON, RIGHT?
SHE'S GLOWING.
ALL DONE!
LONELY CAFE
MATCHA LATTE
IT'S GOOD!
GREAT.
SHE REALLY HADN'T BOUGHT ONE OF THESE BEFORE.
THAT'S SURPRISING. I THOUGHT SHE COULD DO ANY-THING.
WANT SOME? IT'S GOOD!

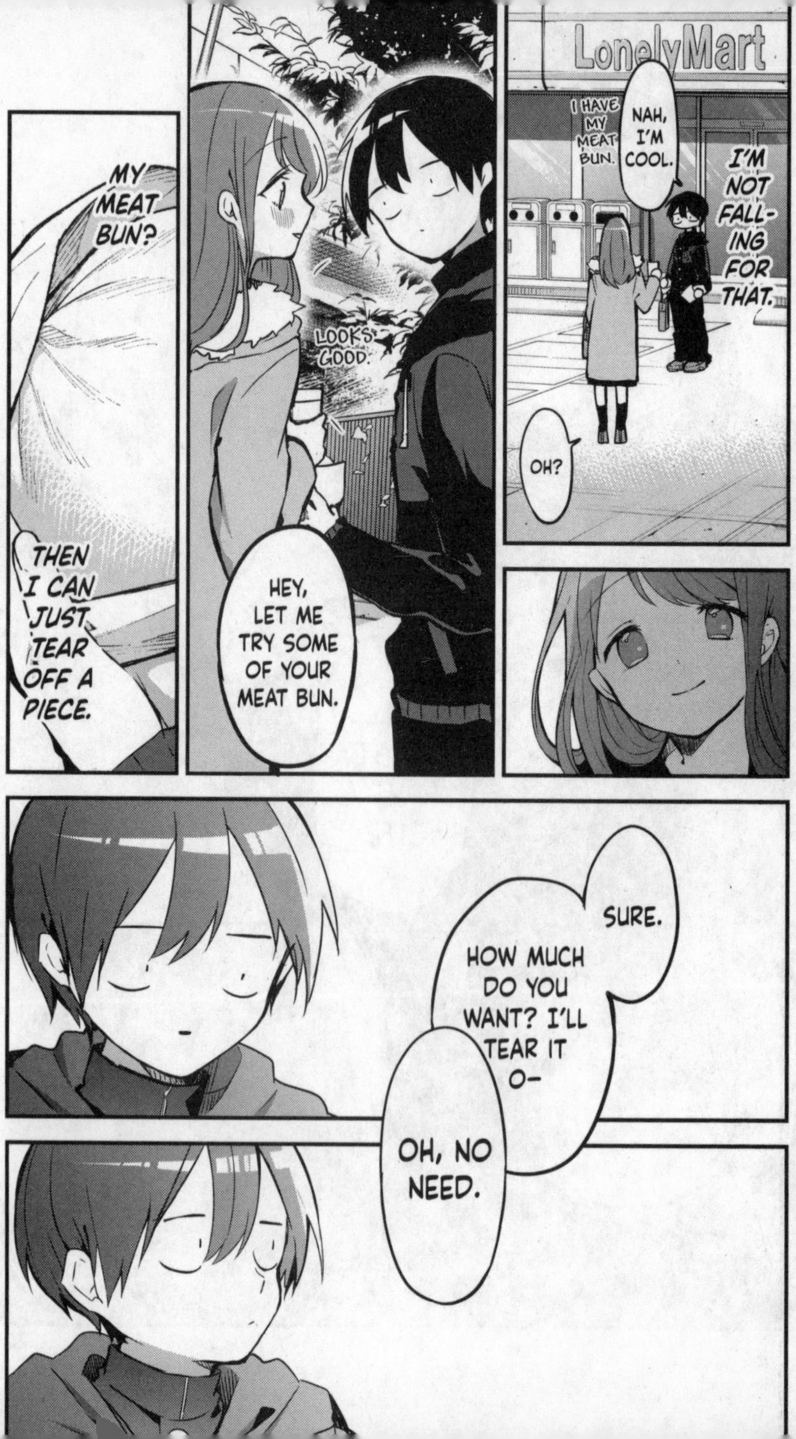
LonelyMart
NAH, I'M COOL.
I HAVE MY MEAT BUN.
I'M NOT FALLING FOR THAT.
OH?
LOOKS GOOD.
HEY, LET ME TRY SOME OF YOUR MEAT BUN.
MY MEAT BUN?
THEN I CAN JUST TEAR OFF A PIECE.
SURE. HOW MUCH DO YOU WANT? I'LL TEAR IT O–
OH, NO NEED.

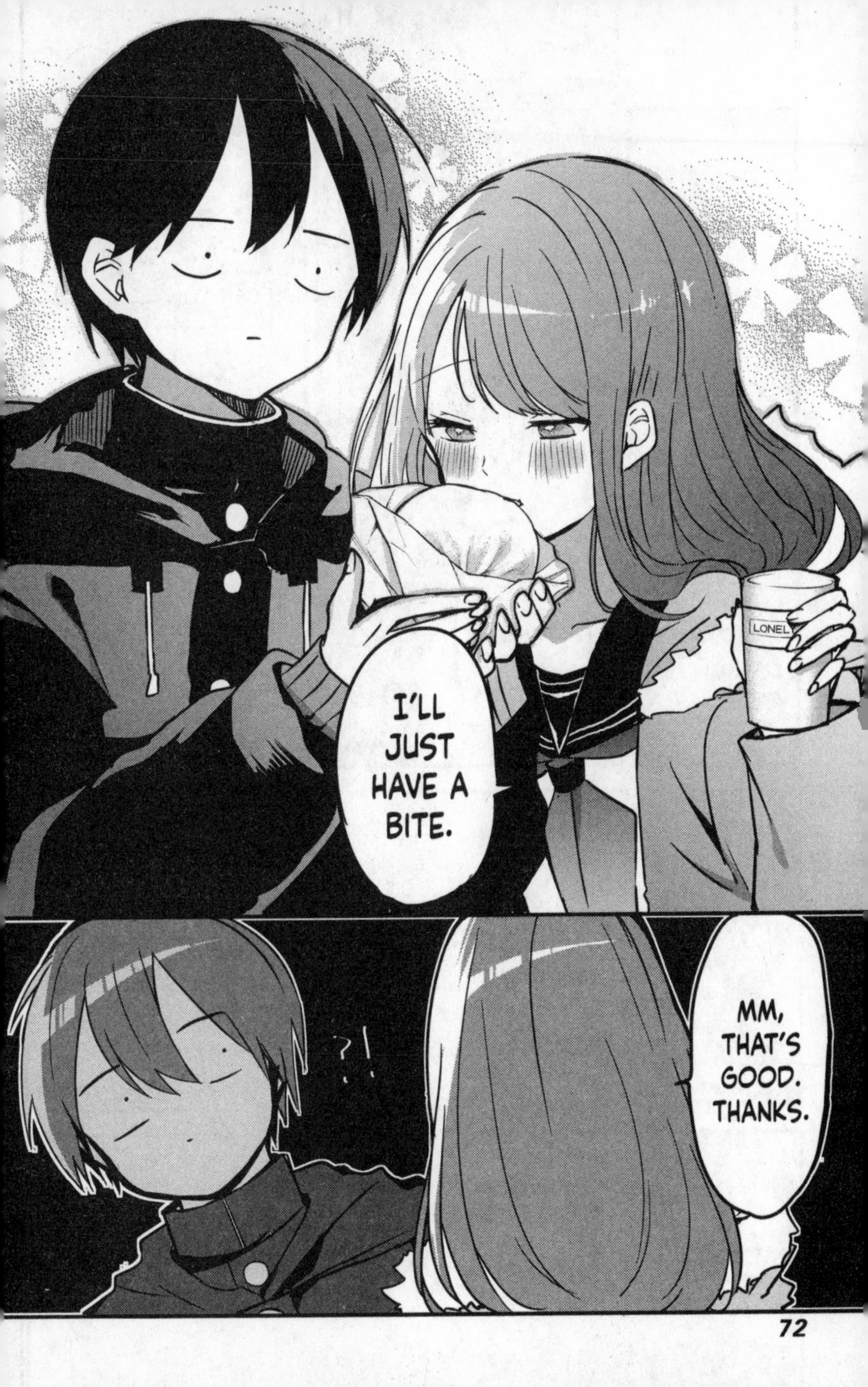
I'LL JUST HAVE A BITE.
?!
MM, THAT'S GOOD. THANKS.

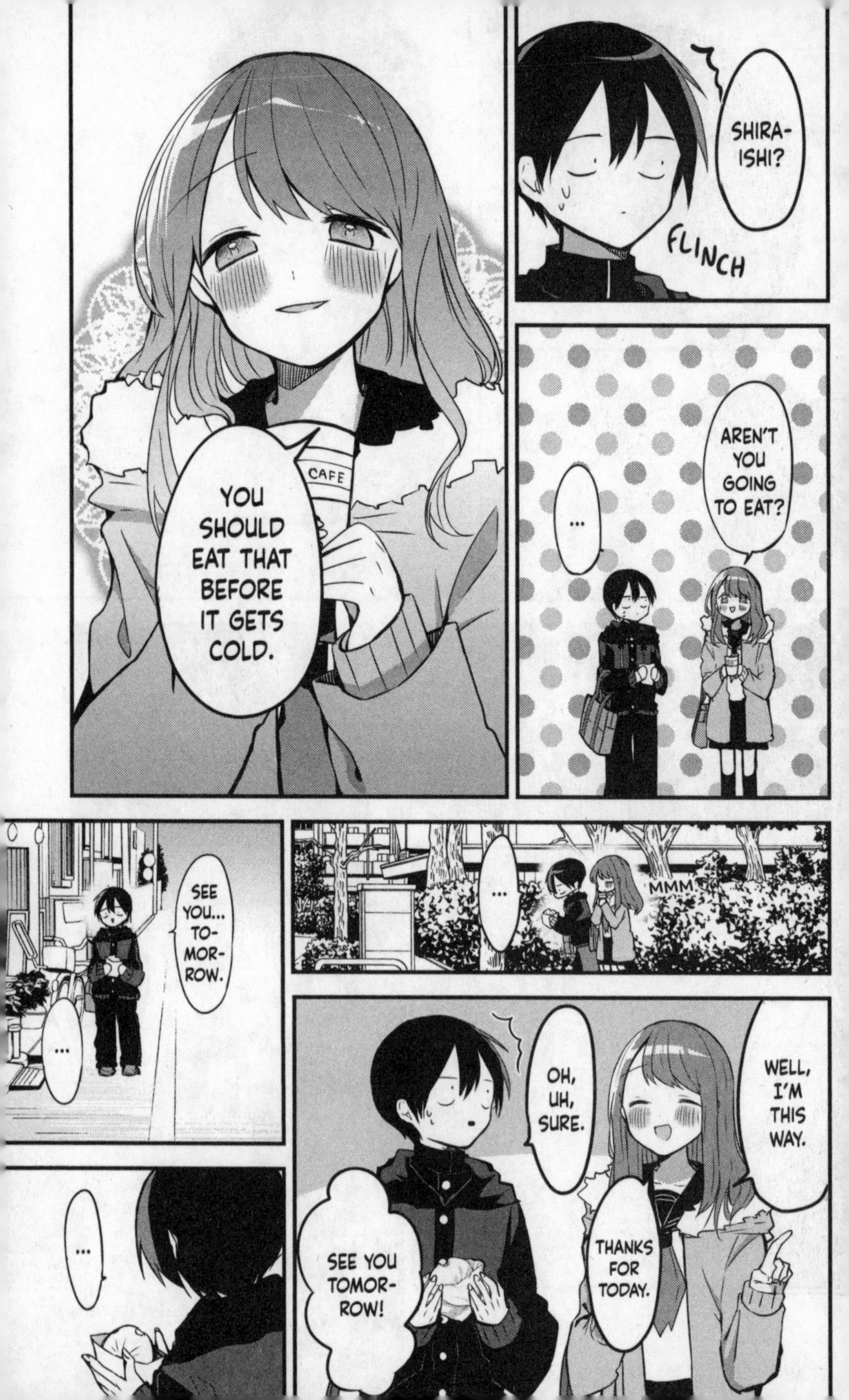
SHIRA-ISHI?
FLINCH
AREN'T YOU GOING TO EAT?
...
CAFE
YOU SHOULD EAT THAT BEFORE IT GETS COLD.
MMM
...
WELL, I'M THIS WAY.
OH, UH, SURE.
THANKS FOR TODAY.
SEE YOU TOMOR-ROW!
SEE YOU... TO-MOR-ROW.
...
...

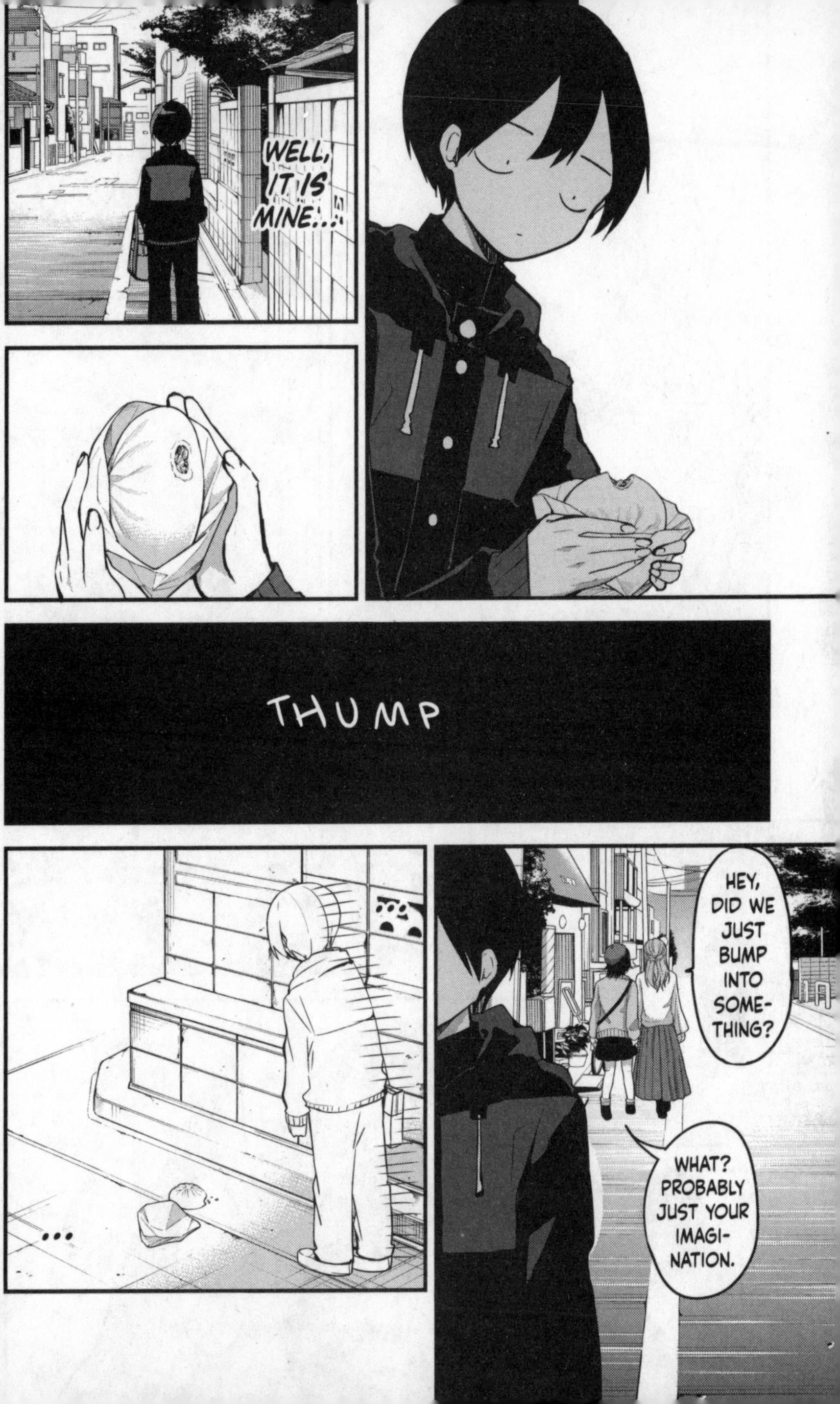
WELL, IT IS MINE...
THUMP
HEY, DID WE JUST BUMP INTO SOME-THING?
WHAT? PROBABLY JUST YOUR IMAGI-NATION.
...

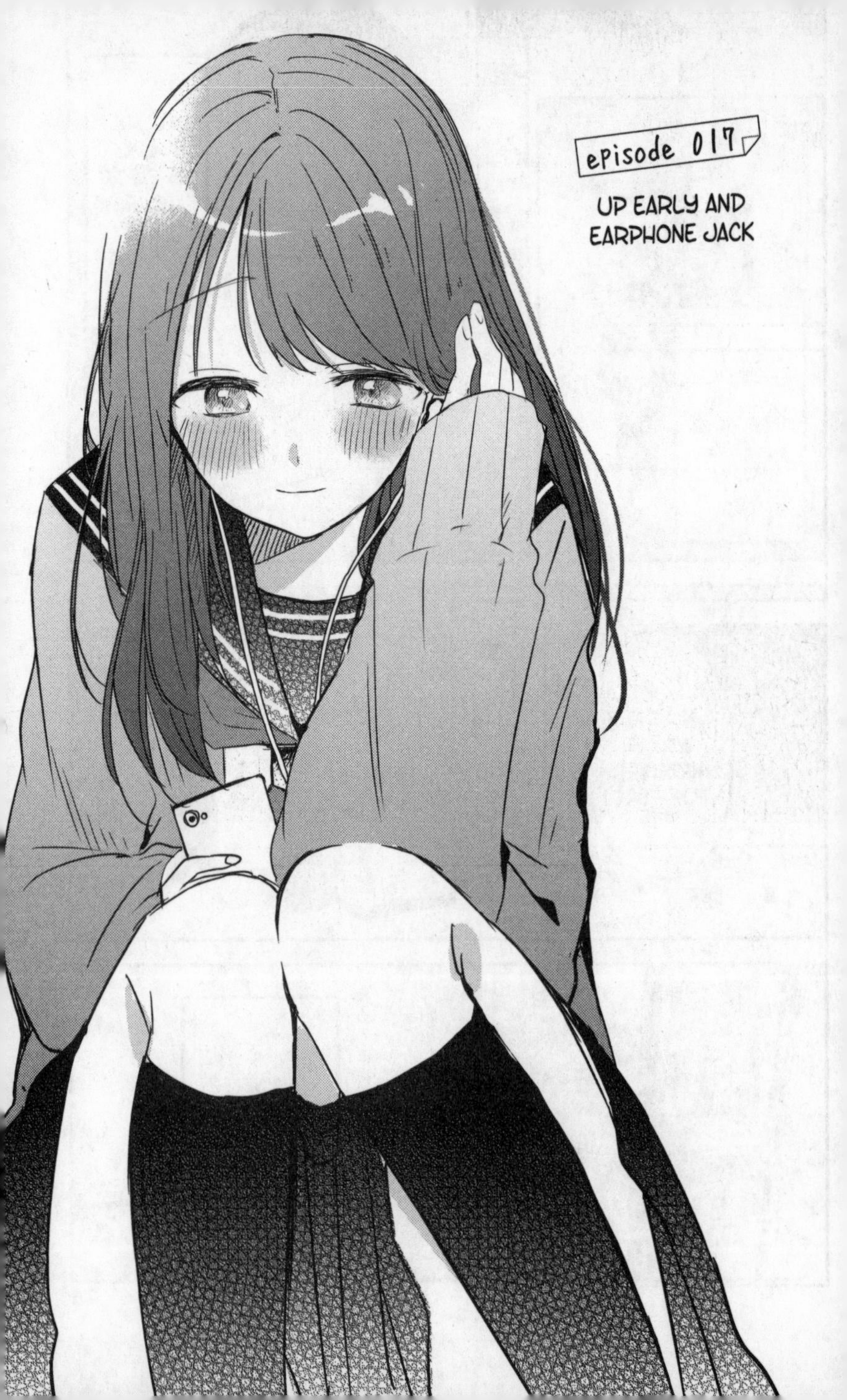
episode 017
UP EARLY AND EARPHONE JACK

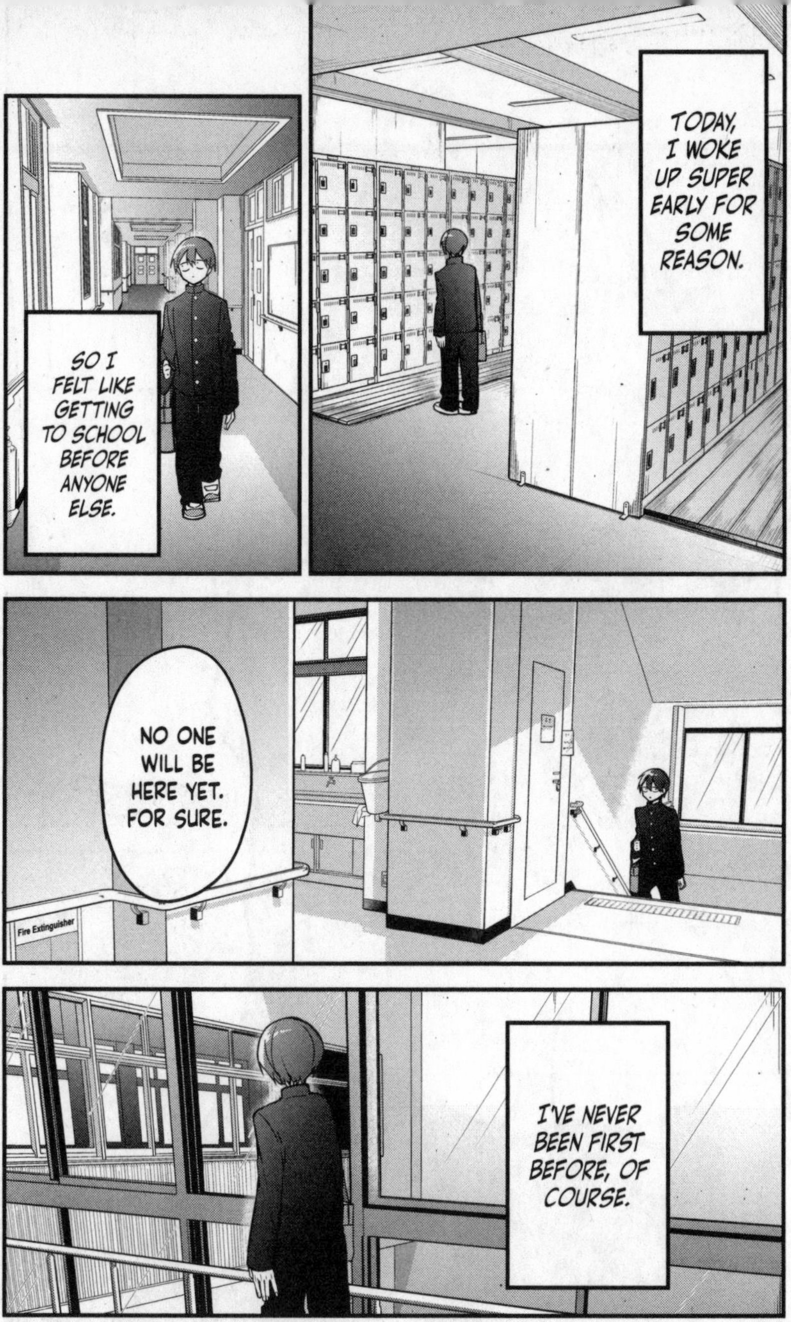
TODAY, I WOKE UP SUPER EARLY FOR SOME REASON.
SO I FELT LIKE GETTING TO SCHOOL BEFORE ANYONE ELSE.
NO ONE WILL BE HERE YET. FOR SURE.
Fire Extinguisher
I'VE NEVER BEEN FIRST BEFORE, OF COURSE.

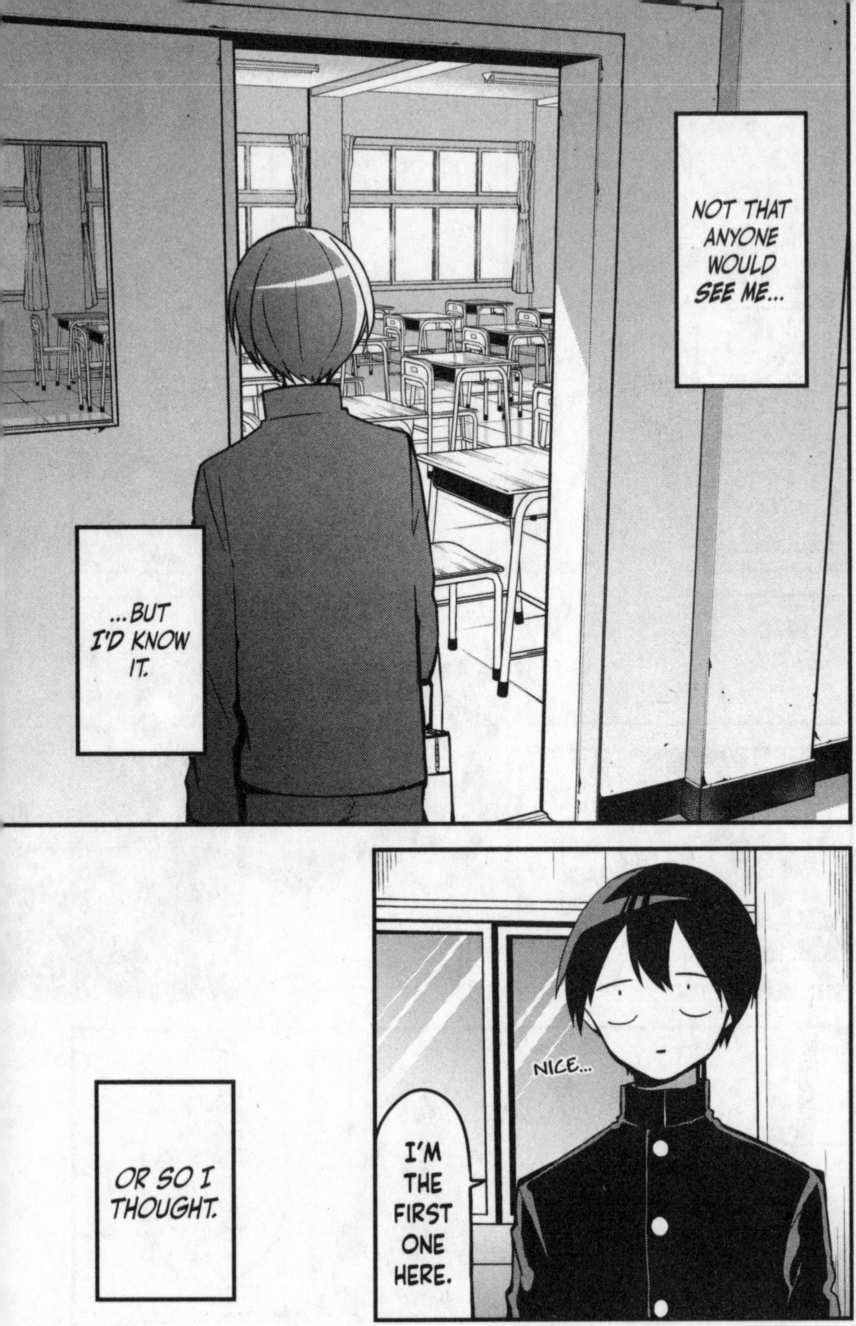
NOT THAT ANYONE WOULD SEE ME...
...BUT I'D KNOW IT.
NICE...
I'M THE FIRST ONE HERE.
OR SO I THOUGHT.

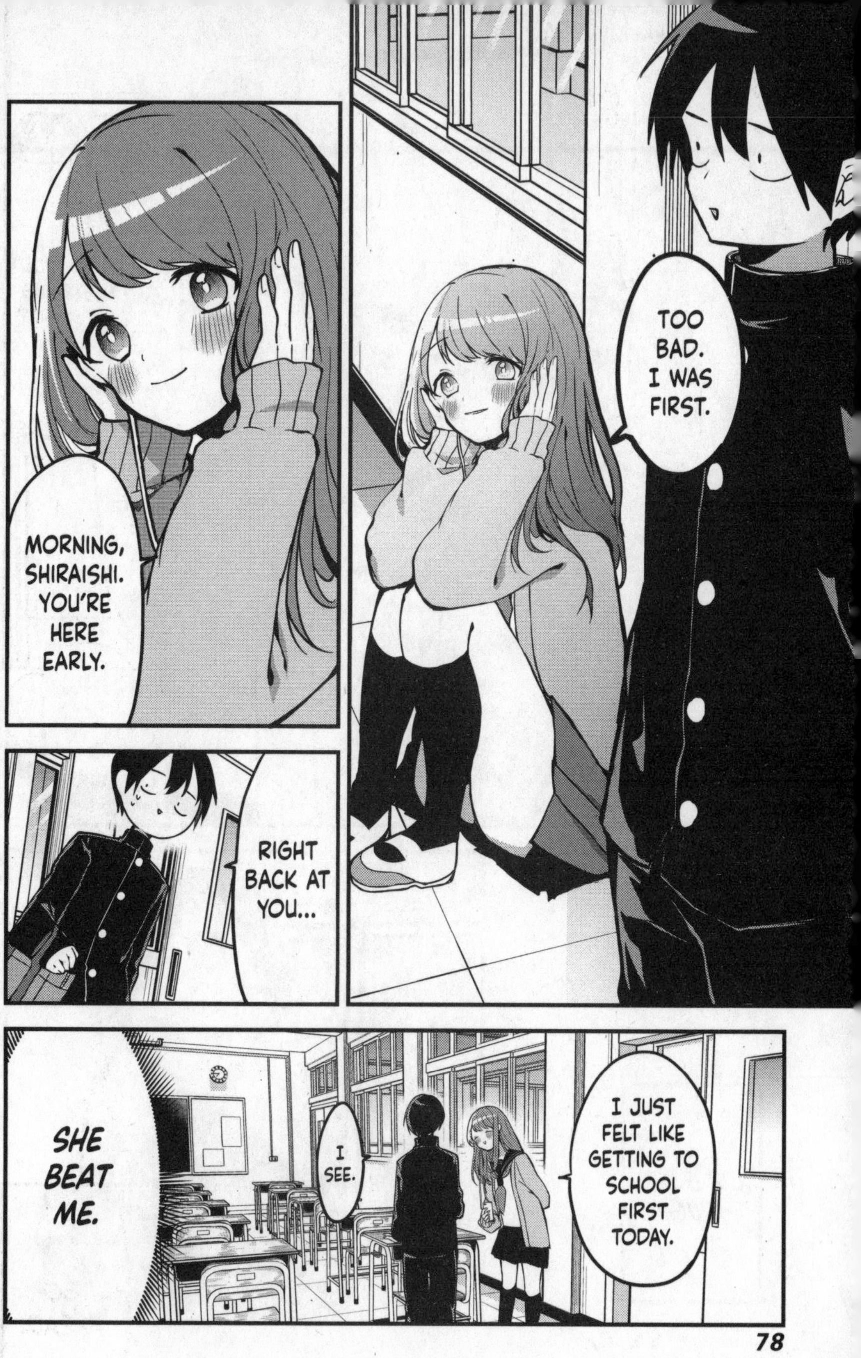
TOO BAD. I WAS FIRST.
MORNING, SHIRAISHI. YOU'RE HERE EARLY.
RIGHT BACK AT YOU...
I JUST FELT LIKE GETTING TO SCHOOL FIRST TODAY.
I SEE.
SHE BEAT ME.

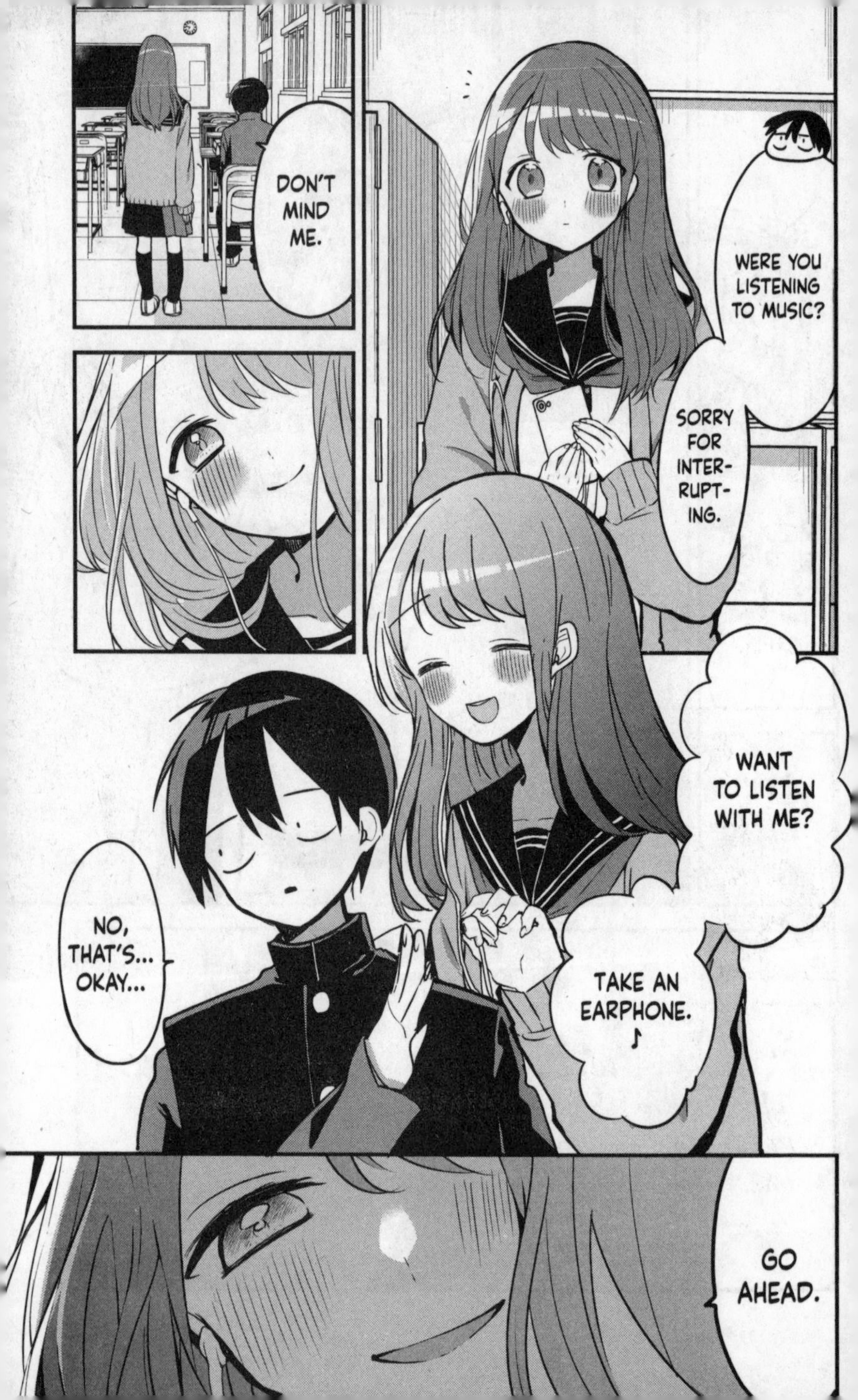
WERE YOU LISTENING TO MUSIC?
SORRY FOR INTER-RUPT-ING.
DON'T MIND ME.
WANT TO LISTEN WITH ME?
TAKE AN EARPHONE. ♪
NO, THAT'S... OKAY...
GO AHEAD.

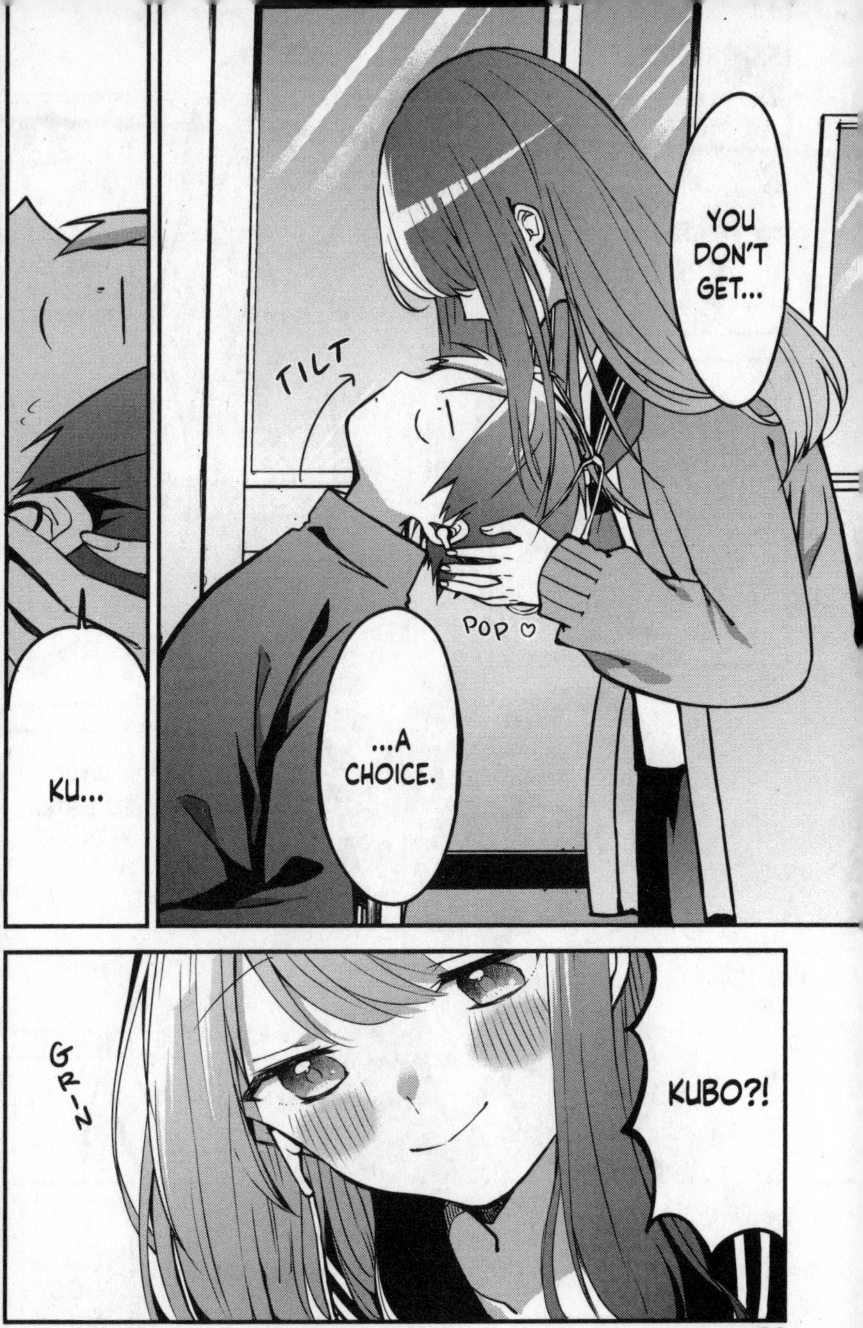
YOU DON'T GET...
TILT
POP ♡
...A CHOICE.
KU...
KUBO?!
GRIN

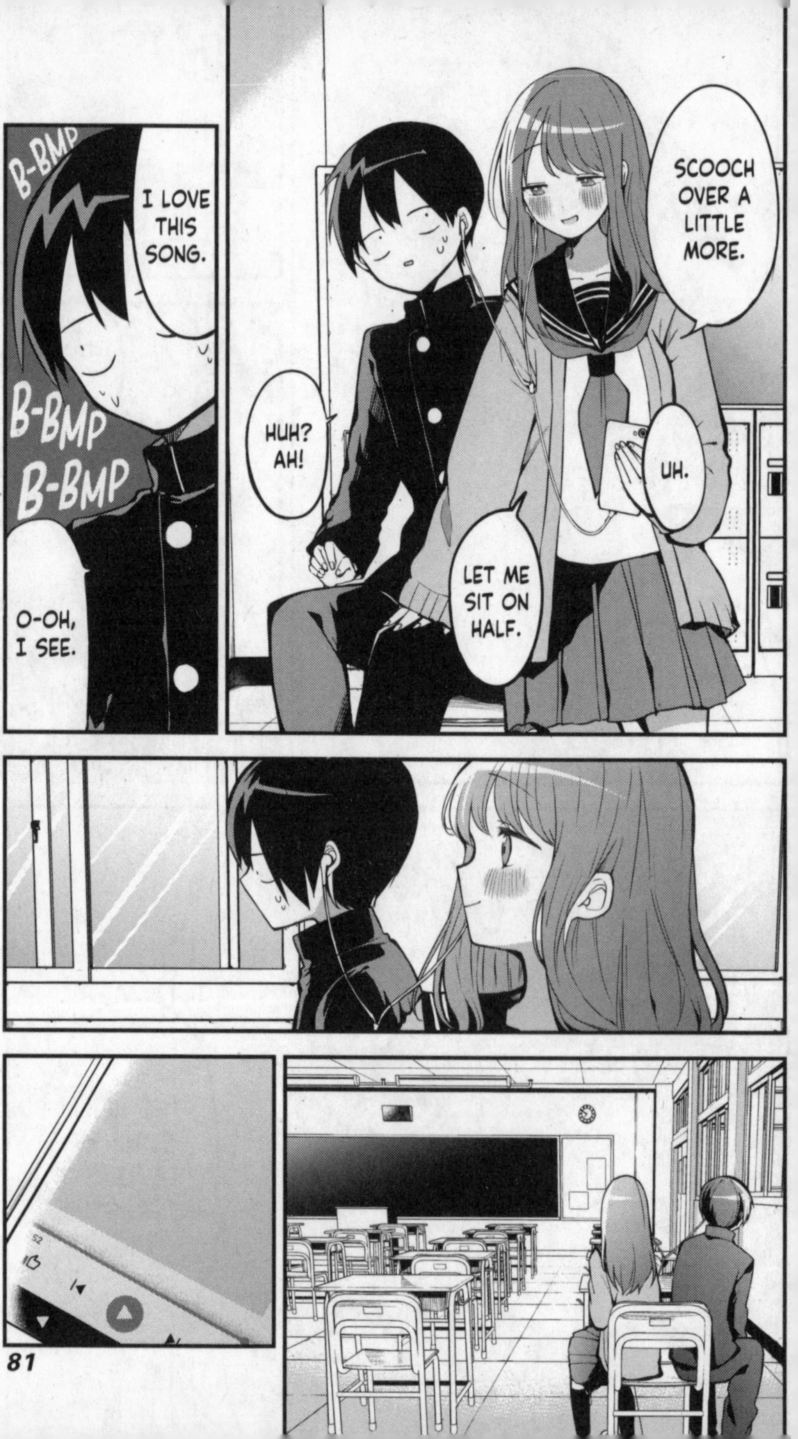
SCOOCH OVER A LITTLE MORE.
UH.
HUH? AH!
LET ME SIT ON HALF.
B-BMP
I LOVE THIS SONG.
B-BMP
B-BMP
O-OH, I SEE.

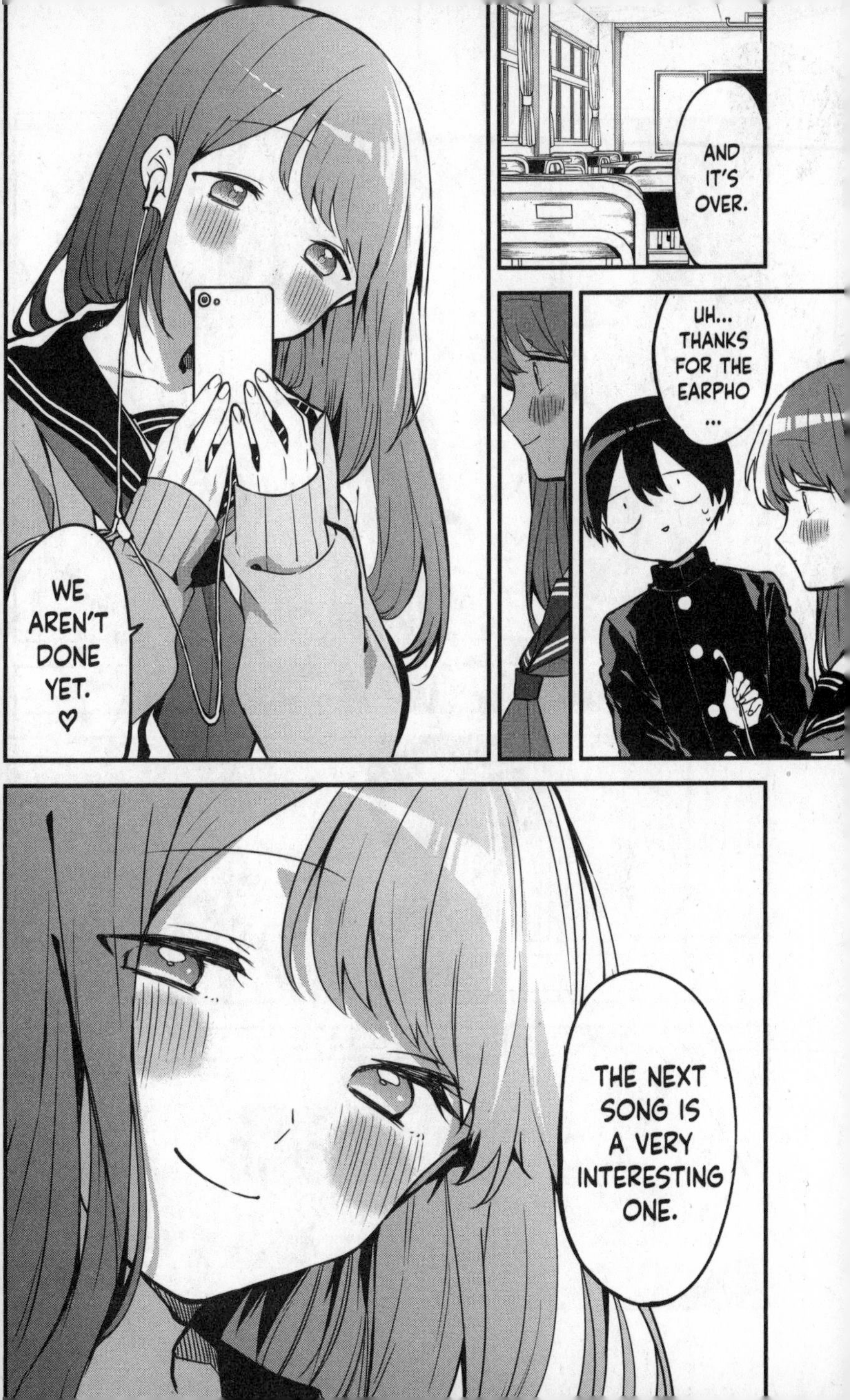
AND IT'S OVER.
UH... THANKS FOR THE EARPHO ...
WE AREN'T DONE YET. ♡
THE NEXT SONG IS A VERY INTERESTING ONE.

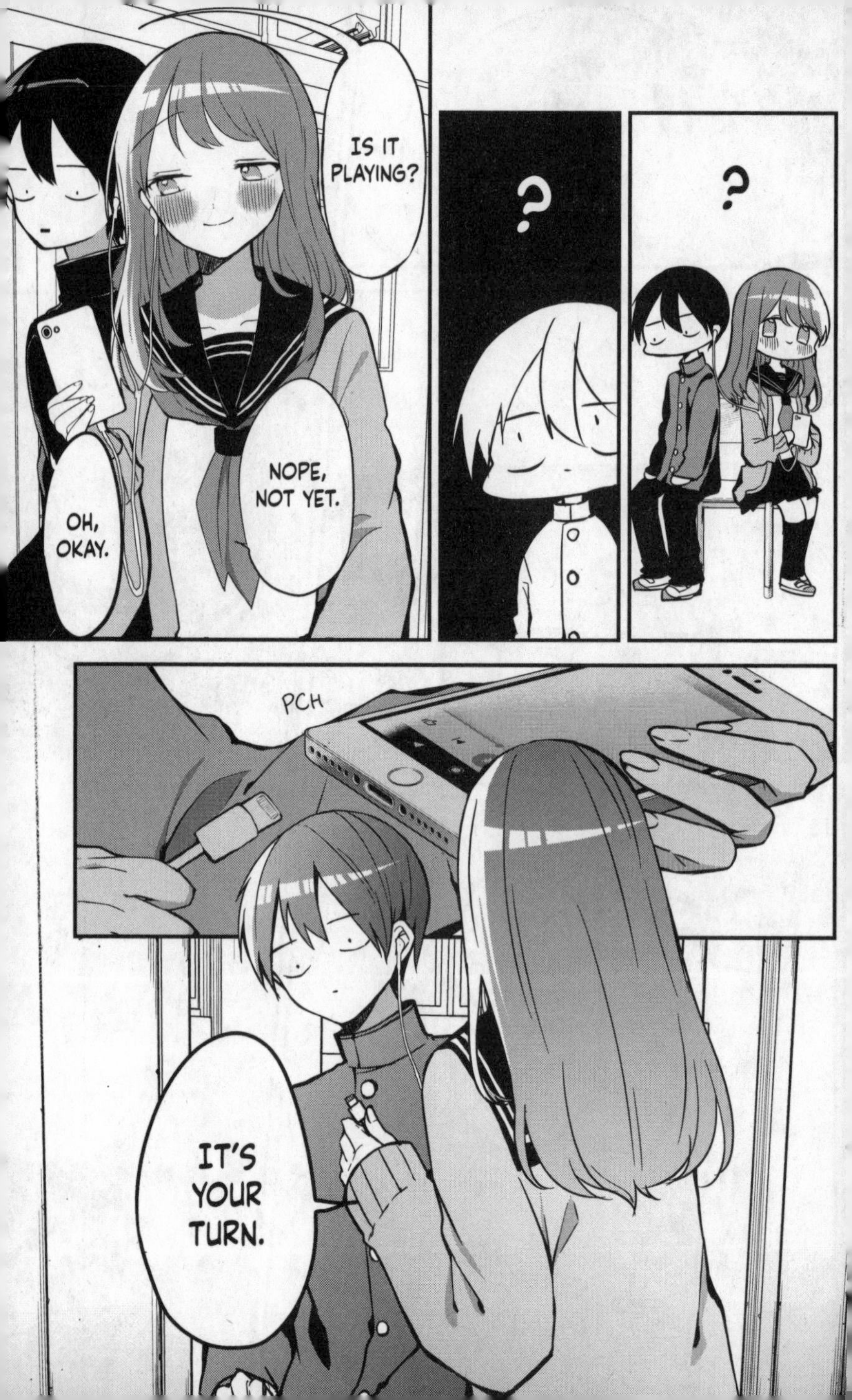
?
?
IS IT PLAYING?
NOPE, NOT YET.
OH, OKAY.
PCH
IT'S YOUR TURN.

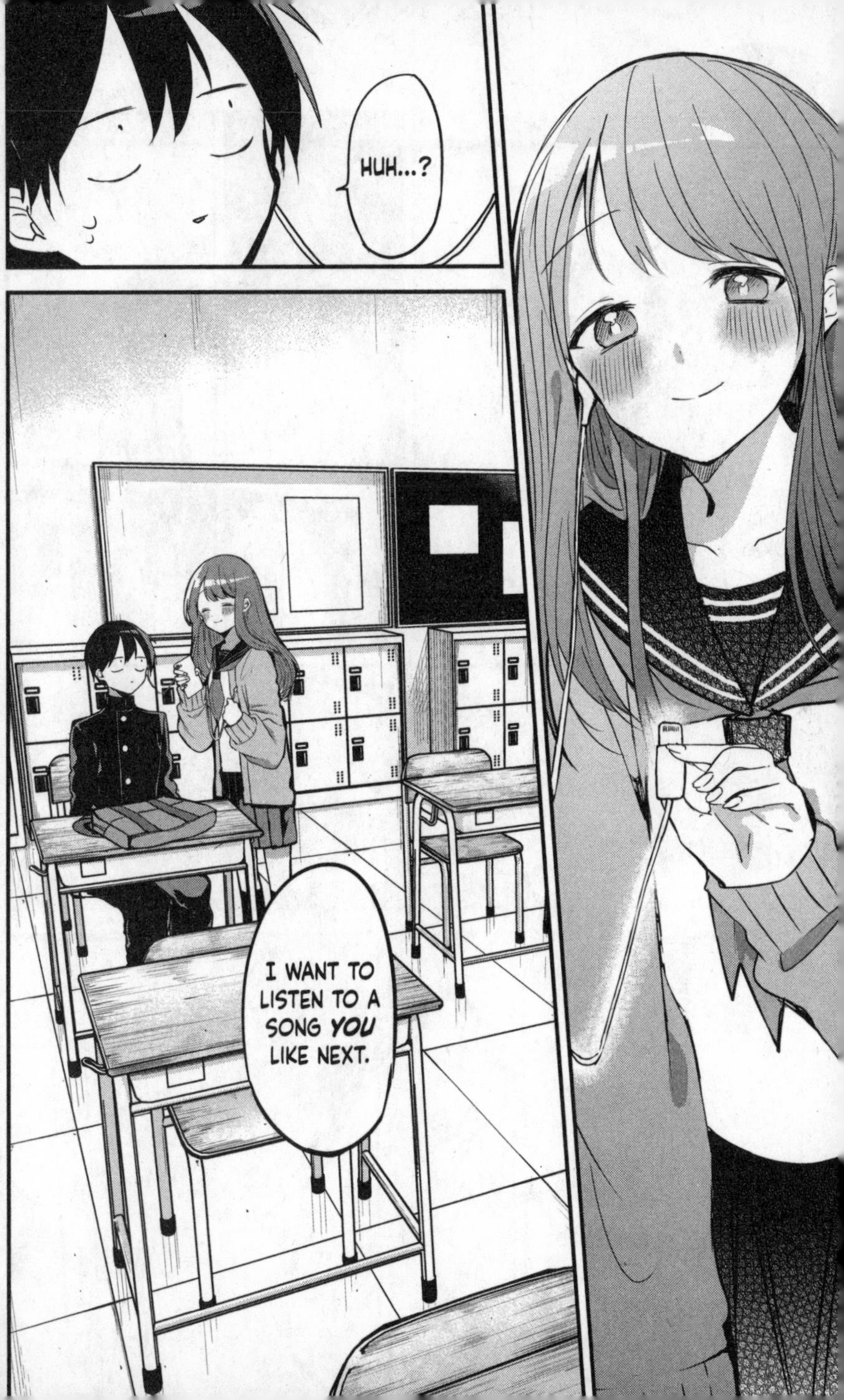
HUH...?
I WANT TO LISTEN TO A SONG YOU LIKE NEXT.

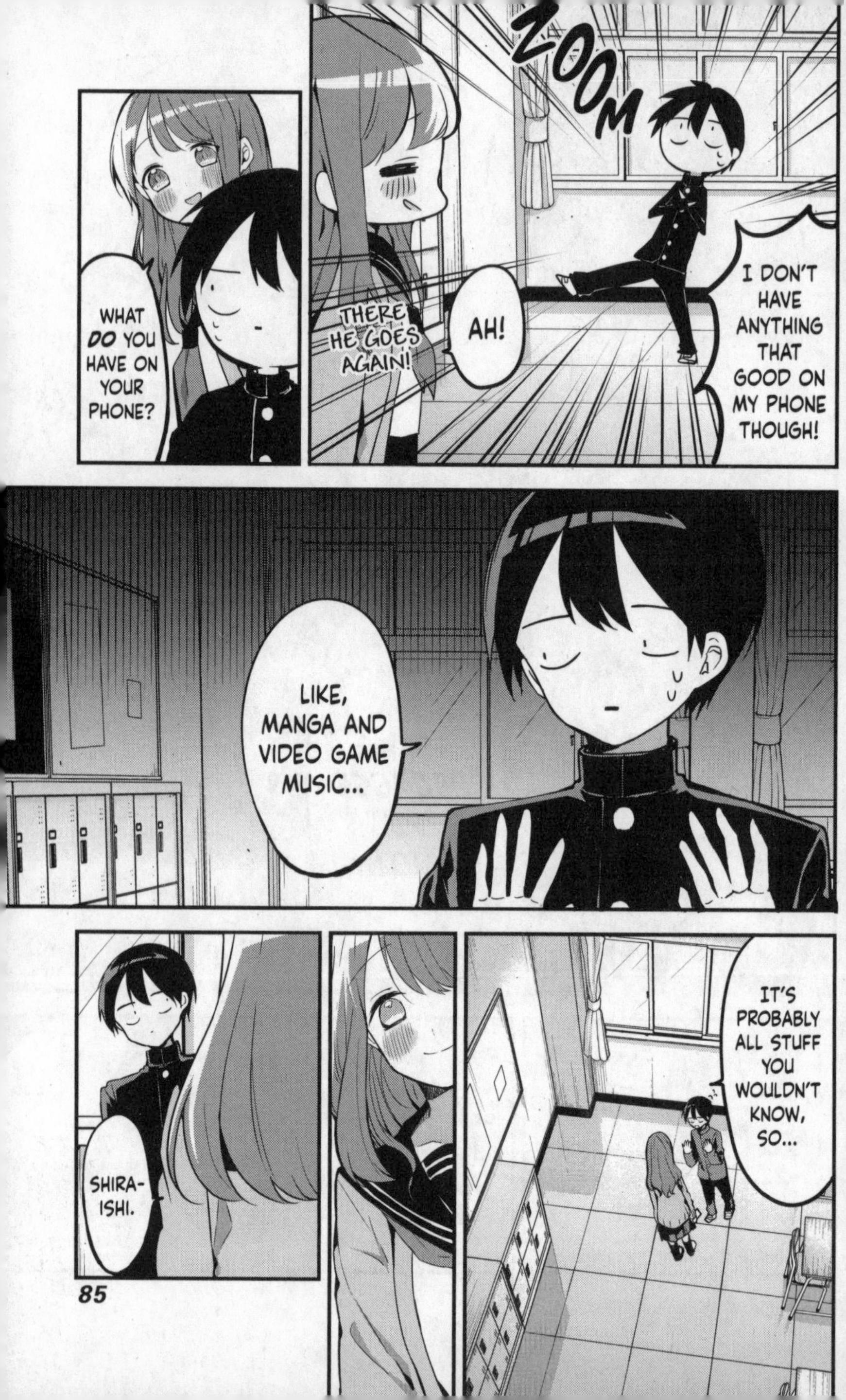
ZOOM
I DON'T HAVE ANYTHING THAT GOOD ON MY PHONE THOUGH!
AH!
THERE HE GOES AGAIN!
WHAT *DO* YOU HAVE ON YOUR PHONE?
LIKE, MANGA AND VIDEO GAME MUSIC...
IT'S PROBABLY ALL STUFF YOU WOULDN'T KNOW, SO...
SHIRA-ISHI.

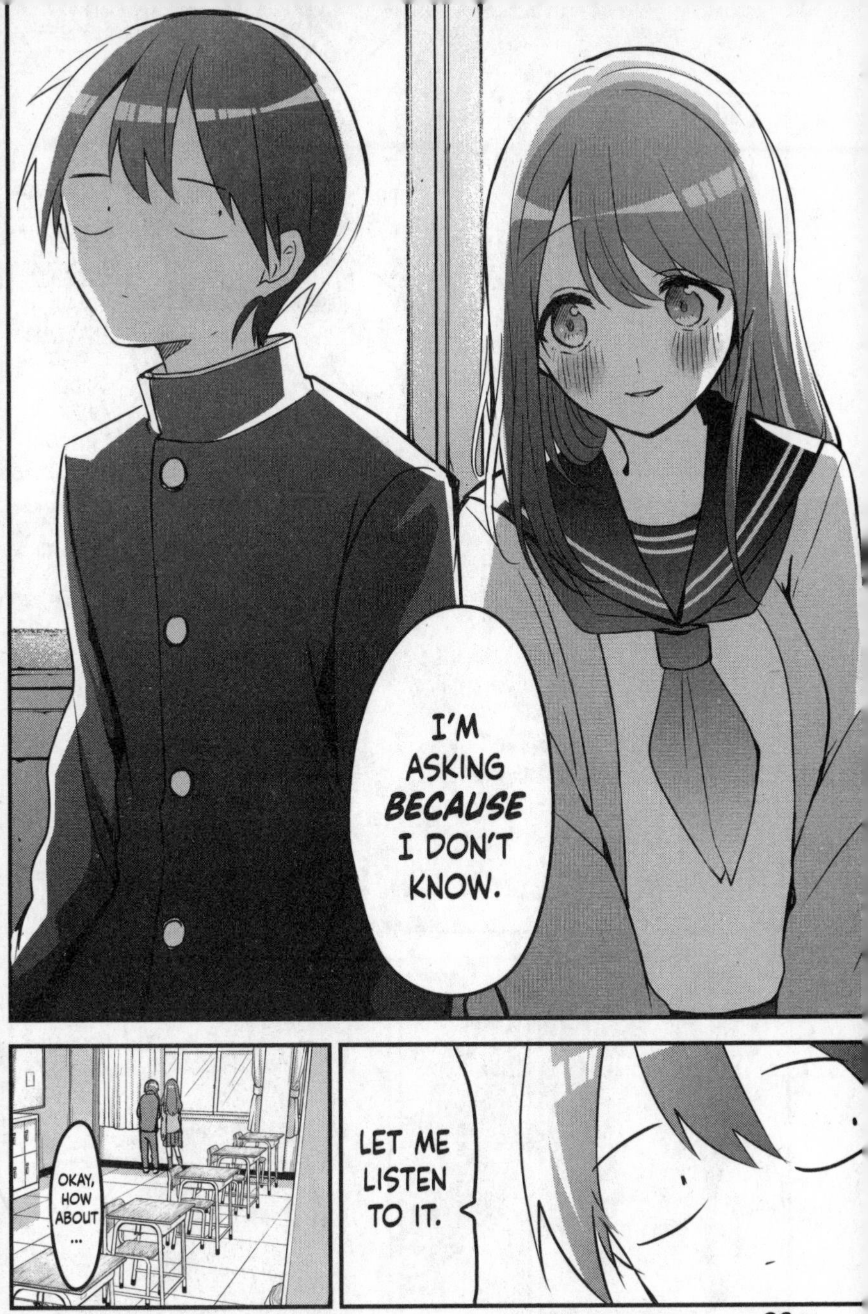
I'M ASKING BECAUSE I DON'T KNOW.
LET ME LISTEN TO IT.
OKAY, HOW ABOUT ...

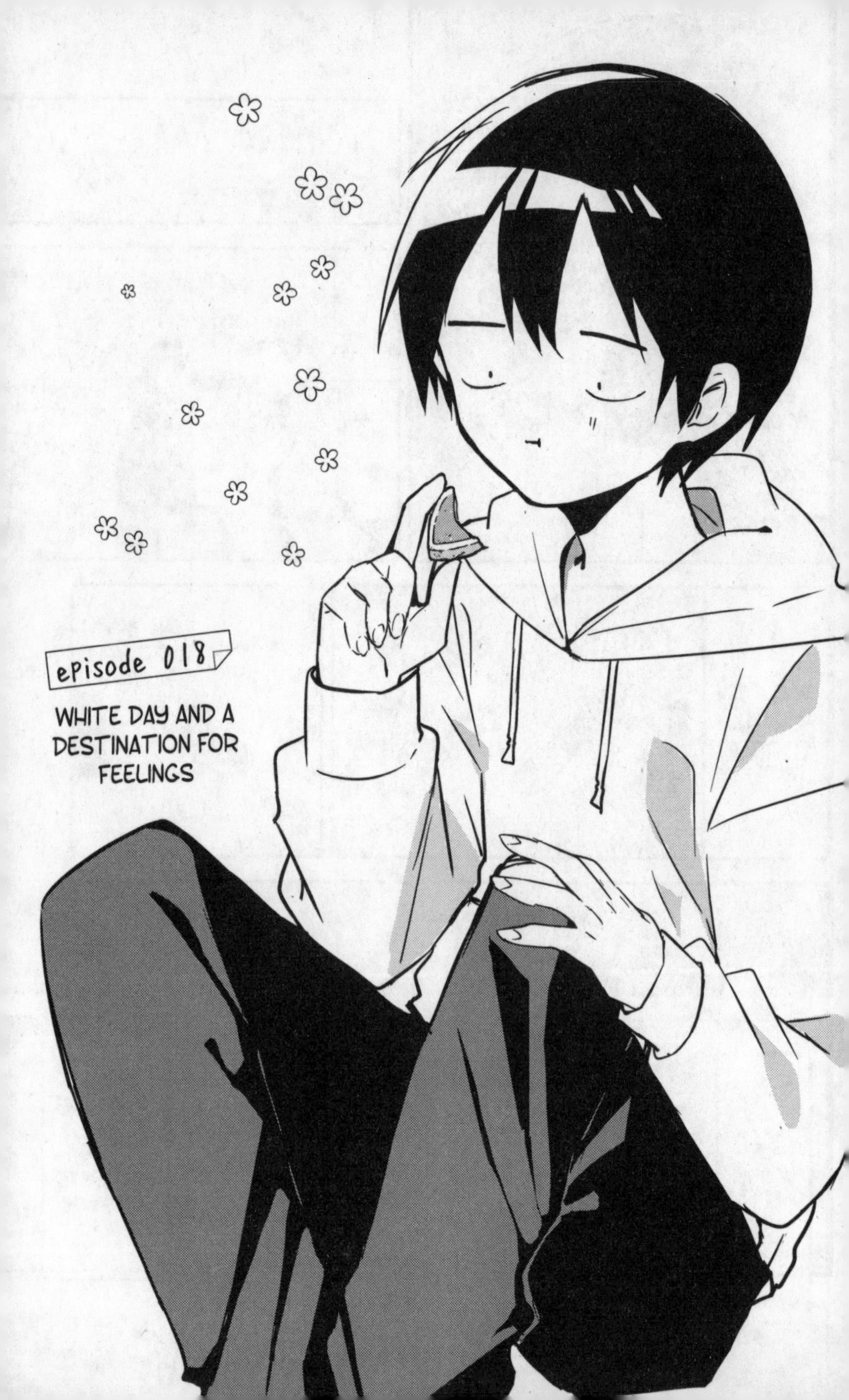
episode 018
WHITE DAY AND A DESTINATION FOR FEELINGS

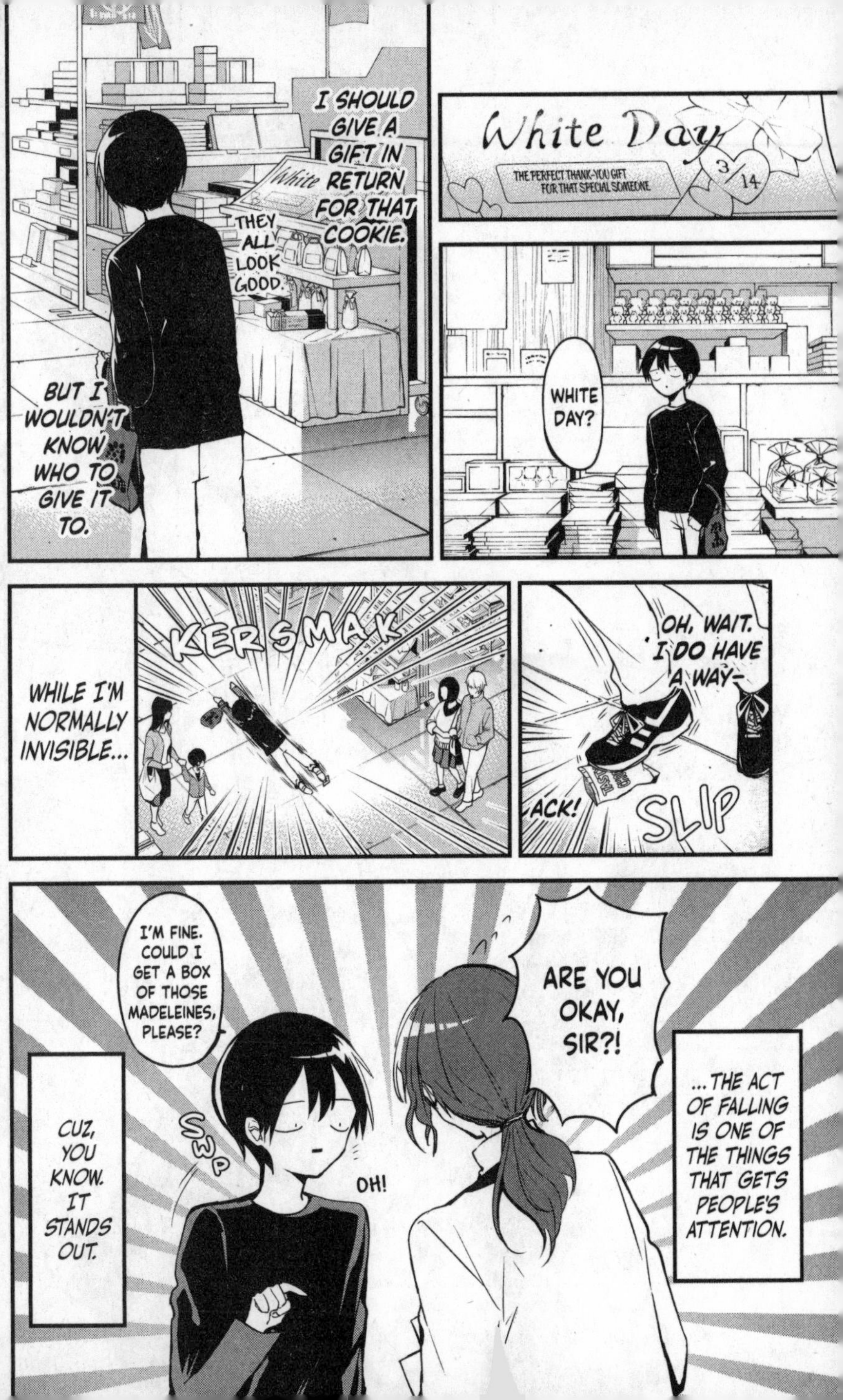
White Day
3/14
THE PERFECT THANK-YOU GIFT FOR THAT SPECIAL SOMEONE
WHITE DAY?
I SHOULD GIVE A GIFT IN RETURN FOR THAT COOKIE.
THEY ALL LOOK GOOD.
BUT I WOULDN'T KNOW WHO TO GIVE IT TO.
OH, WAIT. I DO HAVE A WAY—
ACK!
SLIP
WHILE I'M NORMALLY INVISIBLE...
KERSMAK
...THE ACT OF FALLING IS ONE OF THE THINGS THAT GETS PEOPLE'S ATTENTION.
ARE YOU OKAY, SIR?!
I'M FINE. COULD I GET A BOX OF THOSE MADELEINES, PLEASE?
OH!
SWP
CUZ, YOU KNOW. IT STANDS OUT.

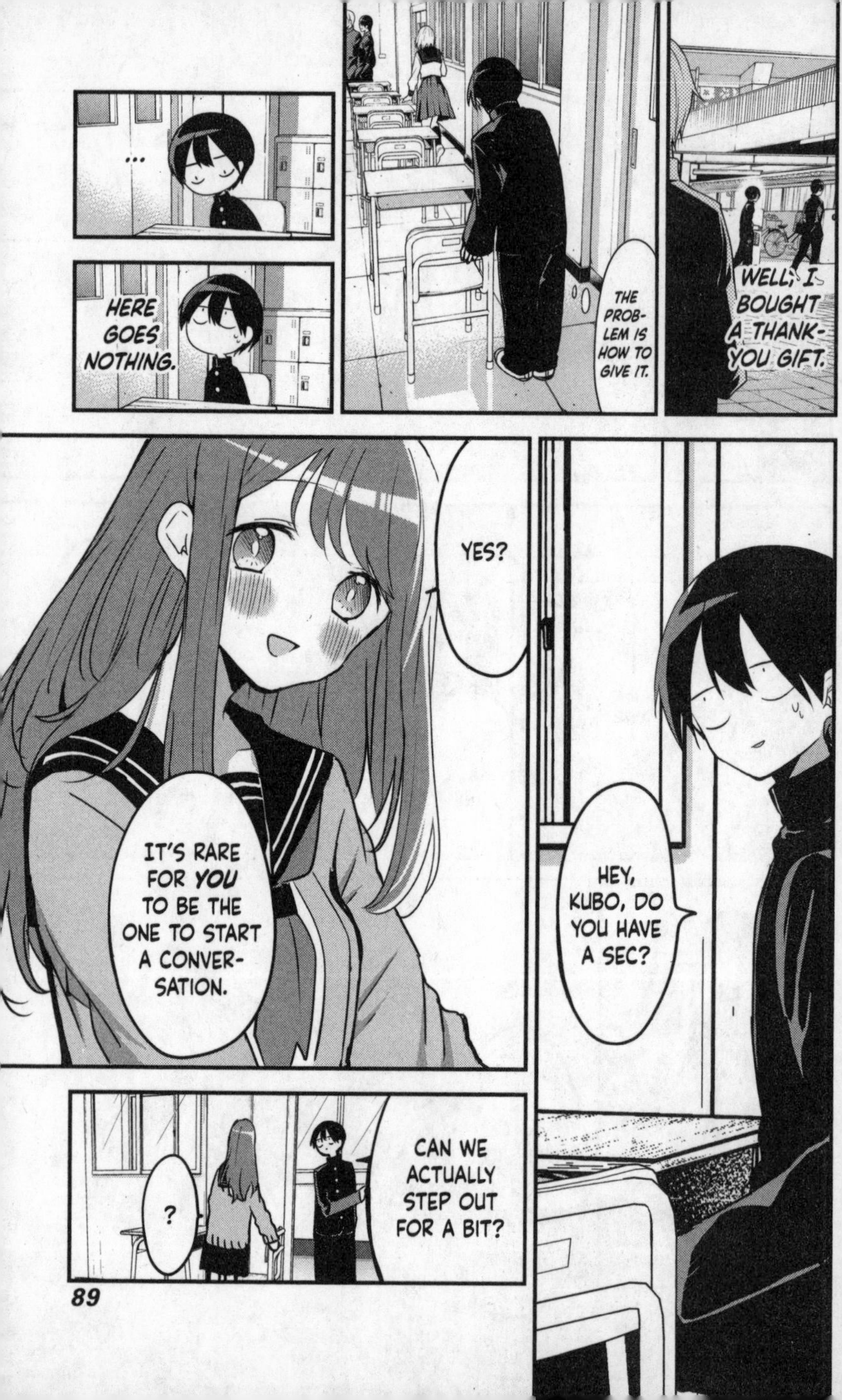
WELL, I BOUGHT A THANK-YOU GIFT.
THE PROBLEM IS HOW TO GIVE IT.
...
HERE GOES NOTHING.
HEY, KUBO, DO YOU HAVE A SEC?
YES?
IT'S RARE FOR *YOU* TO BE THE ONE TO START A CONVERSATION.
CAN WE ACTUALLY STEP OUT FOR A BIT?
?

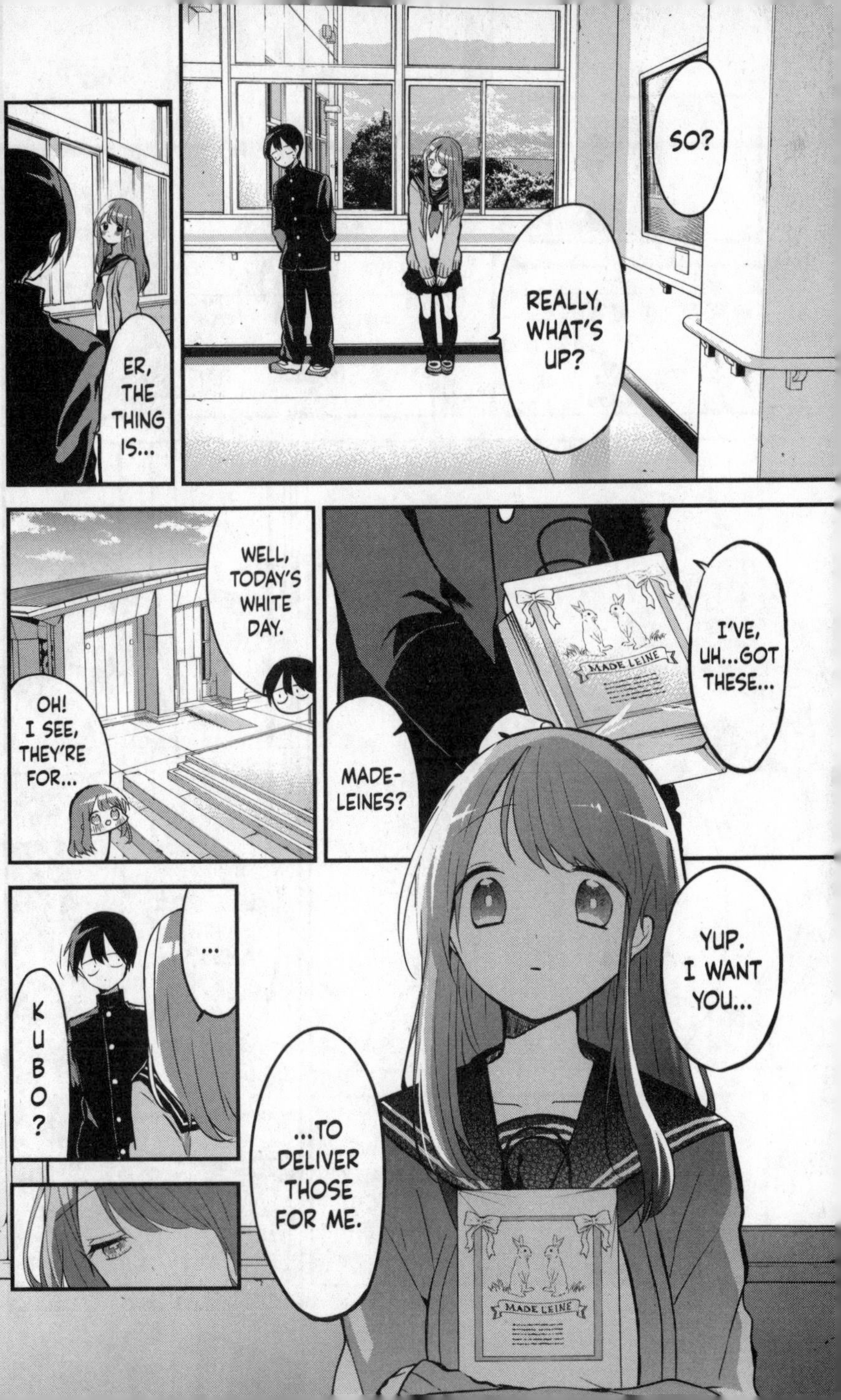
SO?
REALLY, WHAT'S UP?
ER, THE THING IS...
I'VE, UH...GOT THESE...
MADE LEINE
MADE-LEINES?
WELL, TODAY'S WHITE DAY.
OH! I SEE, THEY'RE FOR...
YUP. I WANT YOU...
...TO DELIVER THOSE FOR ME.
MADE LEINE
...
KUBO?

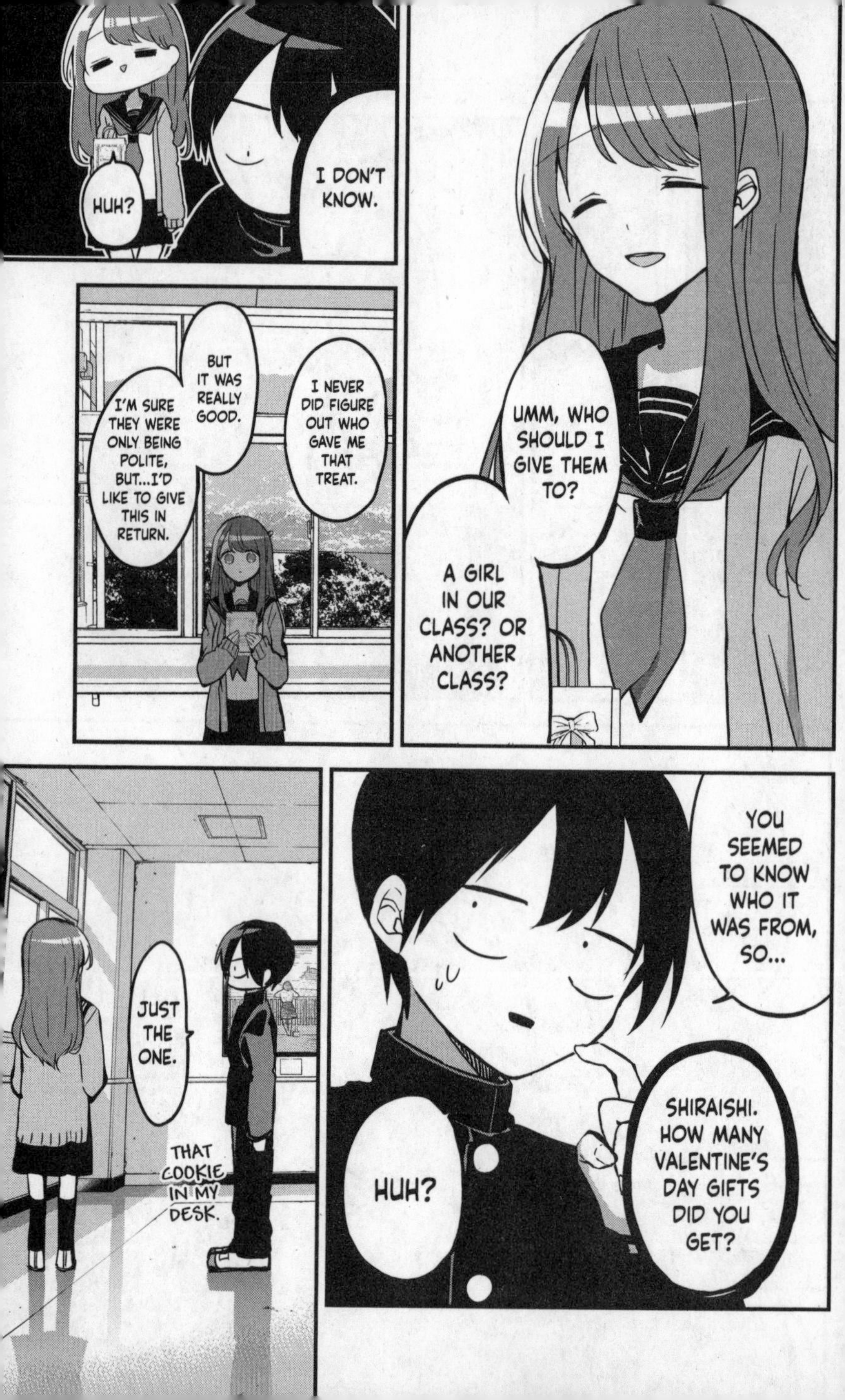
UMM, WHO SHOULD I GIVE THEM TO?
A GIRL IN OUR CLASS? OR ANOTHER CLASS?
I DON'T KNOW.
HUH?
I NEVER DID FIGURE OUT WHO GAVE ME THAT TREAT.
BUT IT WAS REALLY GOOD.
I'M SURE THEY WERE ONLY BEING POLITE, BUT...I'D LIKE TO GIVE THIS IN RETURN.
YOU SEEMED TO KNOW WHO IT WAS FROM, SO...
SHIRAISHI. HOW MANY VALENTINE'S DAY GIFTS DID YOU GET?
HUH?
JUST THE ONE.
THAT COOKIE IN MY DESK.

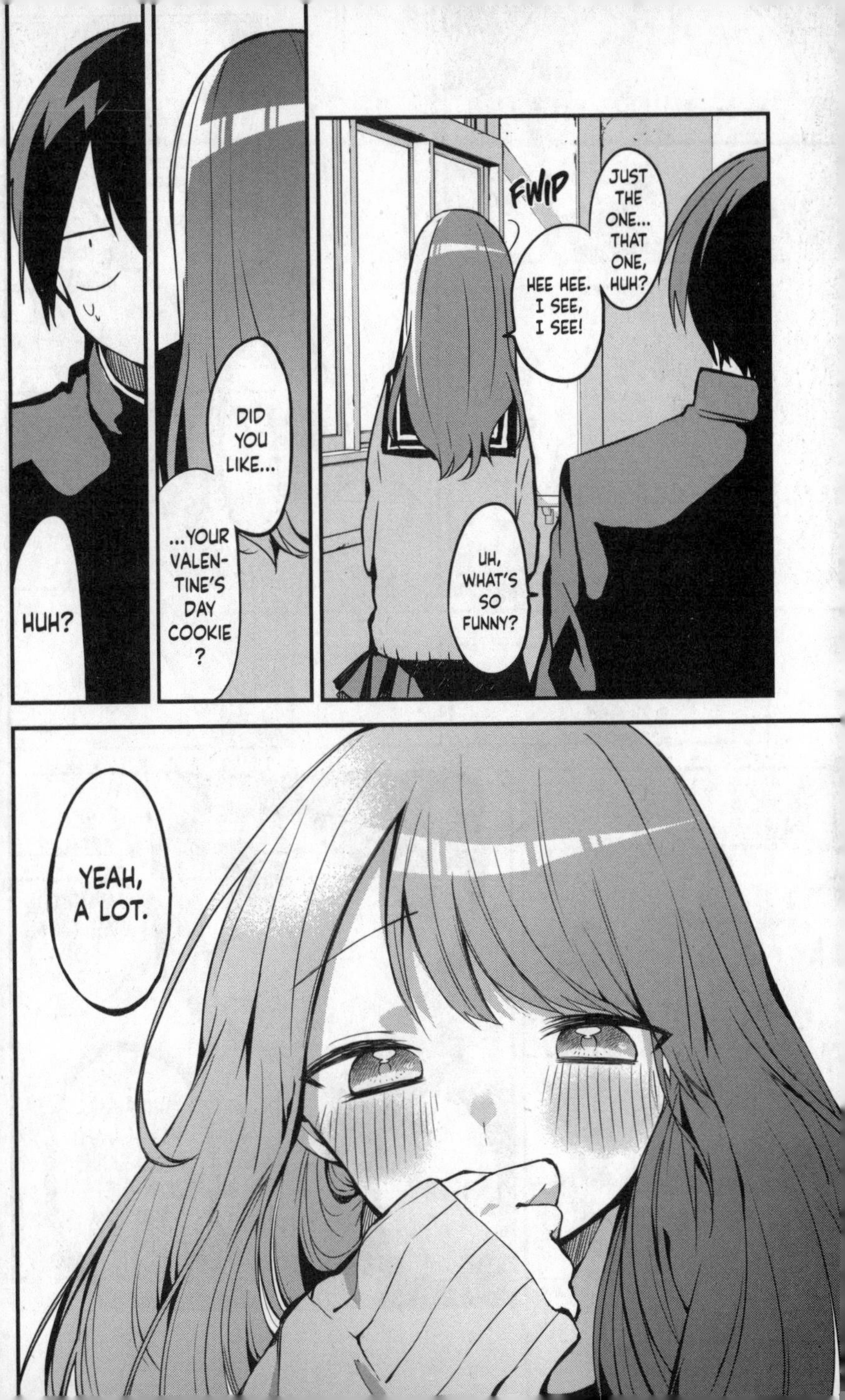
JUST THE ONE... THAT ONE, HUH?
FWIP
HEE HEE. I SEE, I SEE!
UH, WHAT'S SO FUNNY?
DID YOU LIKE...
...YOUR VALENTINE'S DAY COOKIE?
HUH?
YEAH, A LOT.

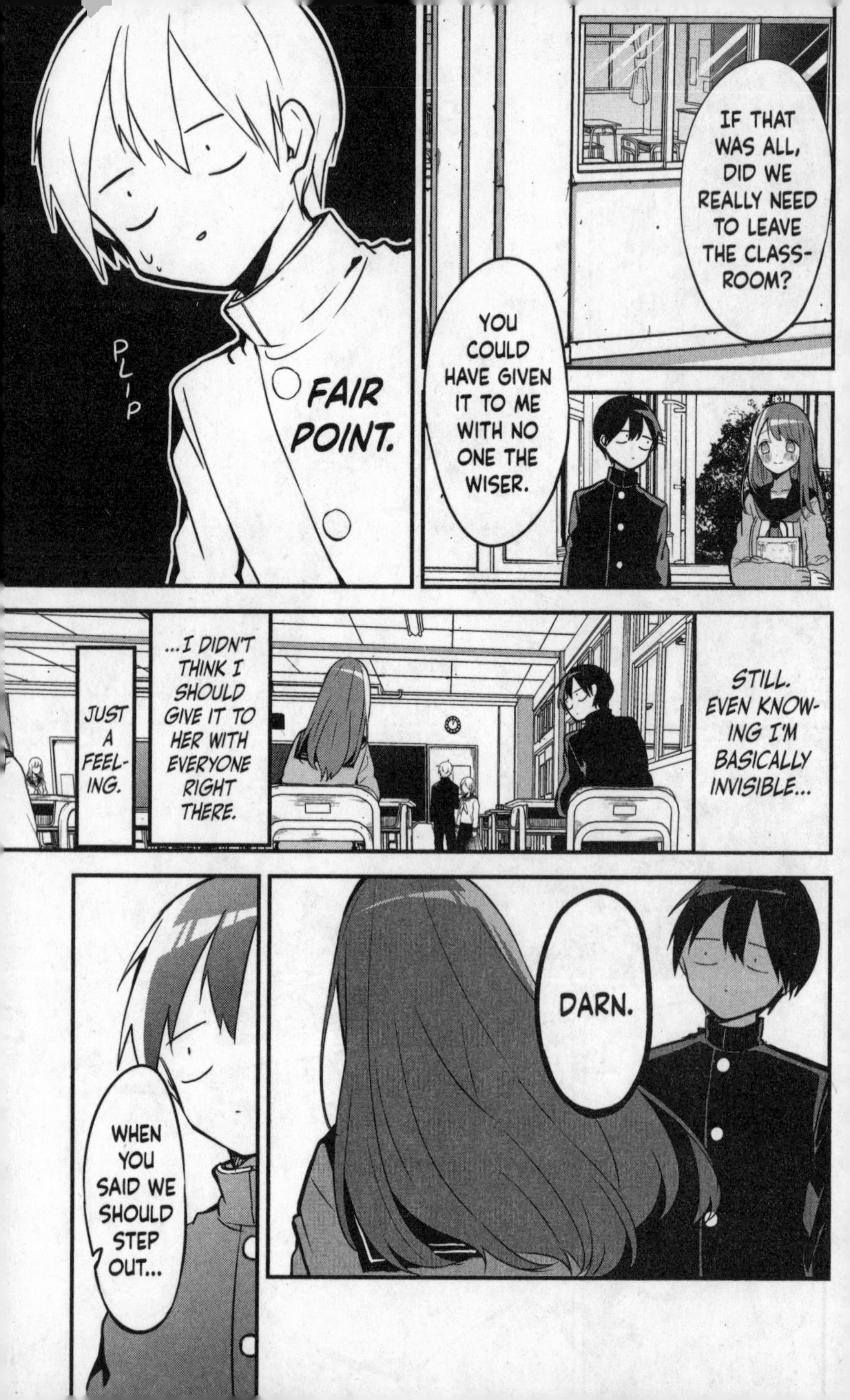
IF THAT WAS ALL, DID WE REALLY NEED TO LEAVE THE CLASSROOM?
YOU COULD HAVE GIVEN IT TO ME WITH NO ONE THE WISER.
FAIR POINT.
PLIP
STILL. EVEN KNOWING I'M BASICALLY INVISIBLE...
...I DIDN'T THINK I SHOULD GIVE IT TO HER WITH EVERYONE RIGHT THERE.
JUST A FEELING.
DARN.
WHEN YOU SAID WE SHOULD STEP OUT...

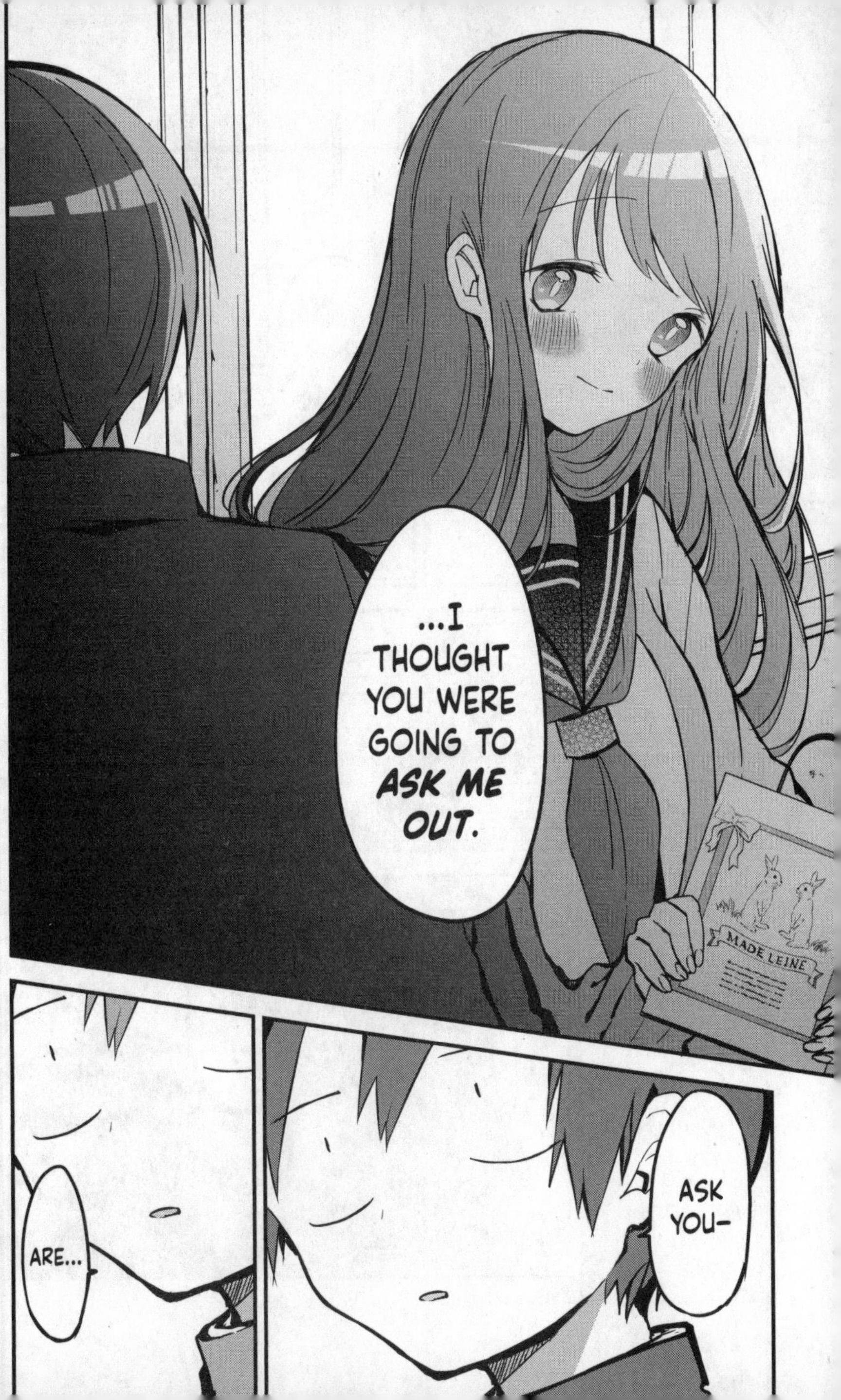
...I THOUGHT YOU WERE GOING TO ASK ME OUT.
MADE LEINE
ASK YOU—
ARE...

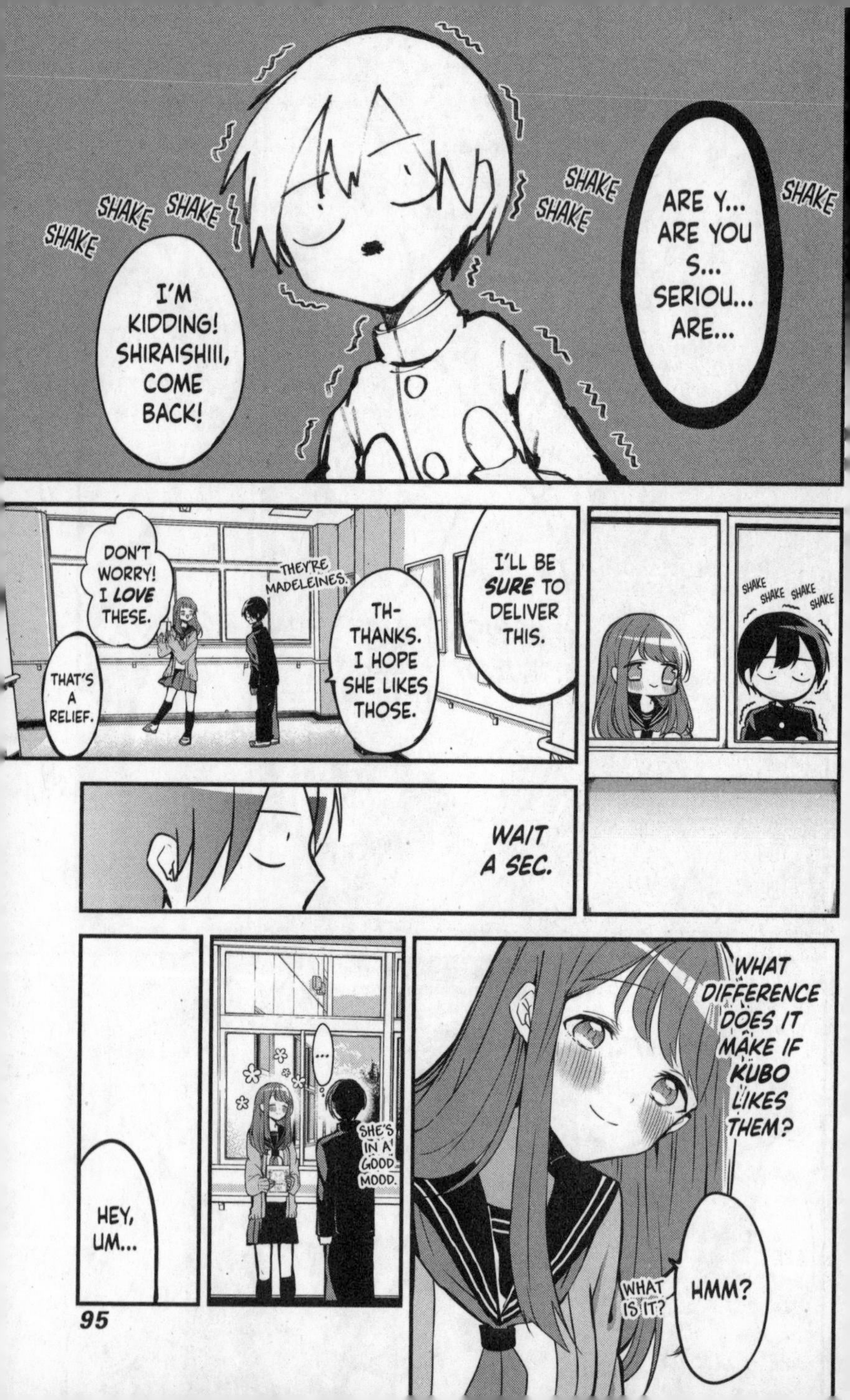
SHAKE
ARE Y... ARE YOU S... SERIOU... ARE...
SHAKE
SHAKE
SHAKE
SHAKE
I'M KIDDING! SHIRAISHIII, COME BACK!
SHAKE
SHAKE SHAKE SHAKE SHAKE
I'LL BE SURE TO DELIVER THIS.
TH- THANKS. I HOPE SHE LIKES THOSE.
THEY'RE MADELEINES.
DON'T WORRY! I LOVE THESE.
THAT'S A RELIEF.
WAIT A SEC.
WHAT DIFFERENCE DOES IT MAKE IF KUBO LIKES THEM?
HMM?
WHAT IS IT?
...
SHE'S IN A GOOD MOOD.
HEY, UM...

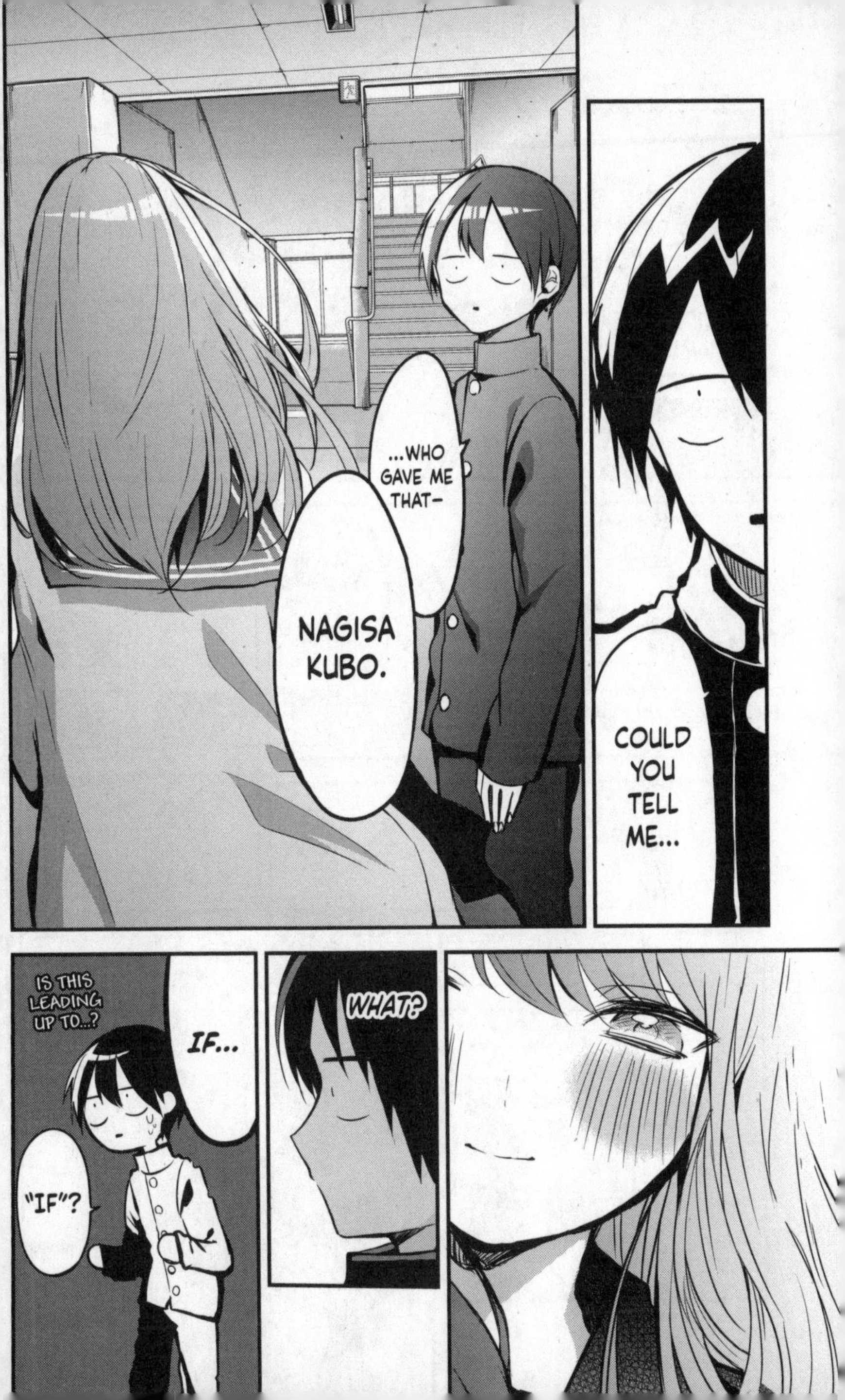
COULD YOU TELL ME...
...WHO GAVE ME THAT—
NAGISA KUBO.
WHAT?
IF...
IS THIS LEADING UP TO...?
"IF"?

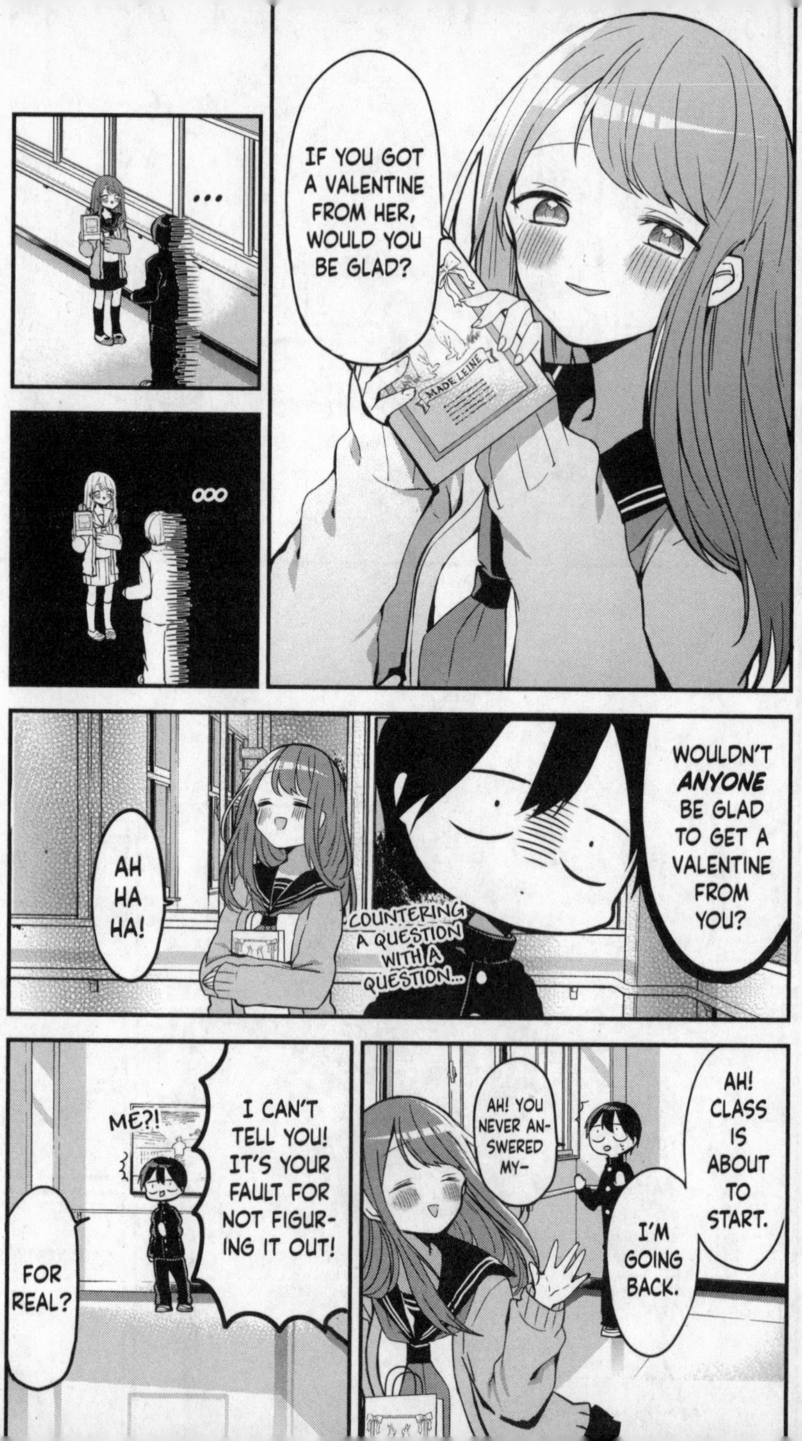
IF YOU GOT A VALENTINE FROM HER, WOULD YOU BE GLAD?
MADE LEINE
...
ooo
WOULDN'T ANYONE BE GLAD TO GET A VALENTINE FROM YOU?
COUNTERING A QUESTION WITH A QUESTION...
AH HA HA!
AH! CLASS IS ABOUT TO START.
I'M GOING BACK.
AH! YOU NEVER AN-SWERED MY–
I CAN'T TELL YOU! IT'S YOUR FAULT FOR NOT FIGUR-ING IT OUT!
ME?!
FOR REAL?

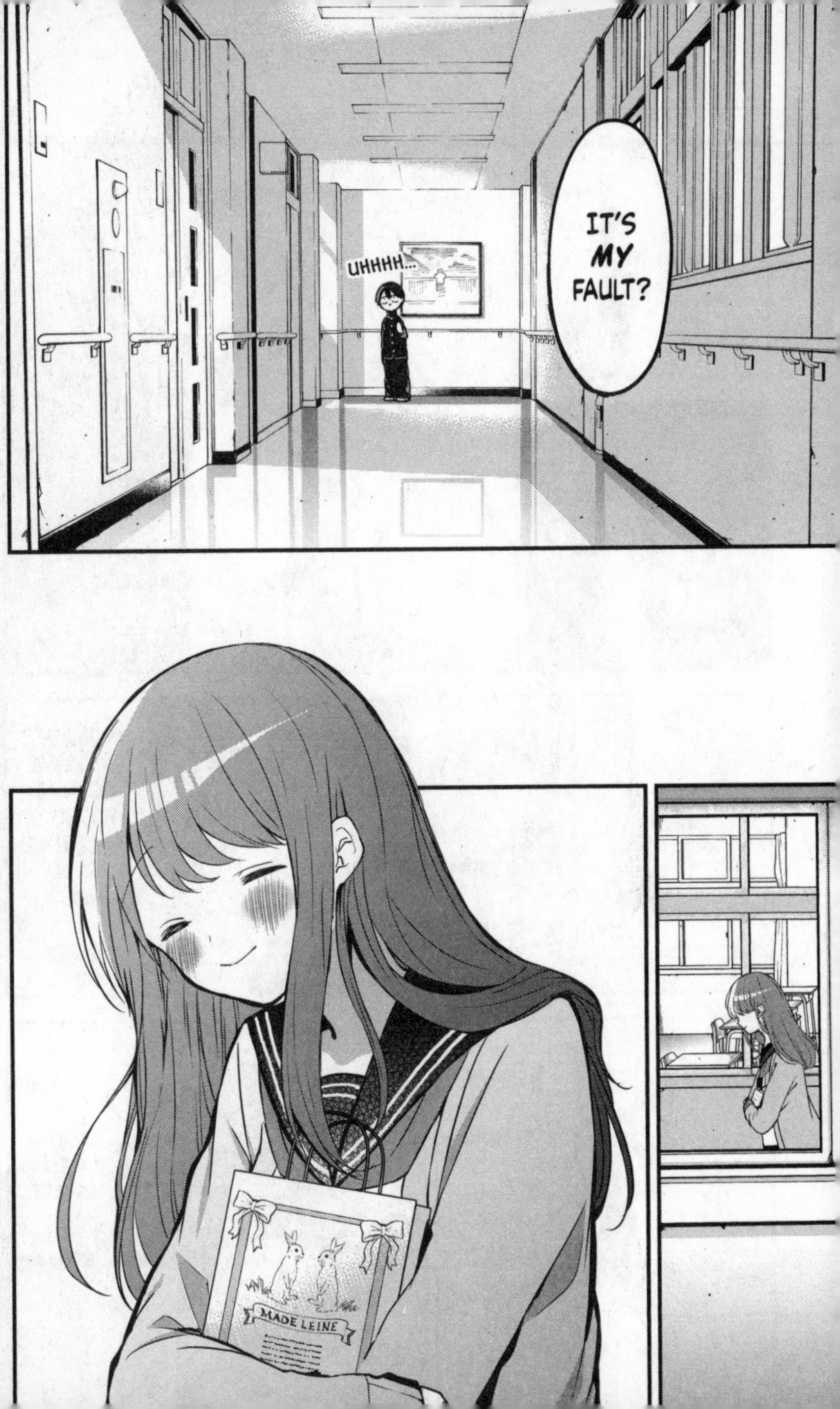
IT'S MY FAULT?
UHHHH...
MADE LEINE

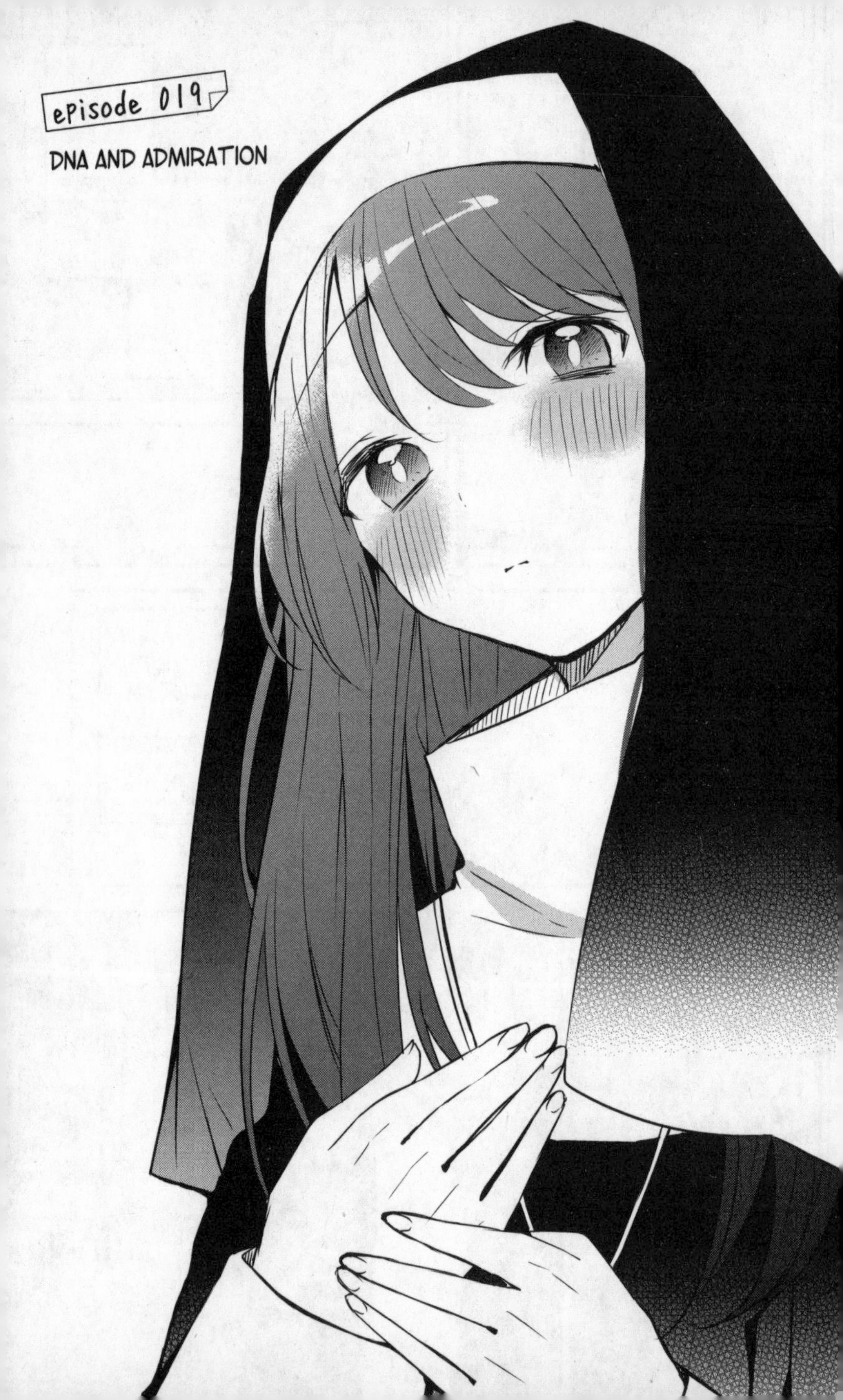
episode 019
DNA AND ADMIRATION

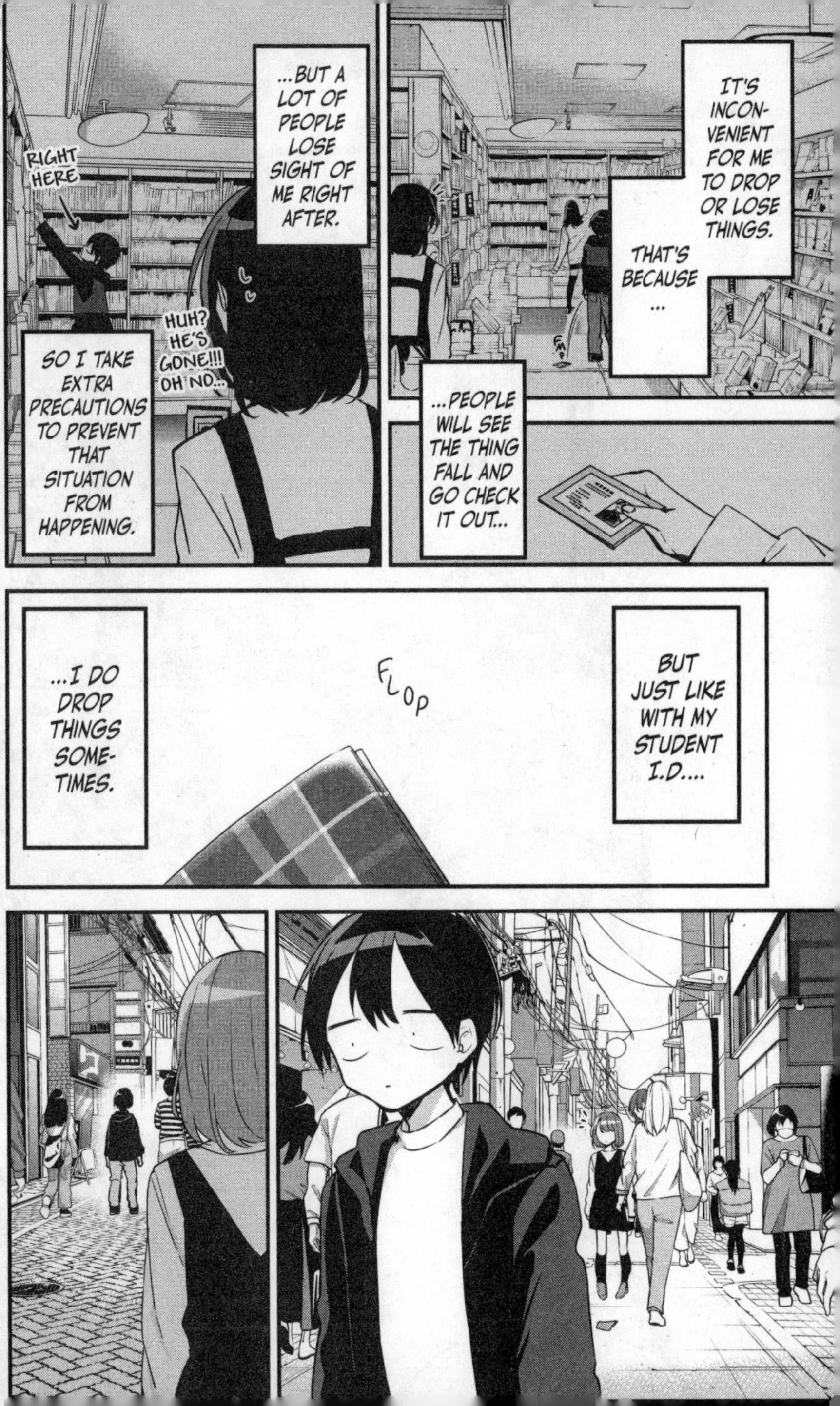
IT'S INCONVENIENT FOR ME TO DROP OR LOSE THINGS.
THAT'S BECAUSE ...
...PEOPLE WILL SEE THE THING FALL AND GO CHECK IT OUT...
...BUT A LOT OF PEOPLE LOSE SIGHT OF ME RIGHT AFTER.
RIGHT HERE
HUH? HE'S GONE!!! OH NO...
SO I TAKE EXTRA PRECAUTIONS TO PREVENT THAT SITUATION FROM HAPPENING.
BUT JUST LIKE WITH MY STUDENT I.D....
FLOP
...I DO DROP THINGS SOME-TIMES.

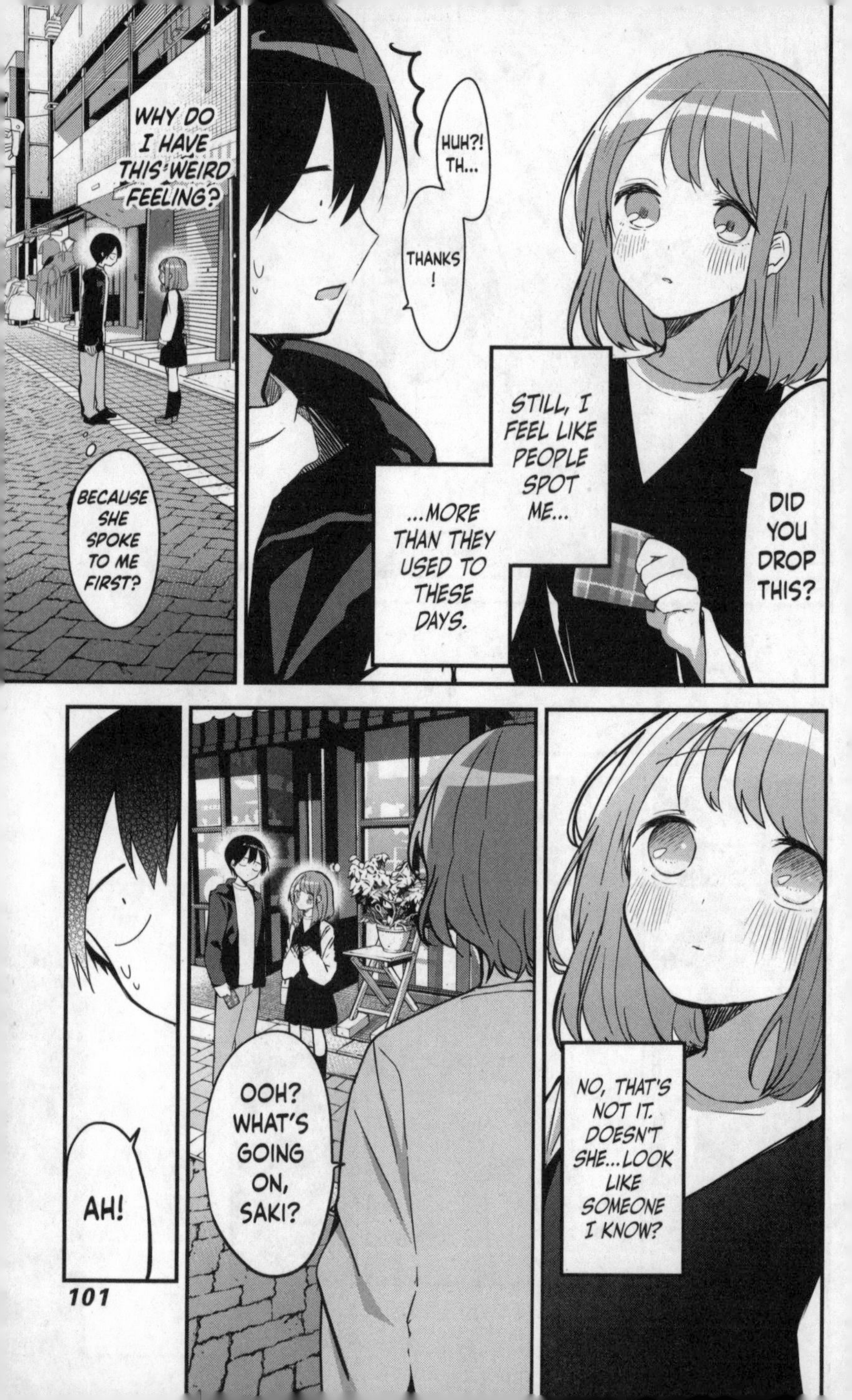
DID YOU DROP THIS?
HUH?! TH...
THANKS!
STILL, I FEEL LIKE PEOPLE SPOT ME...
...MORE THAN THEY USED TO THESE DAYS.
WHY DO I HAVE THIS WEIRD FEELING?
BECAUSE SHE SPOKE TO ME FIRST?
NO, THAT'S NOT IT. DOESN'T SHE...LOOK LIKE SOMEONE I KNOW?
OOH? WHAT'S GOING ON, SAKI?
AH!

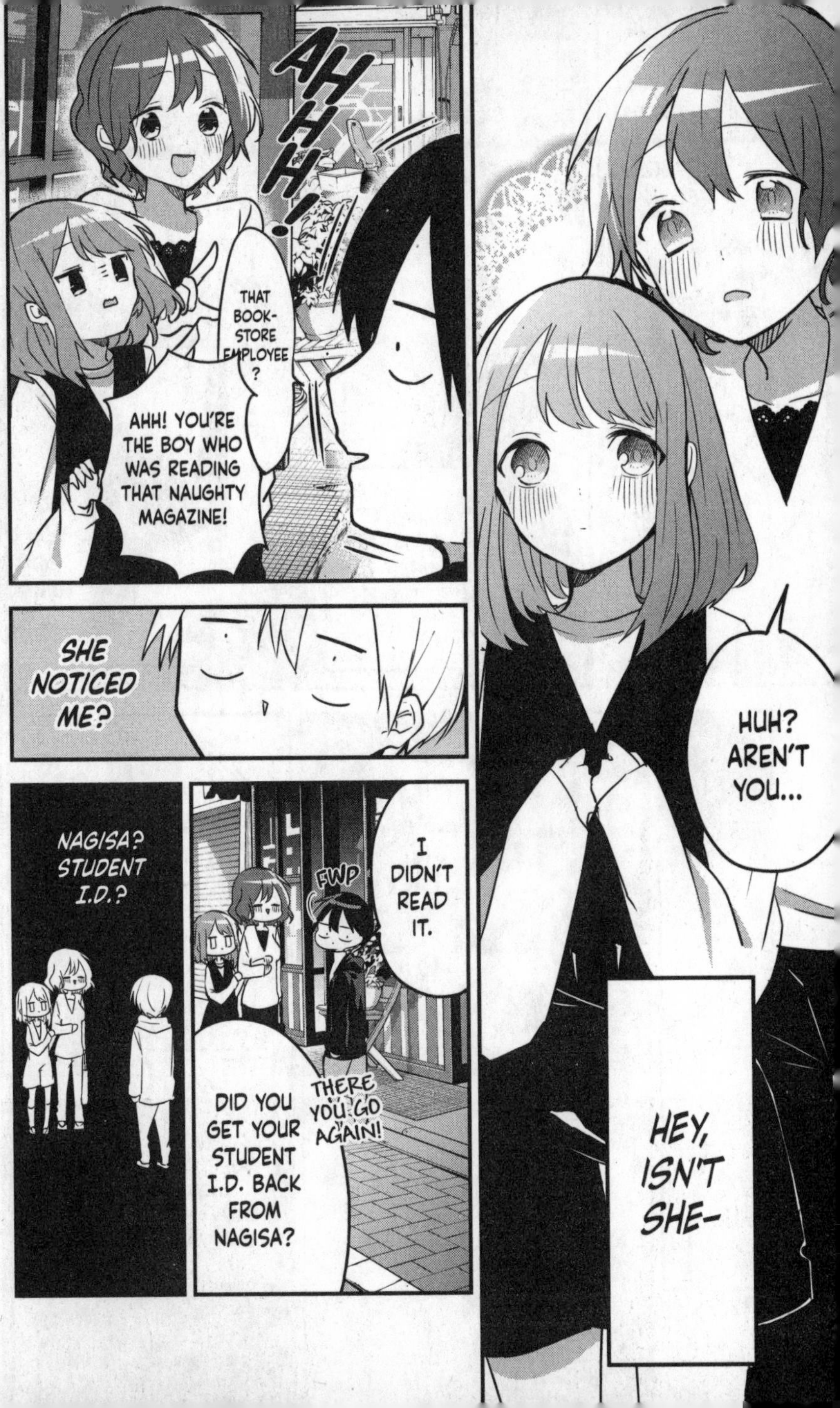
HUH? AREN'T YOU...
HEY, ISN'T SHE–
AHHHH!
THAT BOOK-STORE EMPLOYEE?
AHH! YOU'RE THE BOY WHO WAS READING THAT NAUGHTY MAGAZINE!
SHE NOTICED ME?
I DIDN'T READ IT.
FWP
THERE YOU GO AGAIN!
DID YOU GET YOUR STUDENT I.D. BACK FROM NAGISA?
NAGISA? STUDENT I.D.?

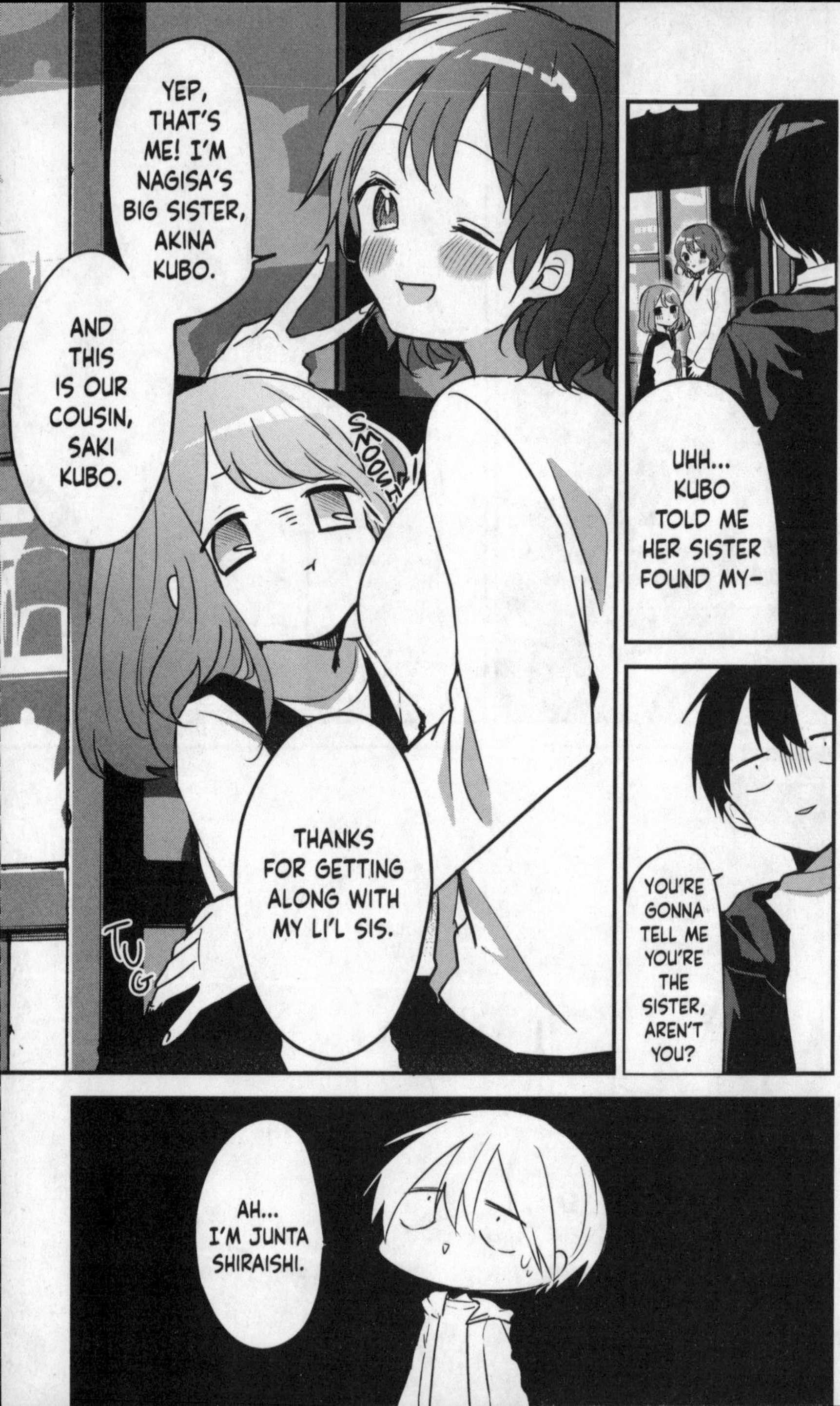
UHH... KUBO TOLD ME HER SISTER FOUND MY–
YOU'RE GONNA TELL ME YOU'RE THE SISTER, AREN'T YOU?
YEP, THAT'S ME! I'M NAGISA'S BIG SISTER, AKINA KUBO.
AND THIS IS OUR COUSIN, SAKI KUBO.
SMOOSH
THANKS FOR GETTING ALONG WITH MY LI'L SIS.
TUG
AH... I'M JUNTA SHIRAISHI.

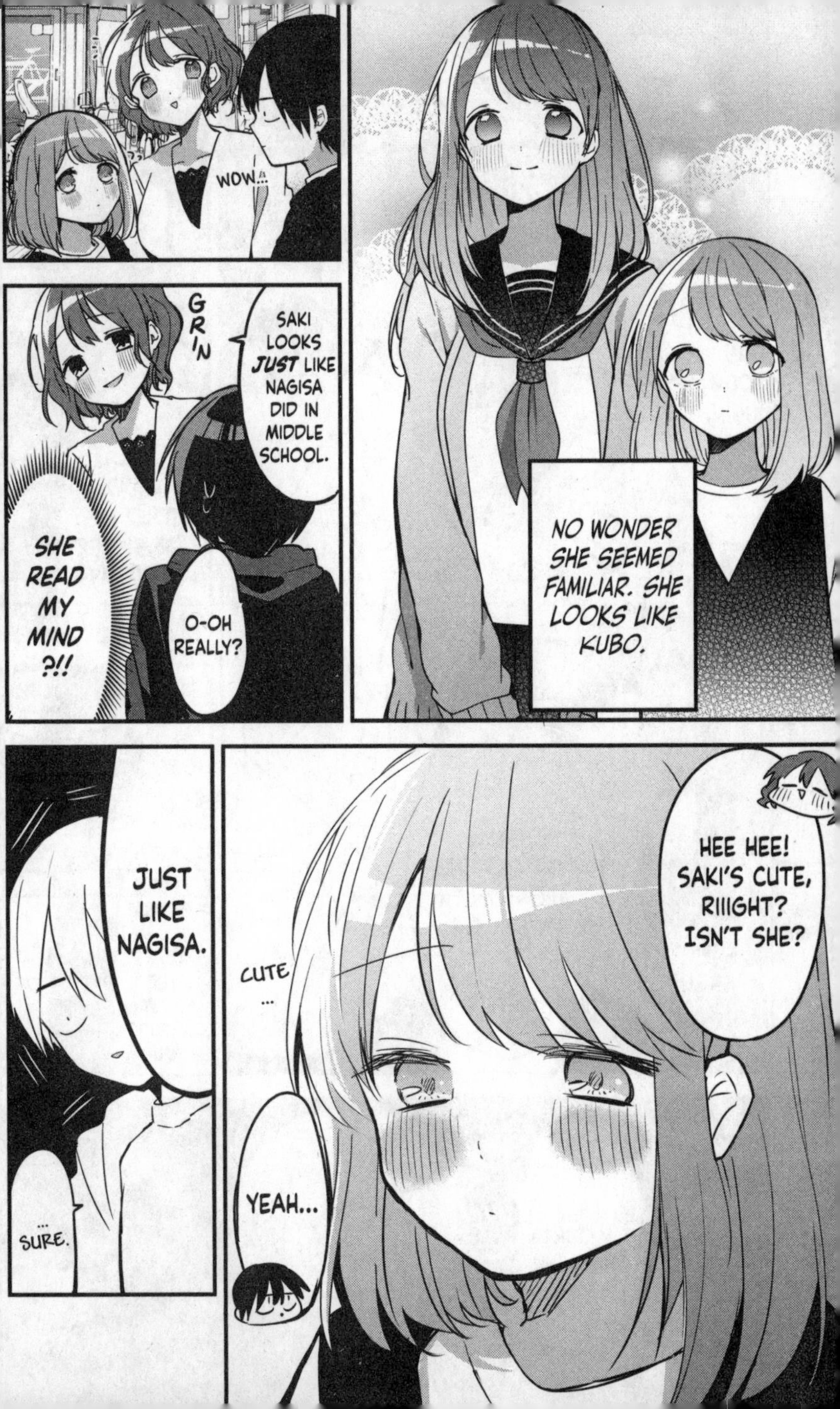
NO WONDER SHE SEEMED FAMILIAR. SHE LOOKS LIKE KUBO.
WOW...
GRIN
SAKI LOOKS JUST LIKE NAGISA DID IN MIDDLE SCHOOL.
SHE READ MY MIND?!!
O-OH REALLY?
HEE HEE! SAKI'S CUTE, RIIIGHT? ISN'T SHE?
CUTE...
YEAH...
JUST LIKE NAGISA.
... SURE.

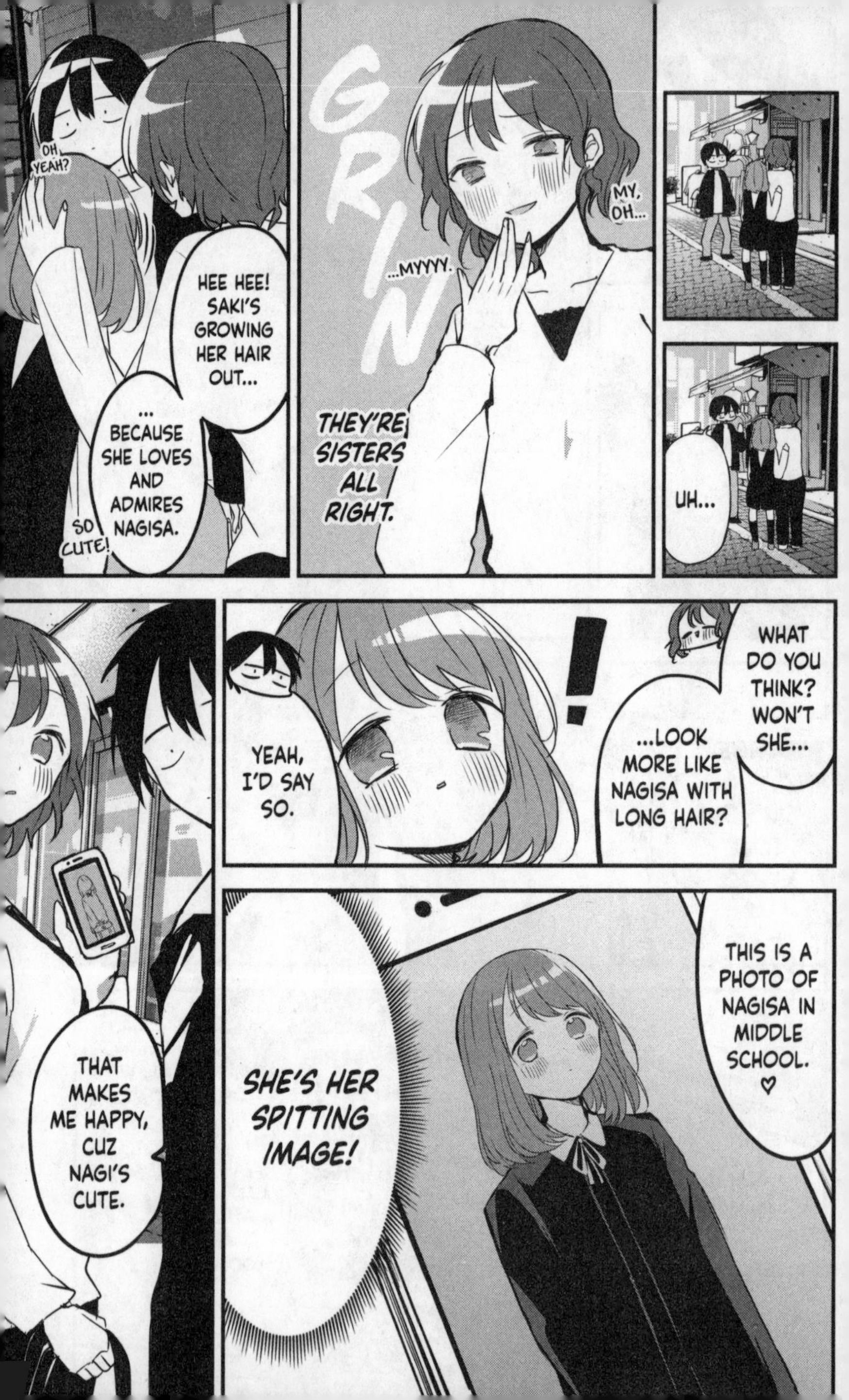
UH...
MY, OH...
GRIN
...MYYYY.
THEY'RE SISTERS ALL RIGHT.
HEE HEE! SAKI'S GROWING HER HAIR OUT...
...BECAUSE SHE LOVES AND ADMIRES NAGISA.
SO CUTE!
OH YEAH?
WHAT DO YOU THINK? WON'T SHE...
...LOOK MORE LIKE NAGISA WITH LONG HAIR?
!
YEAH, I'D SAY SO.
THIS IS A PHOTO OF NAGISA IN MIDDLE SCHOOL. ♡
SHE'S HER SPITTING IMAGE!
THAT MAKES ME HAPPY, CUZ NAGI'S CUTE.

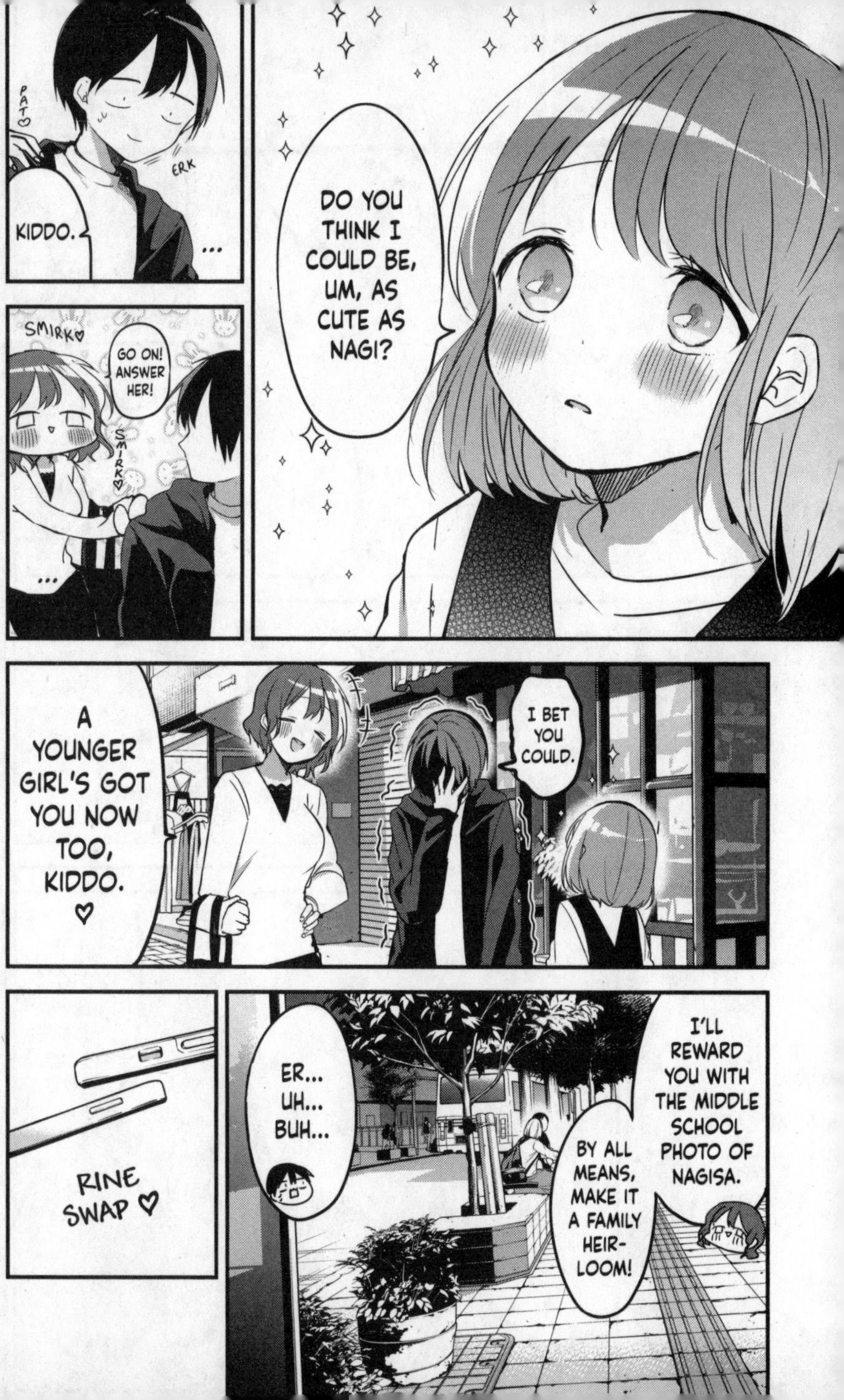
DO YOU THINK I COULD BE, UM, AS CUTE AS NAGI?
PAT ♡
ERK
...
KIDDO.
SMIRK♡
GO ON! ANSWER HER!
SMIRK♡
...
I BET YOU COULD.
A YOUNGER GIRL'S GOT YOU NOW TOO, KIDDO. ♡
I'LL REWARD YOU WITH THE MIDDLE SCHOOL PHOTO OF NAGISA.
BY ALL MEANS, MAKE IT A FAMILY HEIR-LOOM!
ER... UH... BUH...
RINE SWAP ♡

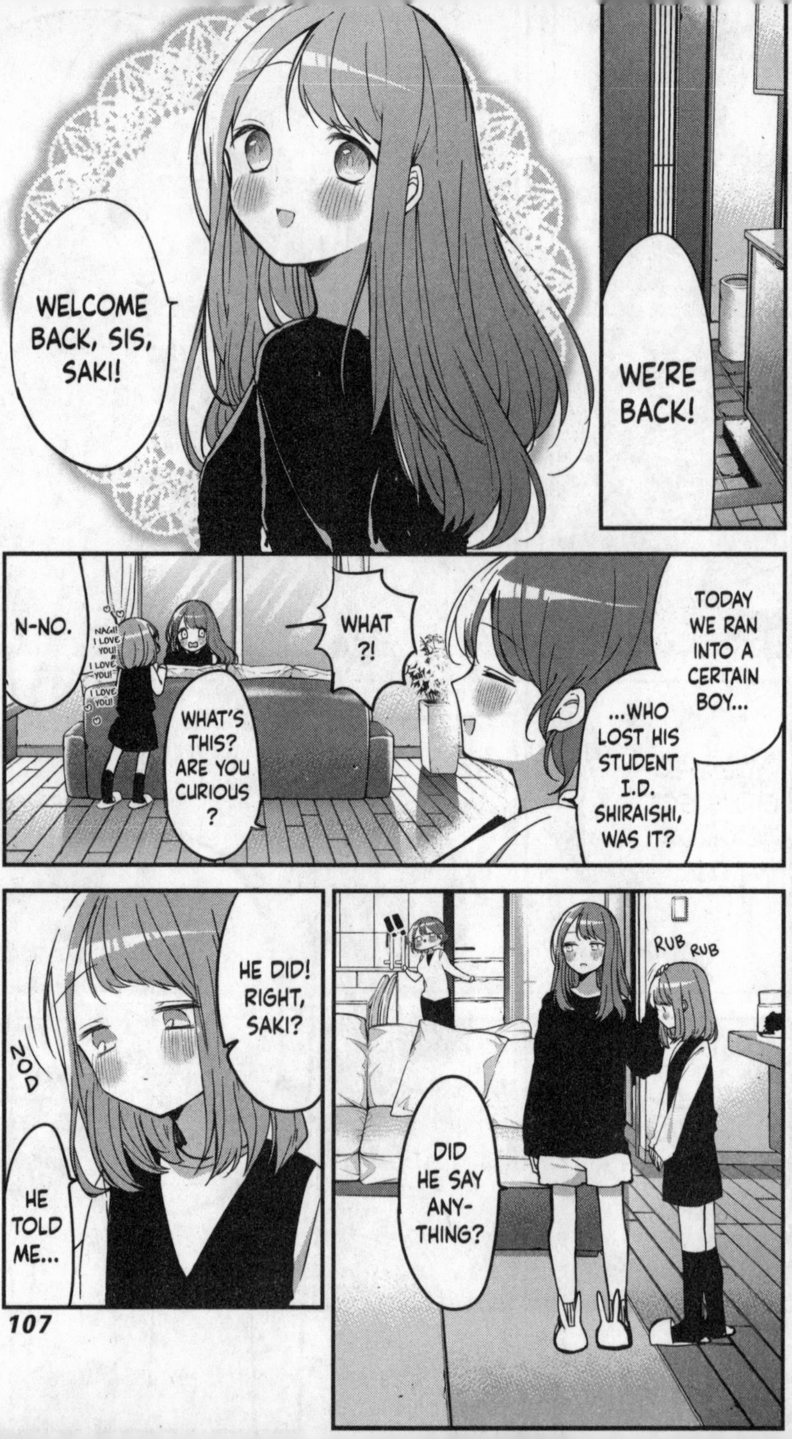
WE'RE BACK!
WELCOME BACK, SIS, SAKI!
TODAY WE RAN INTO A CERTAIN BOY...
...WHO LOST HIS STUDENT I.D. SHIRAISHI, WAS IT?
WHAT ?!
WHAT'S THIS? ARE YOU CURIOUS ?
NAGI! I LOVE YOU! I LOVE YOU! I LOVE YOU!
N-NO.
RUB RUB
DID HE SAY ANY-THING?
HE DID! RIGHT, SAKI?
NOD
HE TOLD ME...

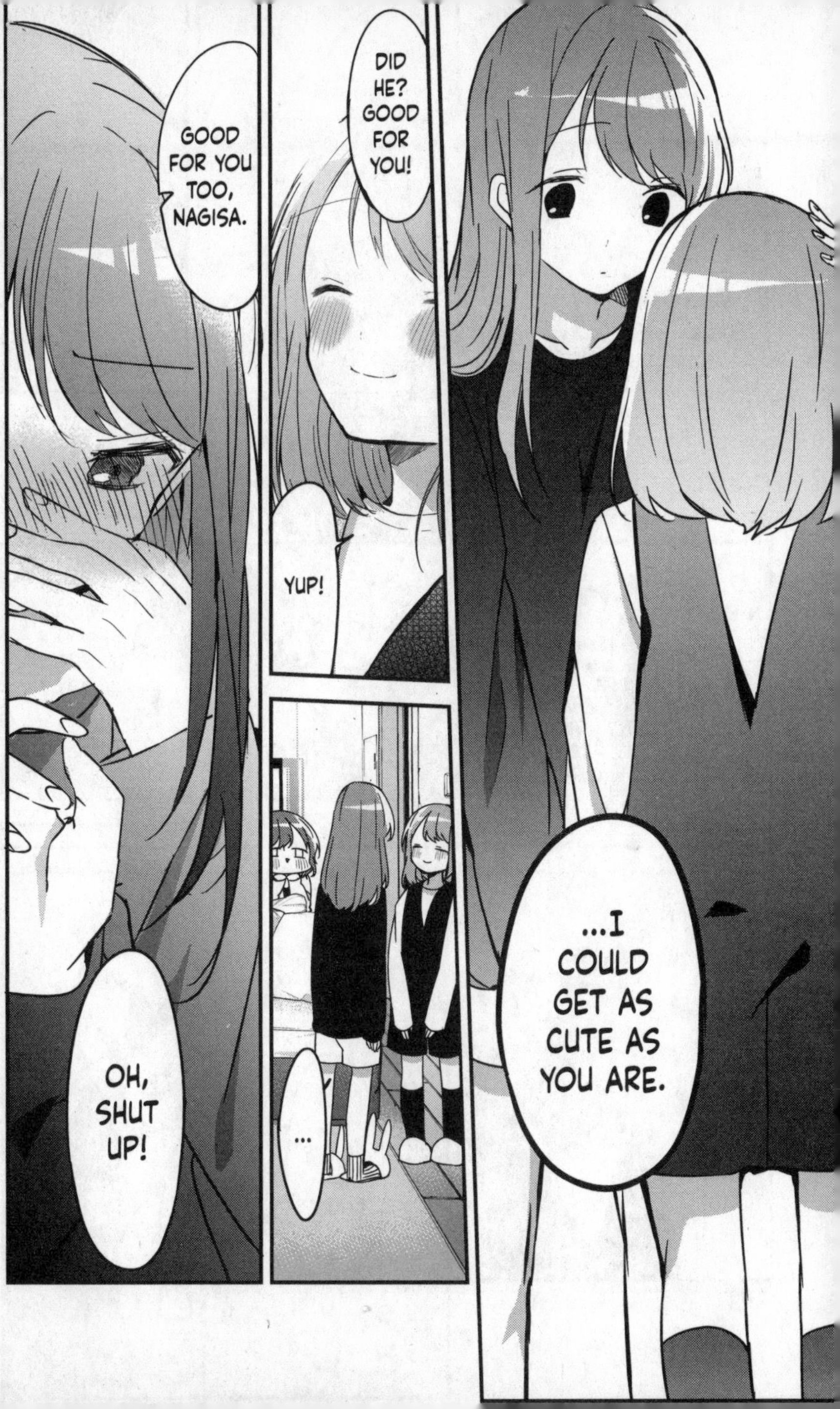
...I COULD GET AS CUTE AS YOU ARE.
DID HE? GOOD FOR YOU!
YUP!
...
GOOD FOR YOU TOO, NAGISA.
OH, SHUT UP!

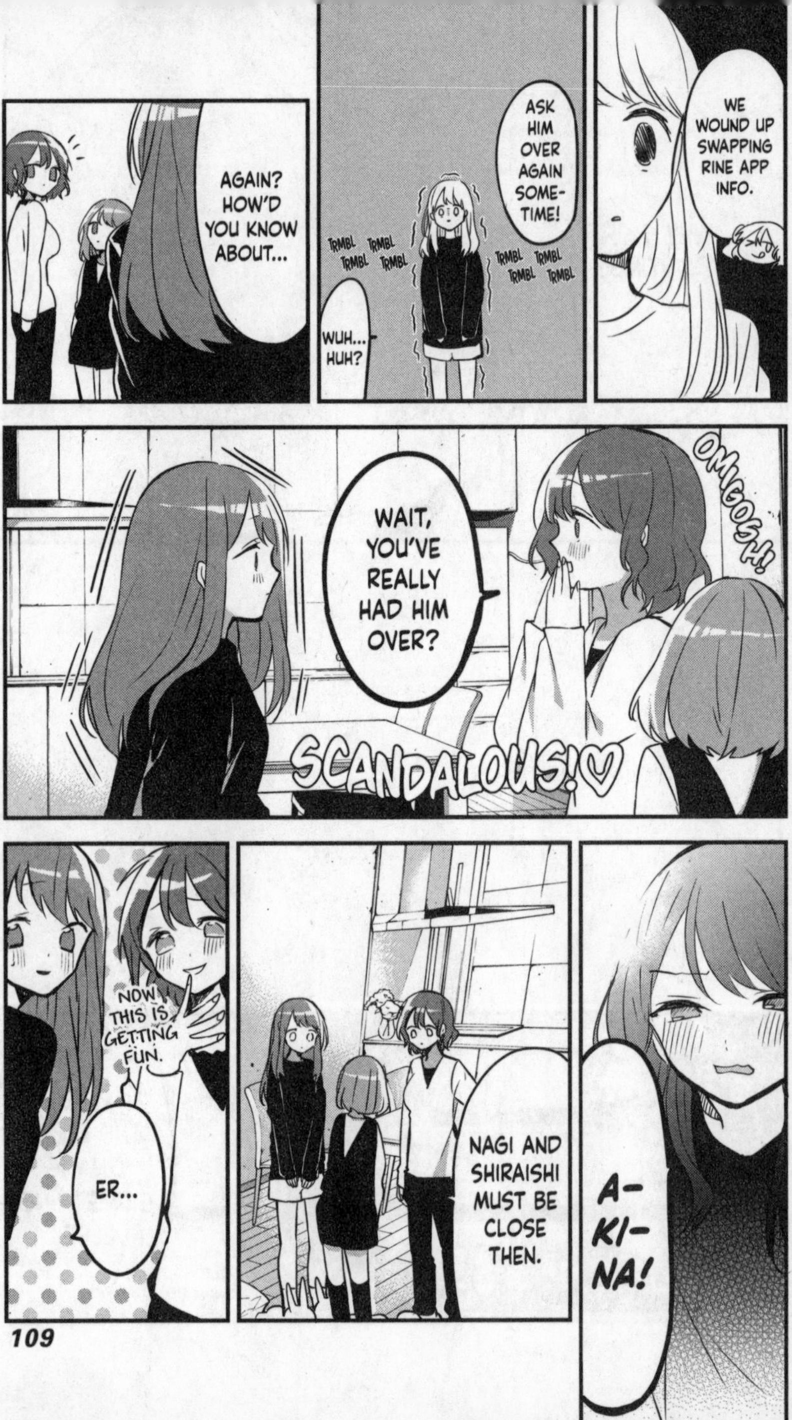
WE WOUND UP SWAPPING RINE APP INFO.
ASK HIM OVER AGAIN SOME-TIME!
TRMBL TRMBL TRMBL TRMBL
TRMBL TRMBL TRMBL TRMBL
WUH... HUH?
AGAIN? HOW'D YOU KNOW ABOUT...
OMGOSH!
WAIT, YOU'VE REALLY HAD HIM OVER?
SCANDALOUS!♡
A-KI-NA!
NAGI AND SHIRAISHI MUST BE CLOSE THEN.
NOW THIS IS GETTING FUN.
ER...

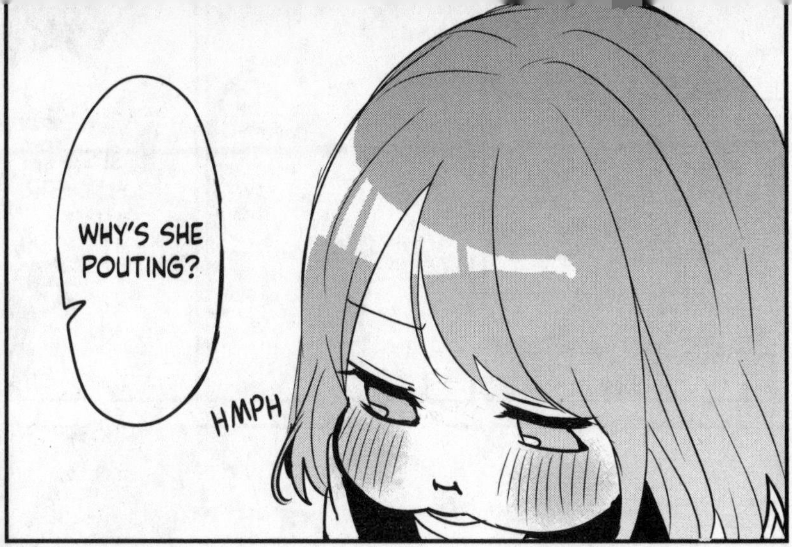
WHY'S SHE POUTING?
HMPH

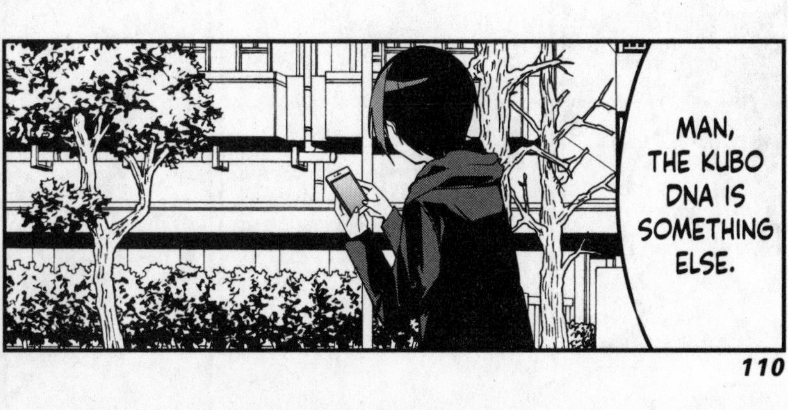
MAN, THE KUBO DNA IS SOMETHING ELSE.

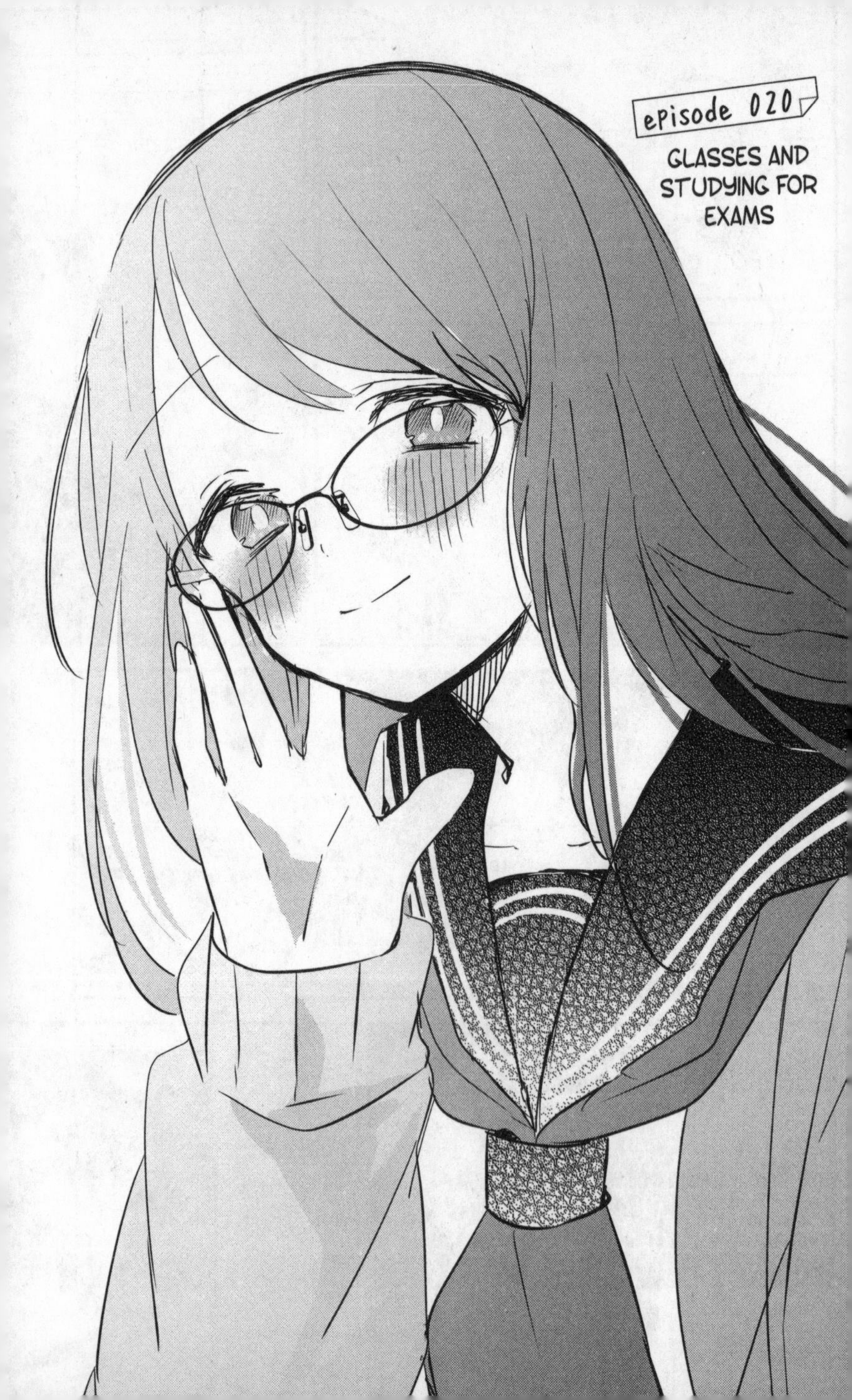
episode 020
GLASSES AND STUDYING FOR EXAMS

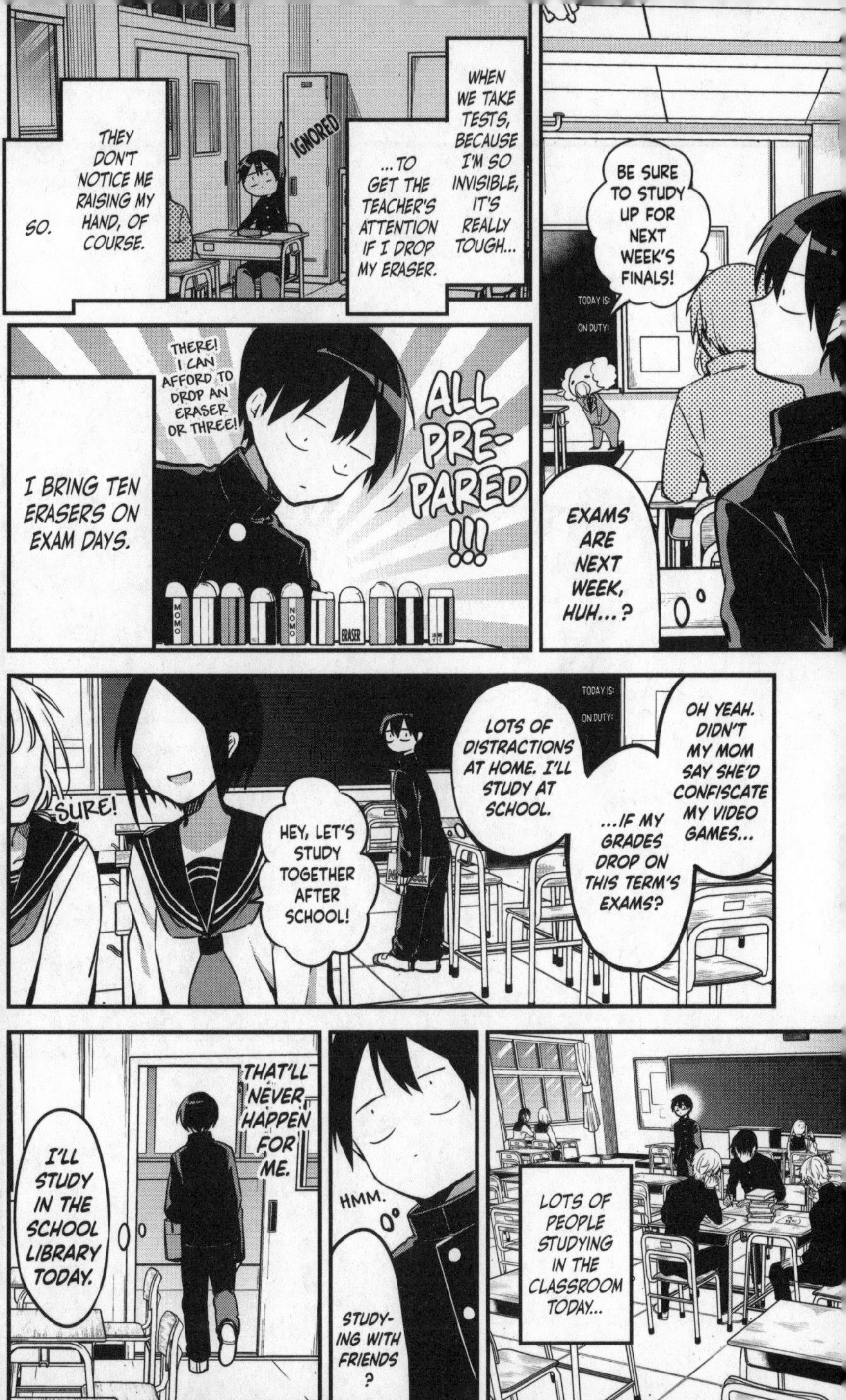
BE SURE TO STUDY UP FOR NEXT WEEK'S FINALS!
TODAY IS:
ON DUTY:
EXAMS ARE NEXT WEEK, HUH...?
WHEN WE TAKE TESTS, BECAUSE I'M SO INVISIBLE, IT'S REALLY TOUGH...
...TO GET THE TEACHER'S ATTENTION IF I DROP MY ERASER.
IGNORED
THEY DON'T NOTICE ME RAISING MY HAND, OF COURSE.
SO.
ALL PRE-PARED!!!
THERE! I CAN AFFORD TO DROP AN ERASER OR THREE!
I BRING TEN ERASERS ON EXAM DAYS.
MOMO
NOMO
ERASER
TODAY IS:
ON DUTY:
OH YEAH. DIDN'T MY MOM SAY SHE'D CONFISCATE MY VIDEO GAMES...
...IF MY GRADES DROP ON THIS TERM'S EXAMS?
LOTS OF DISTRACTIONS AT HOME. I'LL STUDY AT SCHOOL.
HEY, LET'S STUDY TOGETHER AFTER SCHOOL!
SURE!
LOTS OF PEOPLE STUDYING IN THE CLASSROOM TODAY...
HMM.
STUDY-ING WITH FRIENDS ?
THAT'LL NEVER HAPPEN FOR ME.
I'LL STUDY IN THE SCHOOL LIBRARY TODAY.

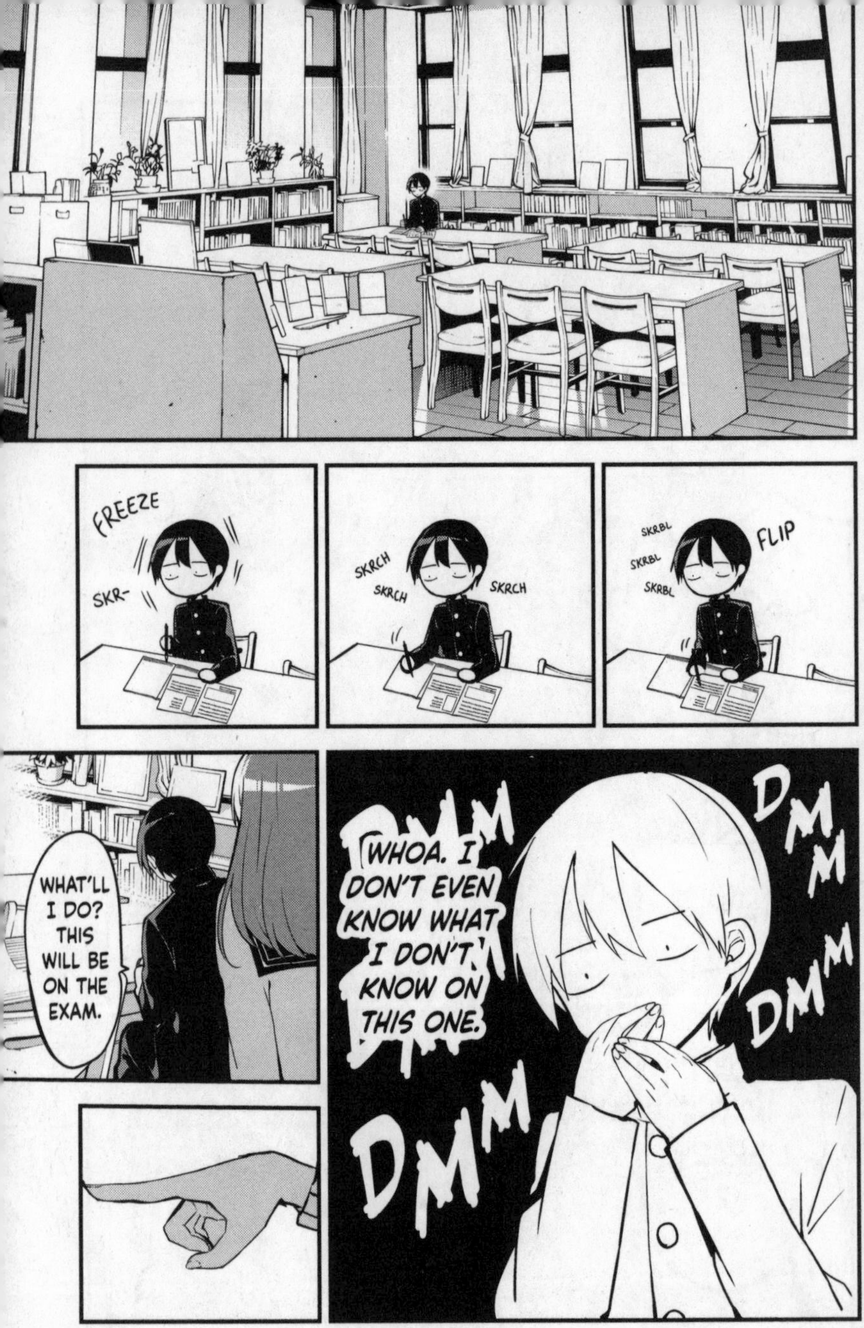
SKRBL
SKRBL
SKRBL
FLIP
SKRCH
SKRCH
SKRCH
FREEZE
SKR-
DMM
DMM
DMM
DMM
WHOA. I DON'T EVEN KNOW WHAT I DON'T KNOW ON THIS ONE.
DMM
WHAT'LL I DO? THIS WILL BE ON THE EXAM.

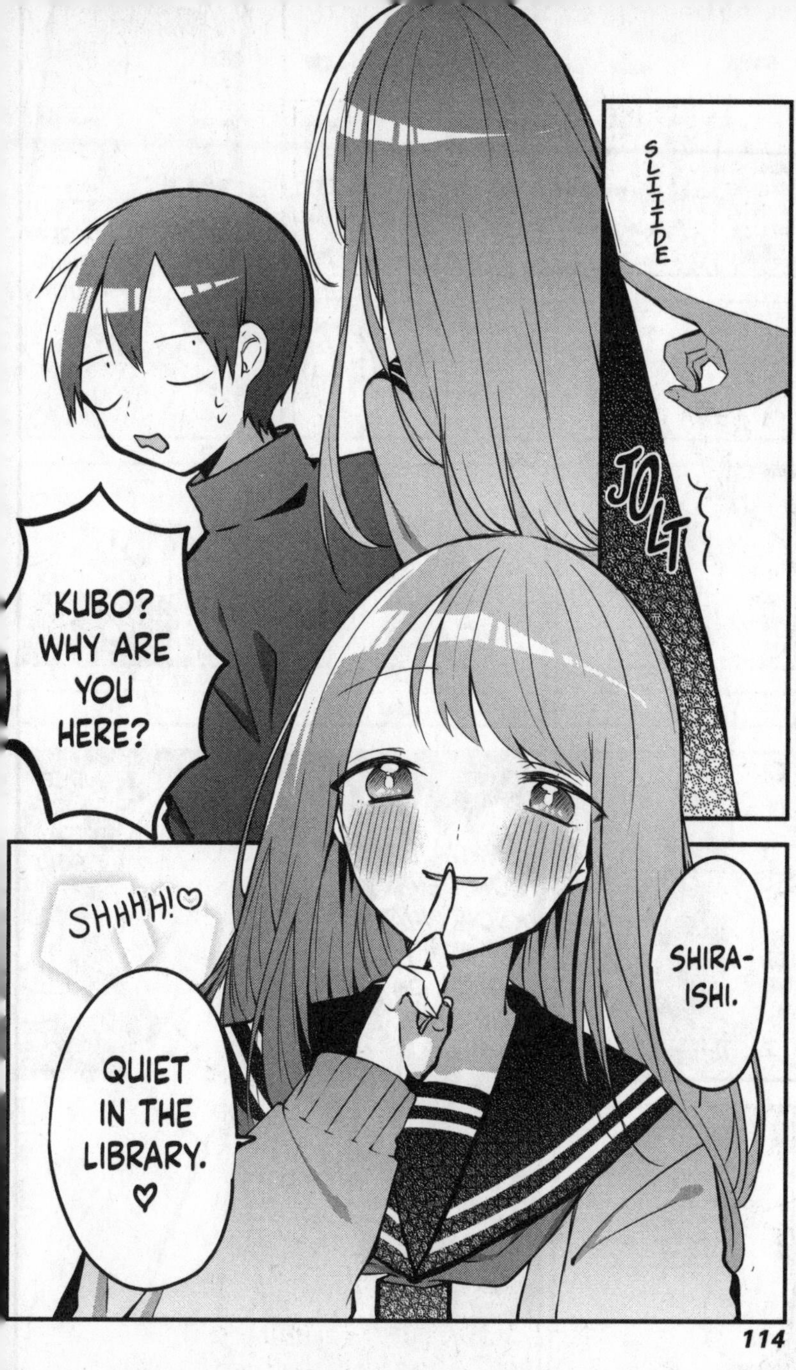
SLIIIDE
JOLT
KUBO? WHY ARE YOU HERE?
SHIRA-ISHI.
SHHHH!♡
QUIET IN THE LIBRARY. ♡

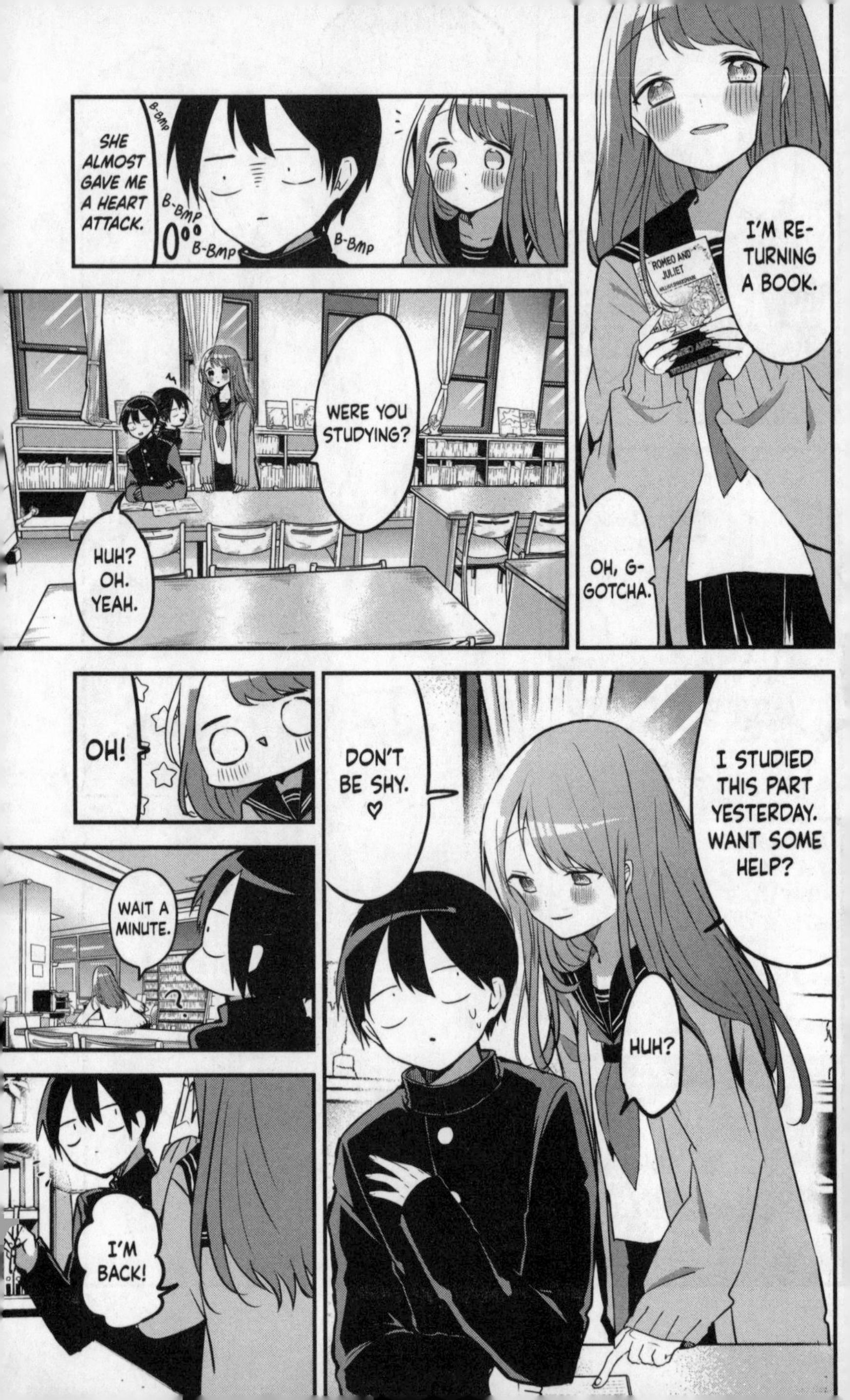
I'M RE-TURNING A BOOK.
ROMEO AND JULIET
OH, G-GOTCHA.
B-BMP
SHE ALMOST GAVE ME A HEART ATTACK.
B-BMP
B-BMP
B-BMP
WERE YOU STUDYING?
HUH? OH. YEAH.
I STUDIED THIS PART YESTERDAY. WANT SOME HELP?
DON'T BE SHY. ♡
HUH?
OH!
WAIT A MINUTE.
I'M BACK!

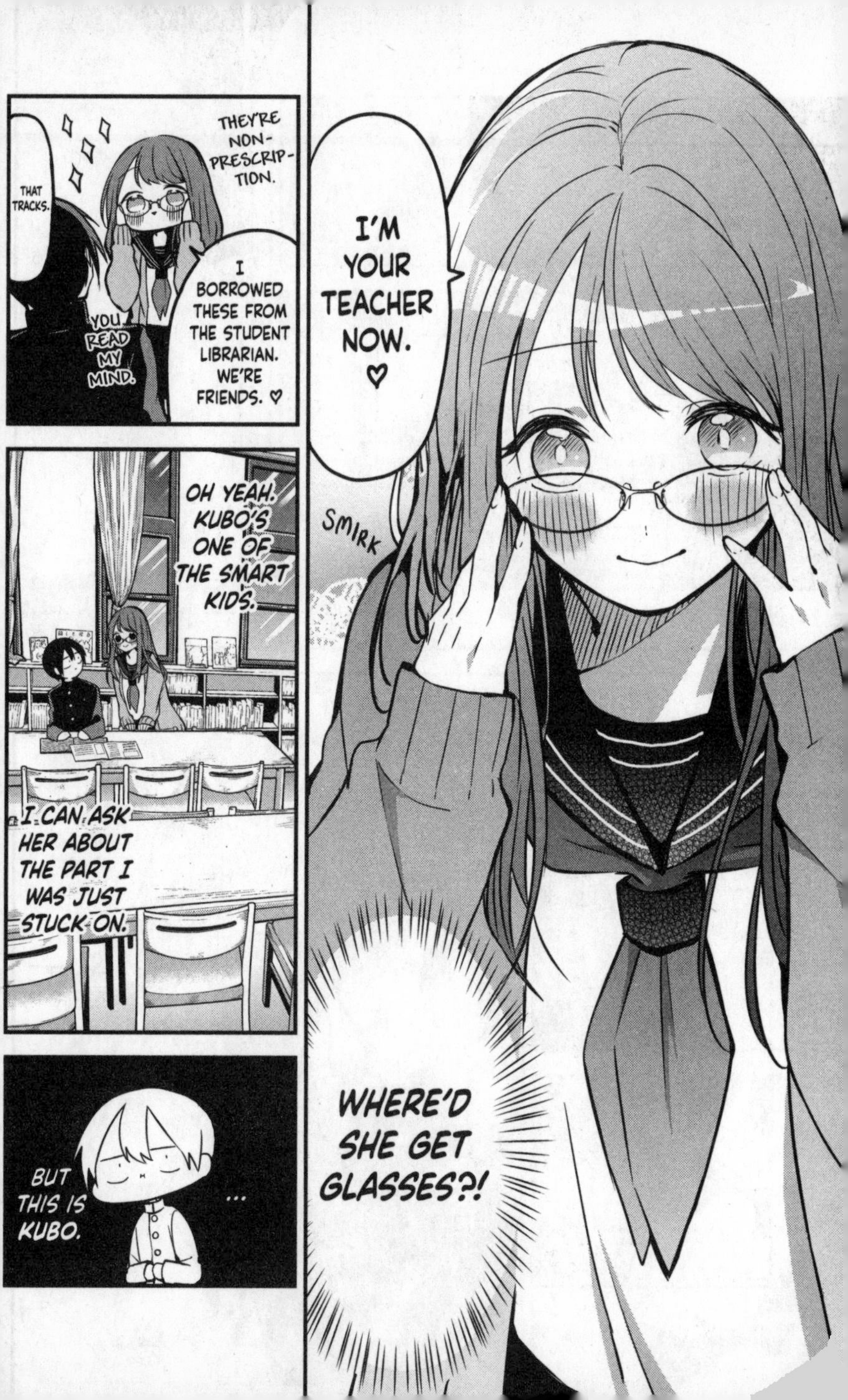
I'M YOUR TEACHER NOW. ♡
SMIRK
WHERE'D SHE GET GLASSES?!
THEY'RE NON-PRESCRIPTION.
THAT TRACKS.
I BORROWED THESE FROM THE STUDENT LIBRARIAN. WE'RE FRIENDS. ♡
YOU READ MY MIND.
OH YEAH. KUBO'S ONE OF THE SMART KIDS.
I CAN ASK HER ABOUT THE PART I WAS JUST STUCK ON.
...
BUT THIS IS KUBO.

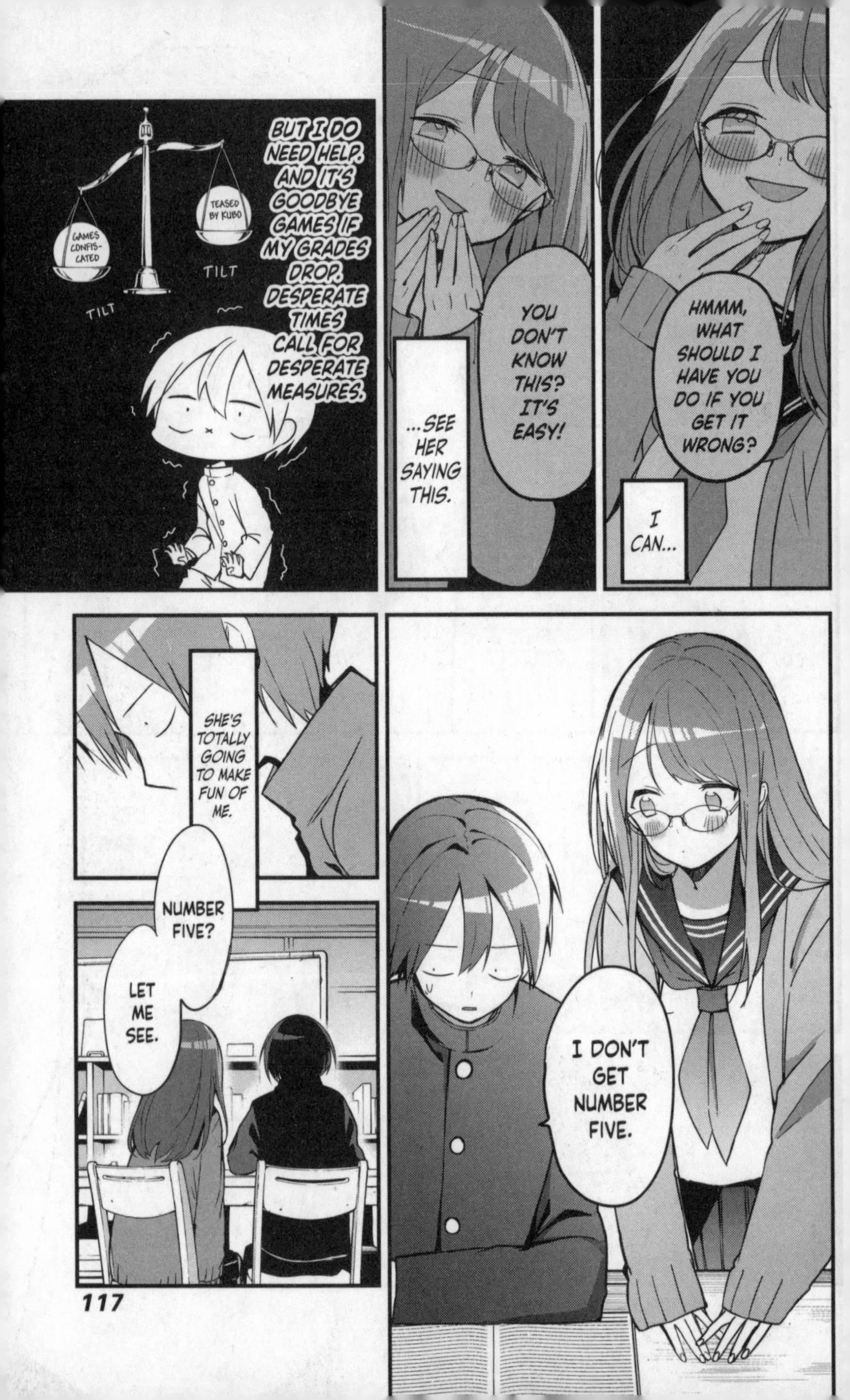
HMMM, WHAT SHOULD I HAVE YOU DO IF YOU GET IT WRONG?
I CAN...
YOU DON'T KNOW THIS? IT'S EASY!
...SEE HER SAYING THIS.
BUT I DO NEED HELP. AND IT'S GOODBYE GAMES IF MY GRADES DROP. DESPERATE TIMES CALL FOR DESPERATE MEASURES.
TEASED BY KUBO
GAMES CONFIS-CATED
TILT
TILT
I DON'T GET NUMBER FIVE.
SHE'S TOTALLY GOING TO MAKE FUN OF ME.
NUMBER FIVE?
LET ME SEE.

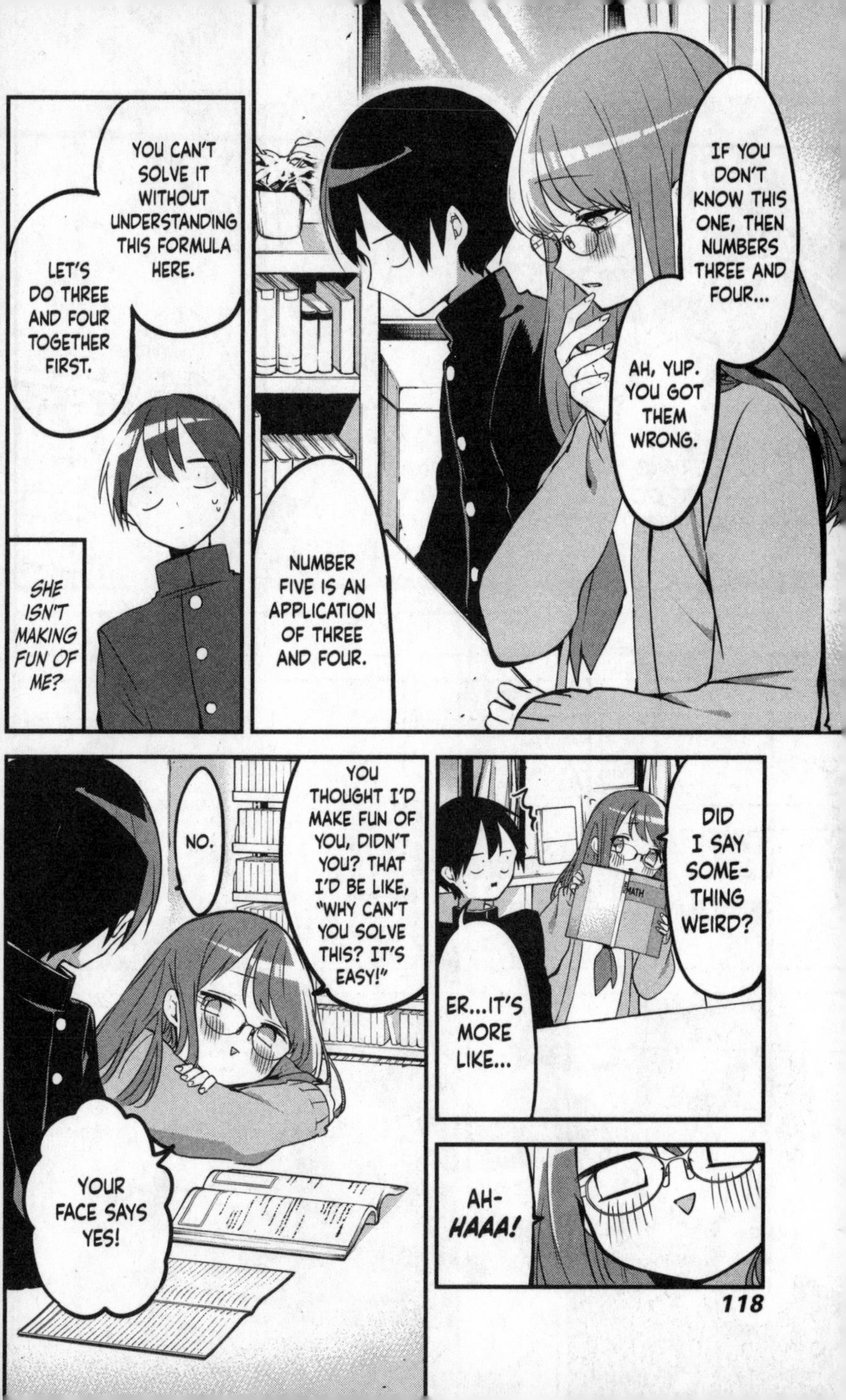
IF YOU DON'T KNOW THIS ONE, THEN NUMBERS THREE AND FOUR...
AH, YUP. YOU GOT THEM WRONG.
NUMBER FIVE IS AN APPLICATION OF THREE AND FOUR.
YOU CAN'T SOLVE IT WITHOUT UNDERSTANDING THIS FORMULA HERE.
LET'S DO THREE AND FOUR TOGETHER FIRST.
SHE ISN'T MAKING FUN OF ME?
DID I SAY SOME-THING WEIRD?
MATH
ER...IT'S MORE LIKE...
AH-HAAA!
YOU THOUGHT I'D MAKE FUN OF YOU, DIDN'T YOU? THAT I'D BE LIKE, "WHY CAN'T YOU SOLVE THIS? IT'S EASY!"
NO.
YOUR FACE SAYS YES!

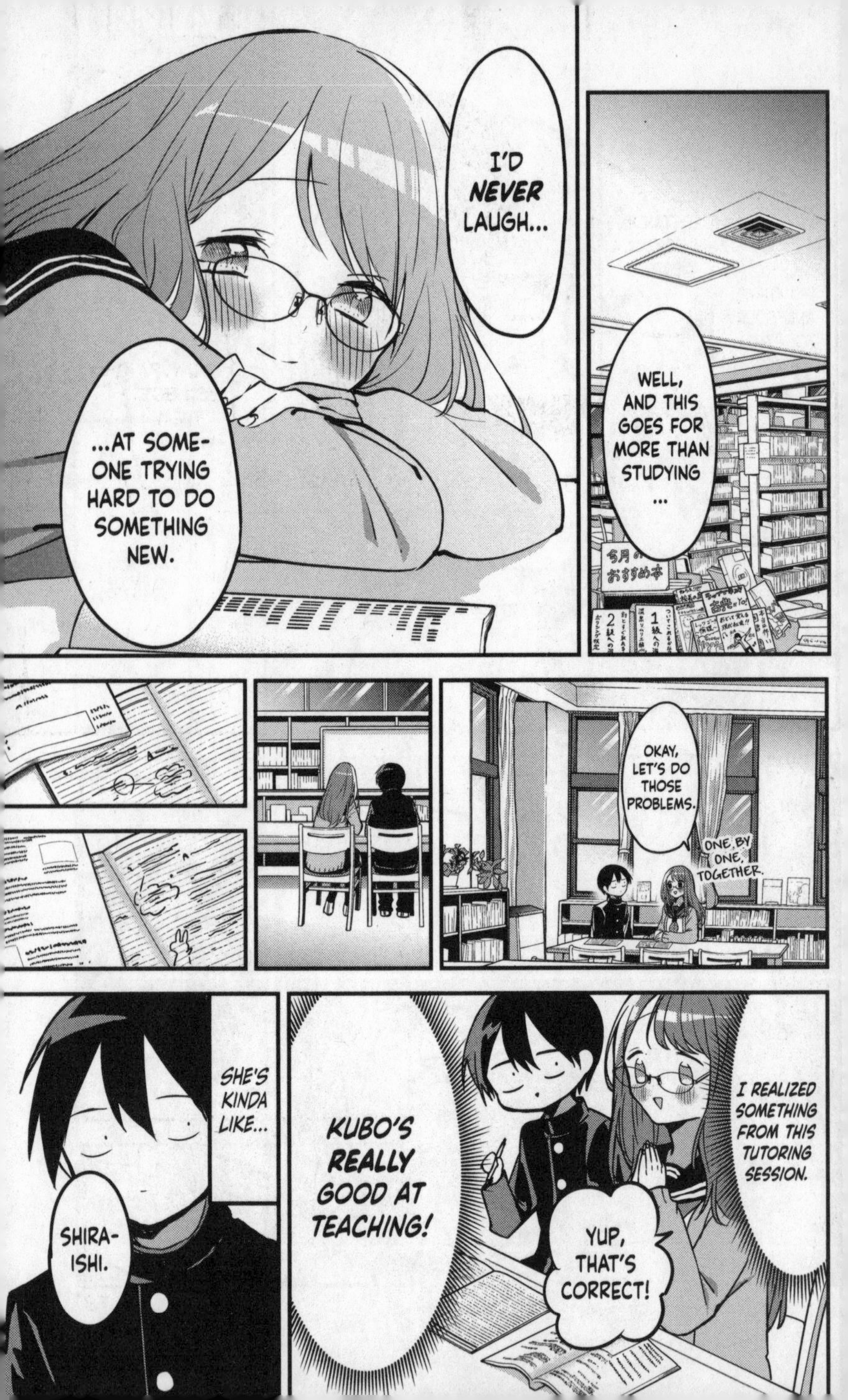
WELL, AND THIS GOES FOR MORE THAN STUDYING ...
I'D NEVER LAUGH...
...AT SOME-ONE TRYING HARD TO DO SOMETHING NEW.
OKAY, LET'S DO THOSE PROBLEMS.
ONE, BY ONE, TOGETHER.
I REALIZED SOMETHING FROM THIS TUTORING SESSION.
KUBO'S REALLY GOOD AT TEACHING!
YUP, THAT'S CORRECT!
SHE'S KINDA LIKE...
SHIRA-ISHI.

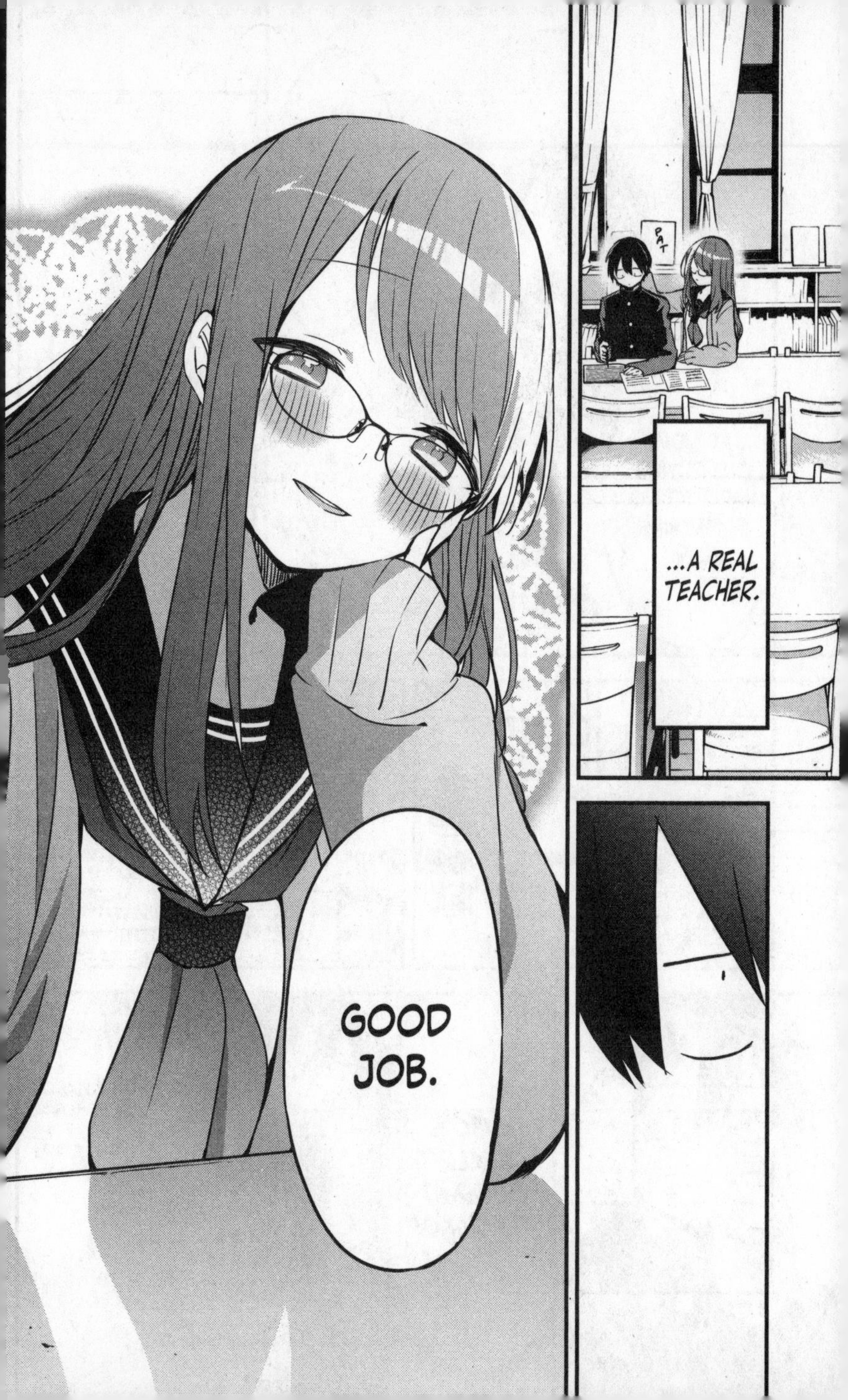
PAT
...A REAL TEACHER.
GOOD JOB.

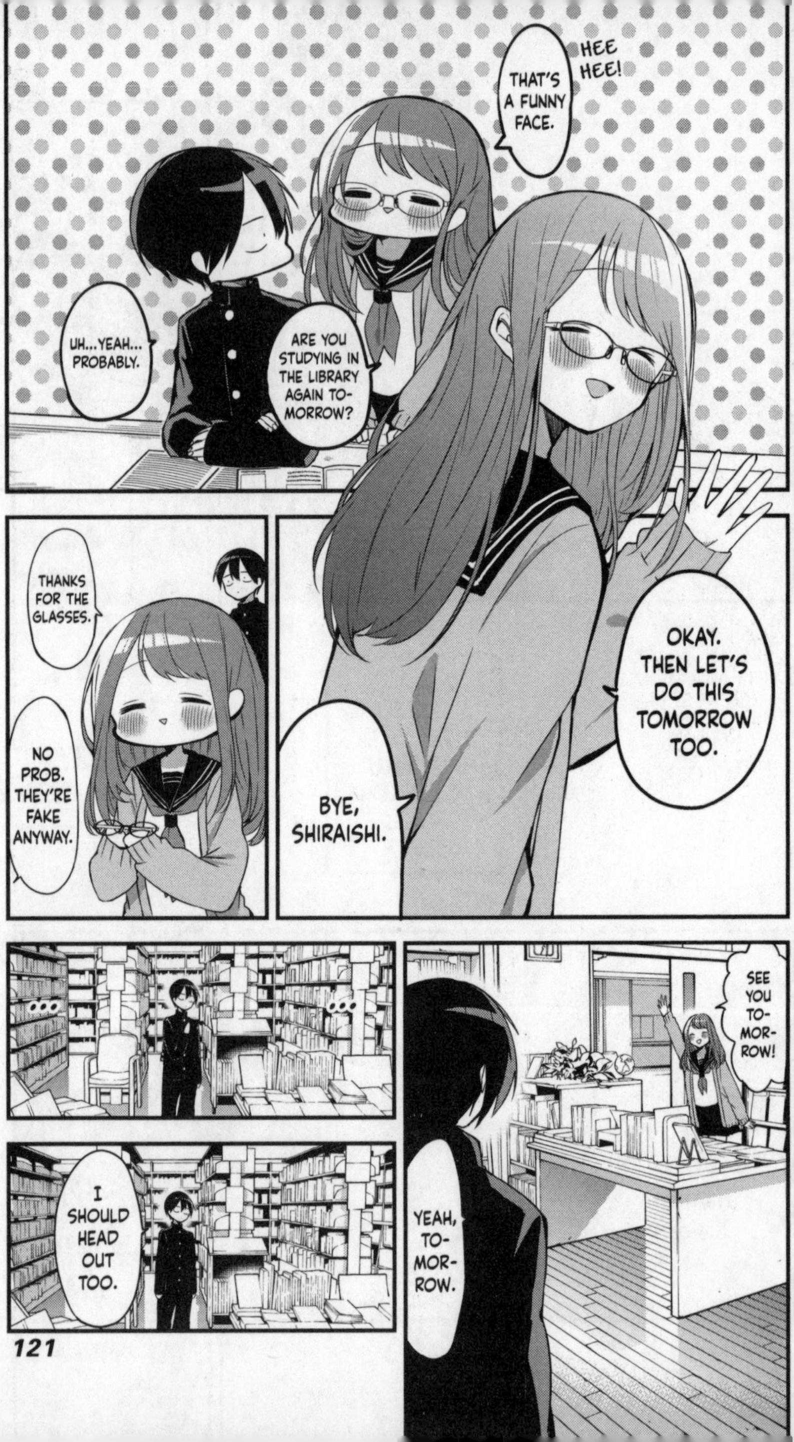
HEE HEE!
THAT'S A FUNNY FACE.
ARE YOU STUDYING IN THE LIBRARY AGAIN TO-MORROW?
UH...YEAH... PROBABLY.
OKAY. THEN LET'S DO THIS TOMORROW TOO.
BYE, SHIRAISHI.
THANKS FOR THE GLASSES.
NO PROB. THEY'RE FAKE ANYWAY.
SEE YOU TO-MOR-ROW!
YEAH, TO-MOR-ROW.
...
...
I SHOULD HEAD OUT TOO.

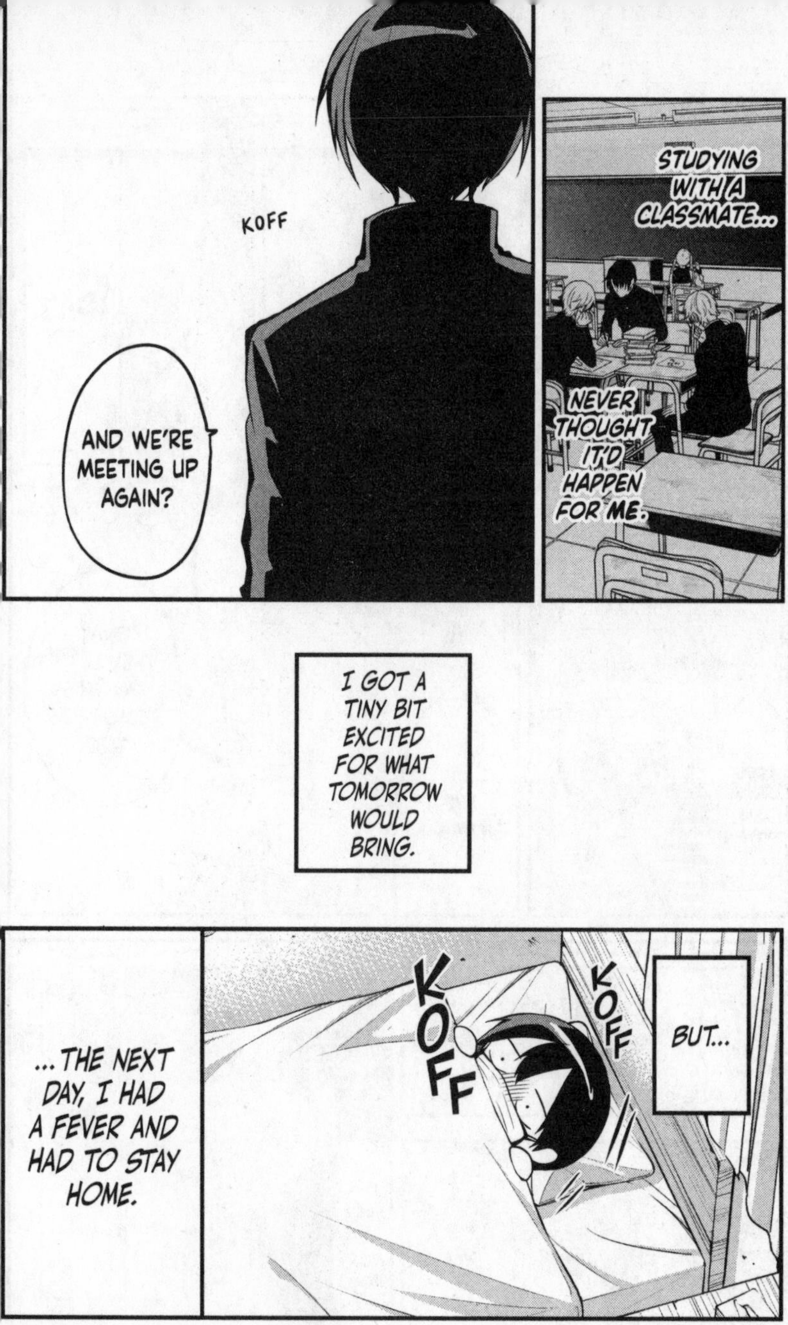
STUDYING WITH A CLASSMATE...
NEVER THOUGHT IT'D HAPPEN FOR ME.
KOFF
AND WE'RE MEETING UP AGAIN?
I GOT A TINY BIT EXCITED FOR WHAT TOMORROW WOULD BRING.
BUT...
KOFF
KOFF
...THE NEXT DAY, I HAD A FEVER AND HAD TO STAY HOME.

special episode FREQUENCY OF YOUR VOICE

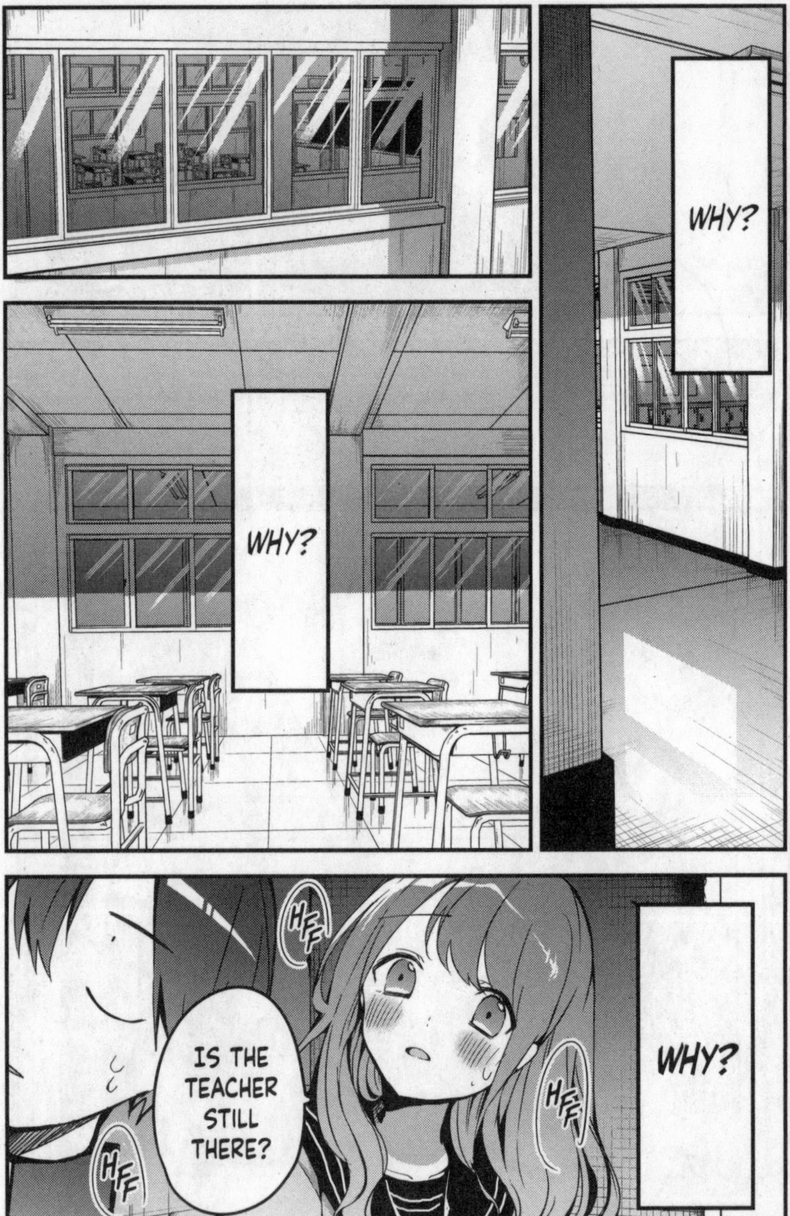
WHY?
WHY?
WHY?
HFF
HFF
IS THE TEACHER STILL THERE?
HFF

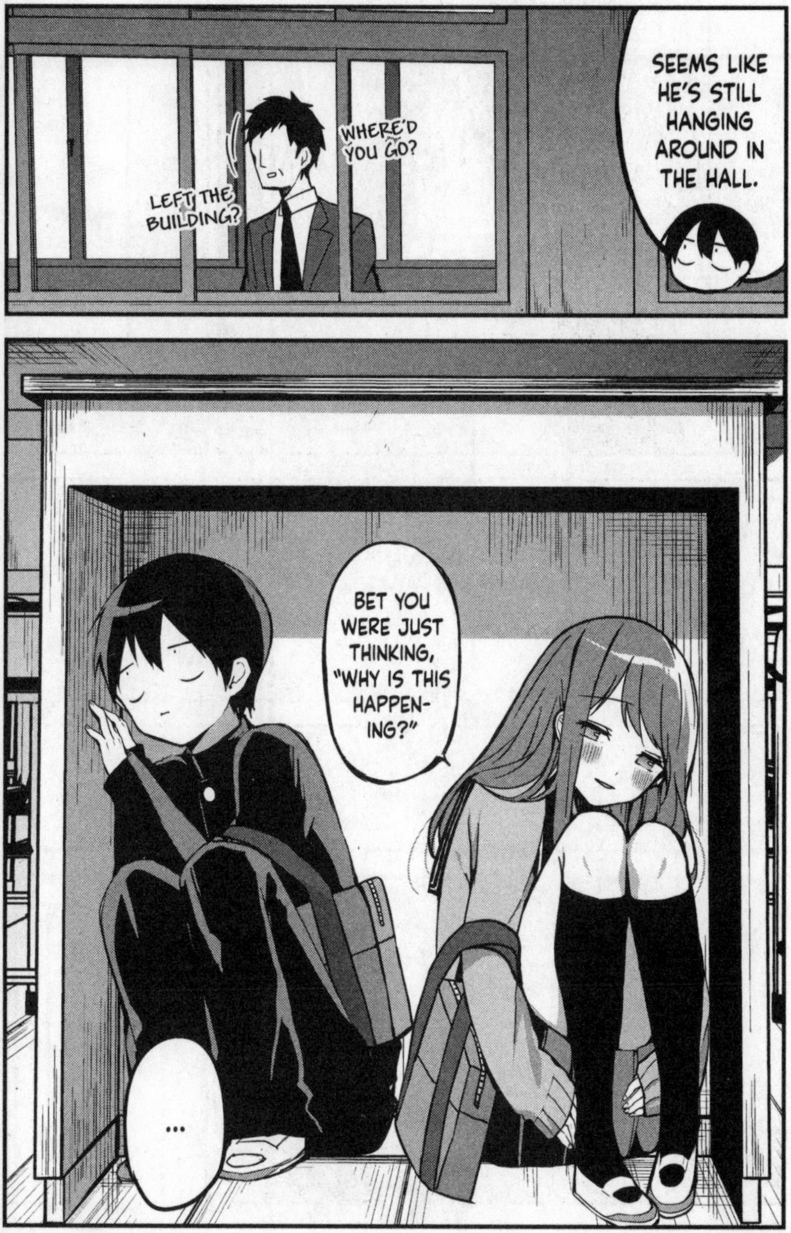
SEEMS LIKE HE'S STILL HANGING AROUND IN THE HALL.
WHERE'D YOU GO?
LEFT THE BUILDING?
BET YOU WERE JUST THINKING, "WHY IS THIS HAPPEN-ING?"
...

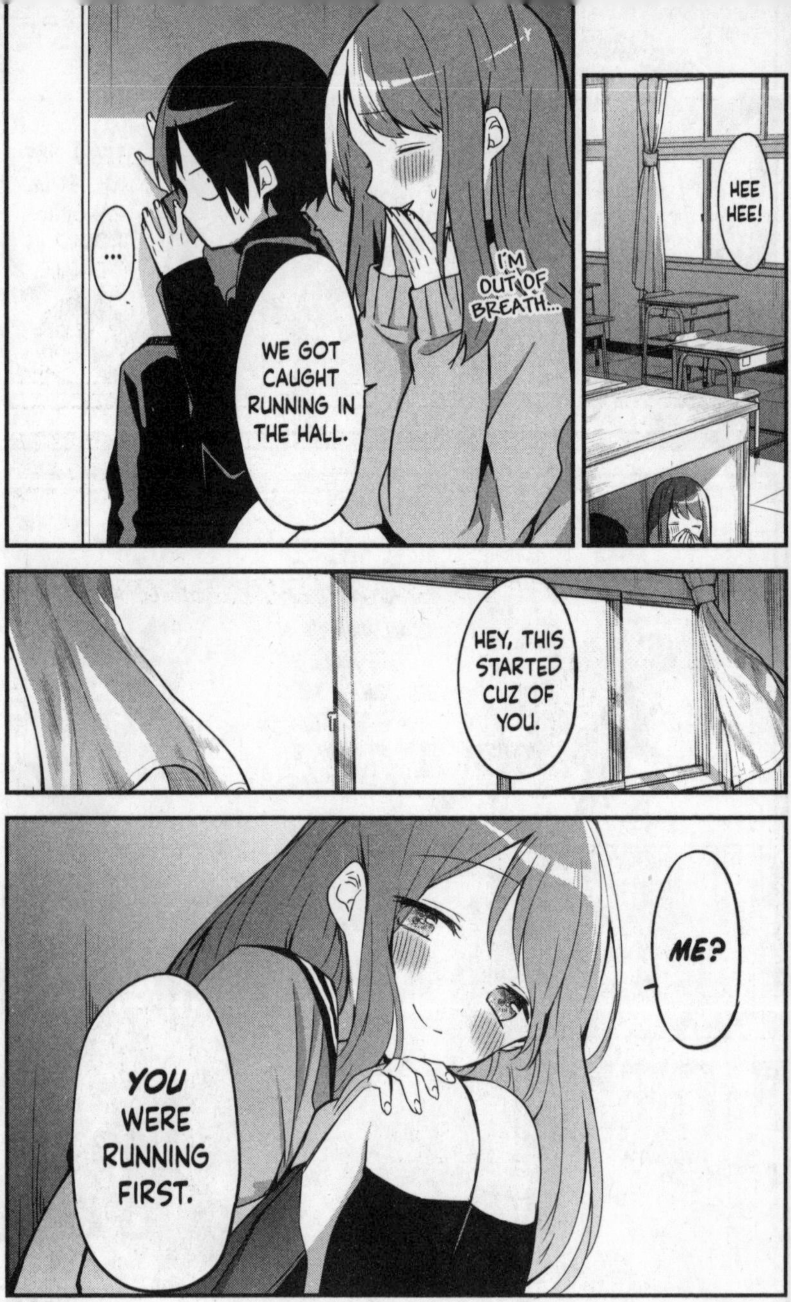
HEE HEE!
I'M OUT OF BREATH...
WE GOT CAUGHT RUNNING IN THE HALL.
...
HEY, THIS STARTED CUZ OF YOU.
ME?
YOU WERE RUNNING FIRST.

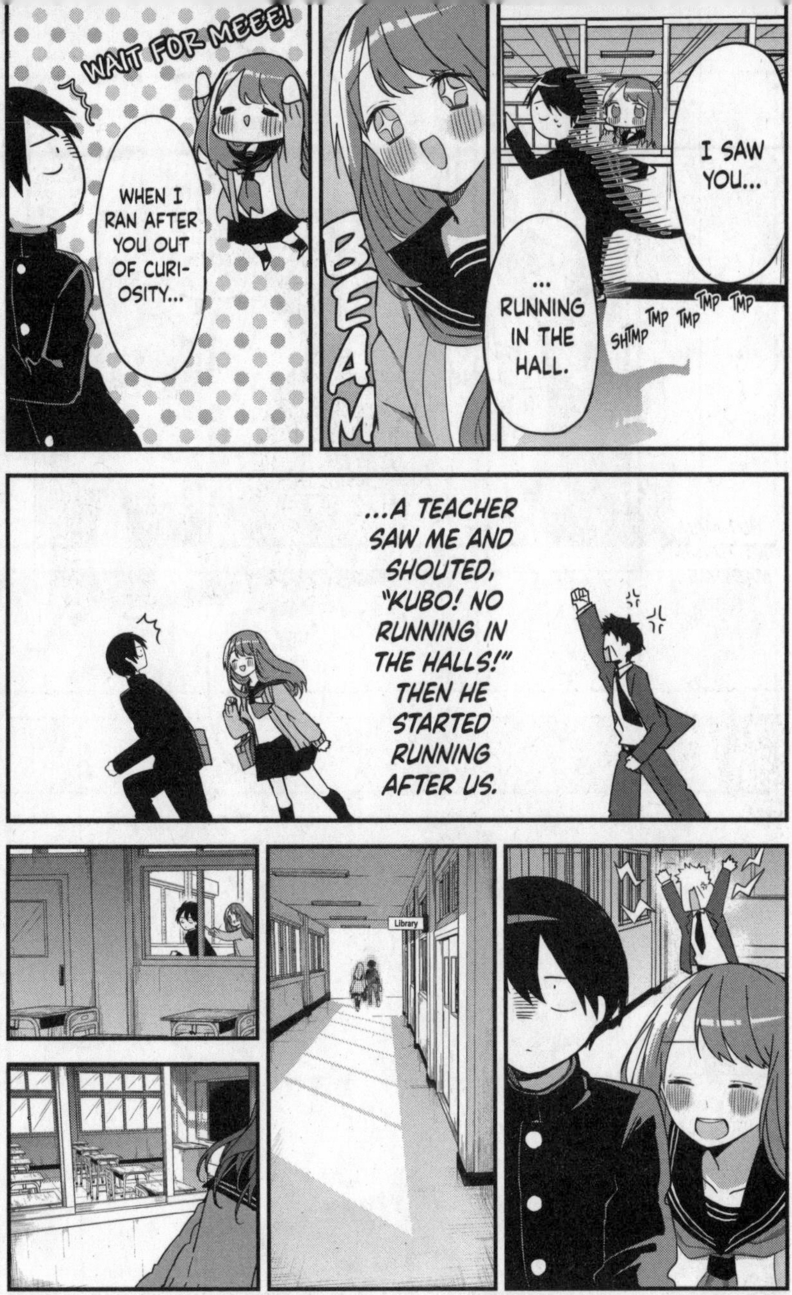
I SAW YOU...
... RUNNING IN THE HALL.
SHTMP TMP TMP TMP TMP
BEAM
WAIT FOR MEEE!
WHEN I RAN AFTER YOU OUT OF CURI-OSITY...
...A TEACHER SAW ME AND SHOUTED, "KUBO! NO RUNNING IN THE HALLS!" THEN HE STARTED RUNNING AFTER US.
Library

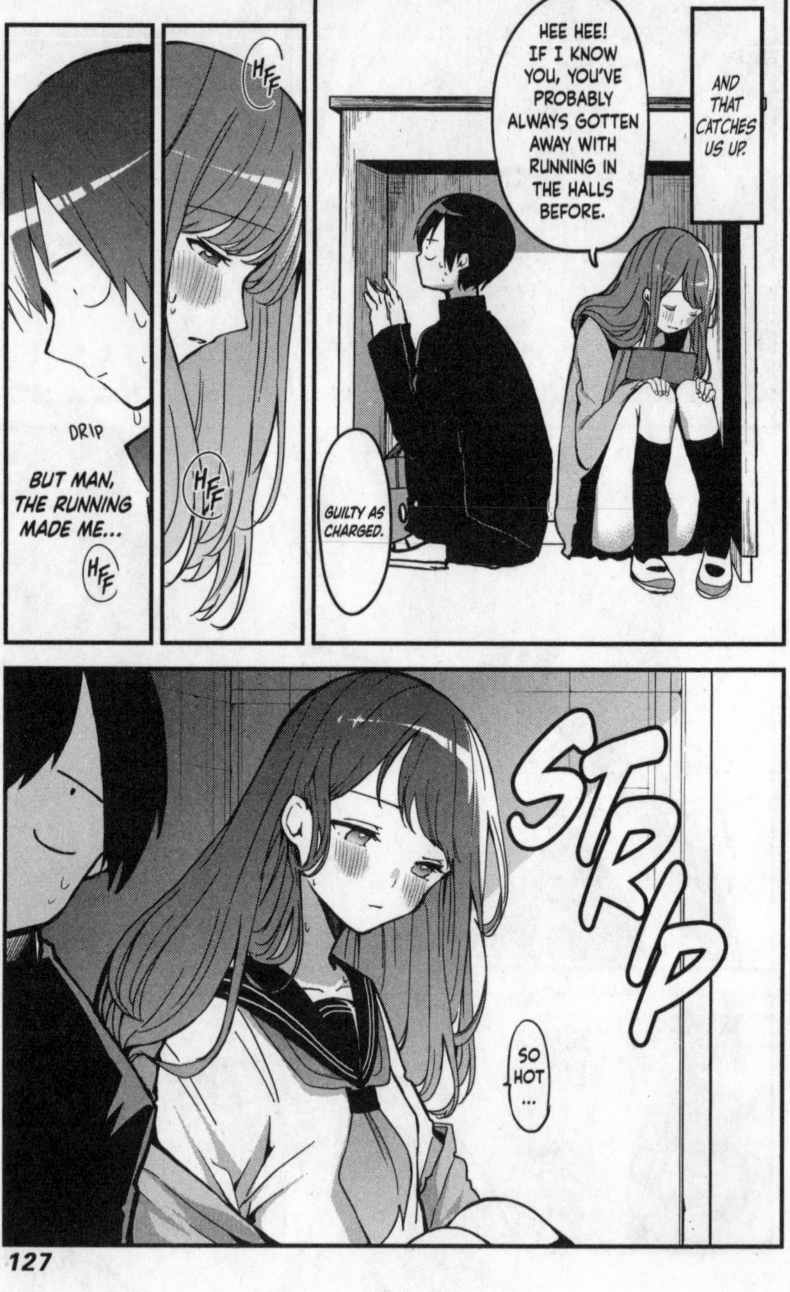
AND THAT CATCHES US UP.
HEE HEE! IF I KNOW YOU, YOU'VE PROBABLY ALWAYS GOTTEN AWAY WITH RUNNING IN THE HALLS BEFORE.
GUILTY AS CHARGED.
HFF
HFF
DRIP
BUT MAN, THE RUNNING MADE ME...
HFF
STRIP
SO HOT...

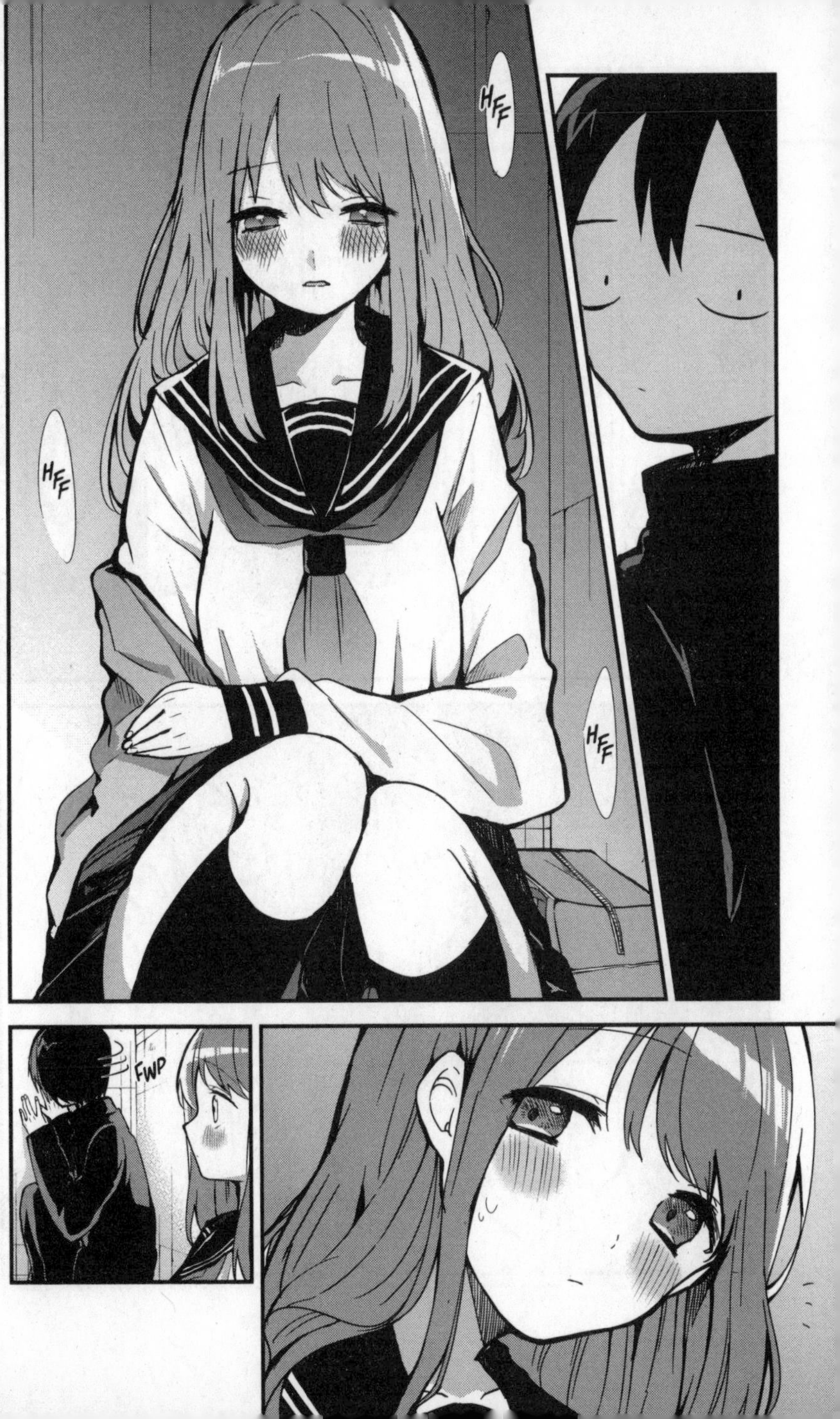
HFF
HFF
HFF
FWP

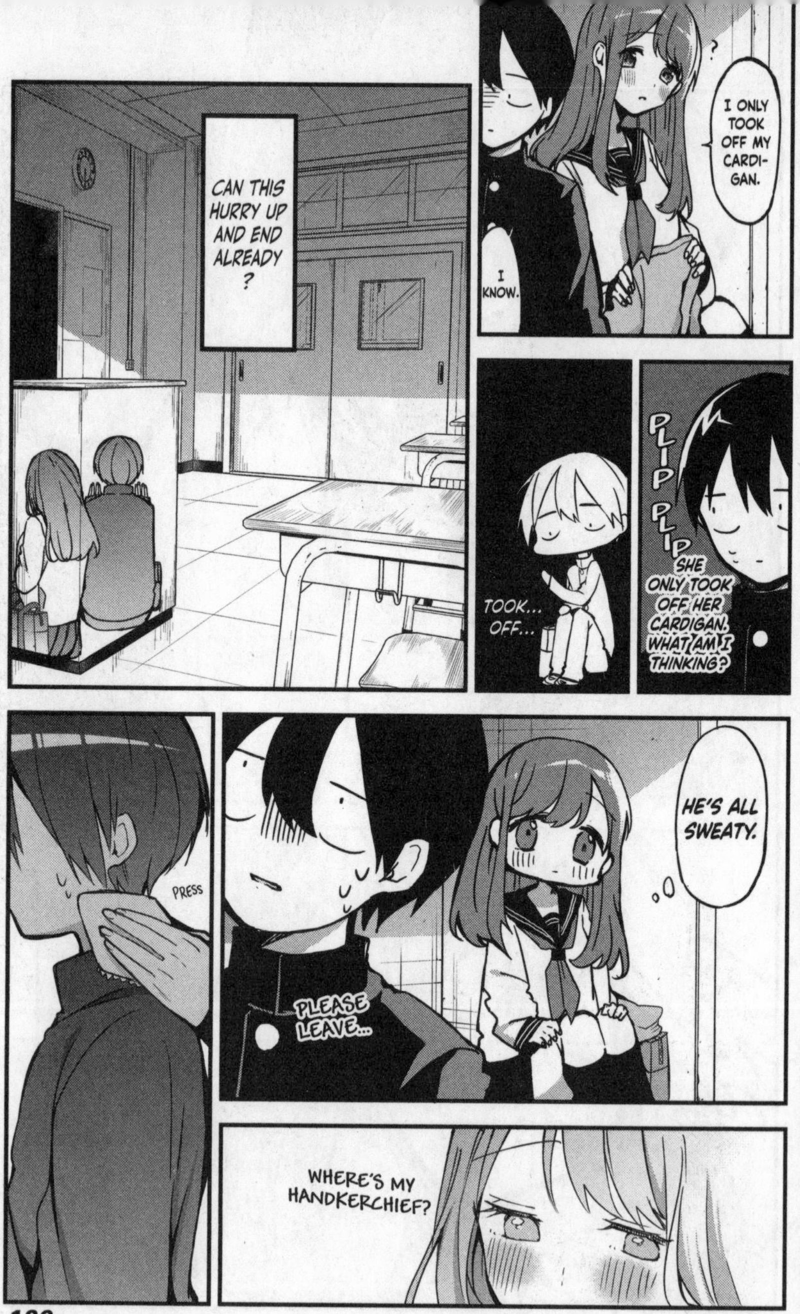
?
I ONLY TOOK OFF MY CARDI-GAN.
I KNOW.
PLIP PLIP PLIP
SHE ONLY TOOK OFF HER CARDIGAN. WHAT AM I THINKING?
TOOK... OFF...
CAN THIS HURRY UP AND END ALREADY ?
HE'S ALL SWEATY.
PLEASE LEAVE...
WHERE'S MY HANDKERCHIEF?
PRESS

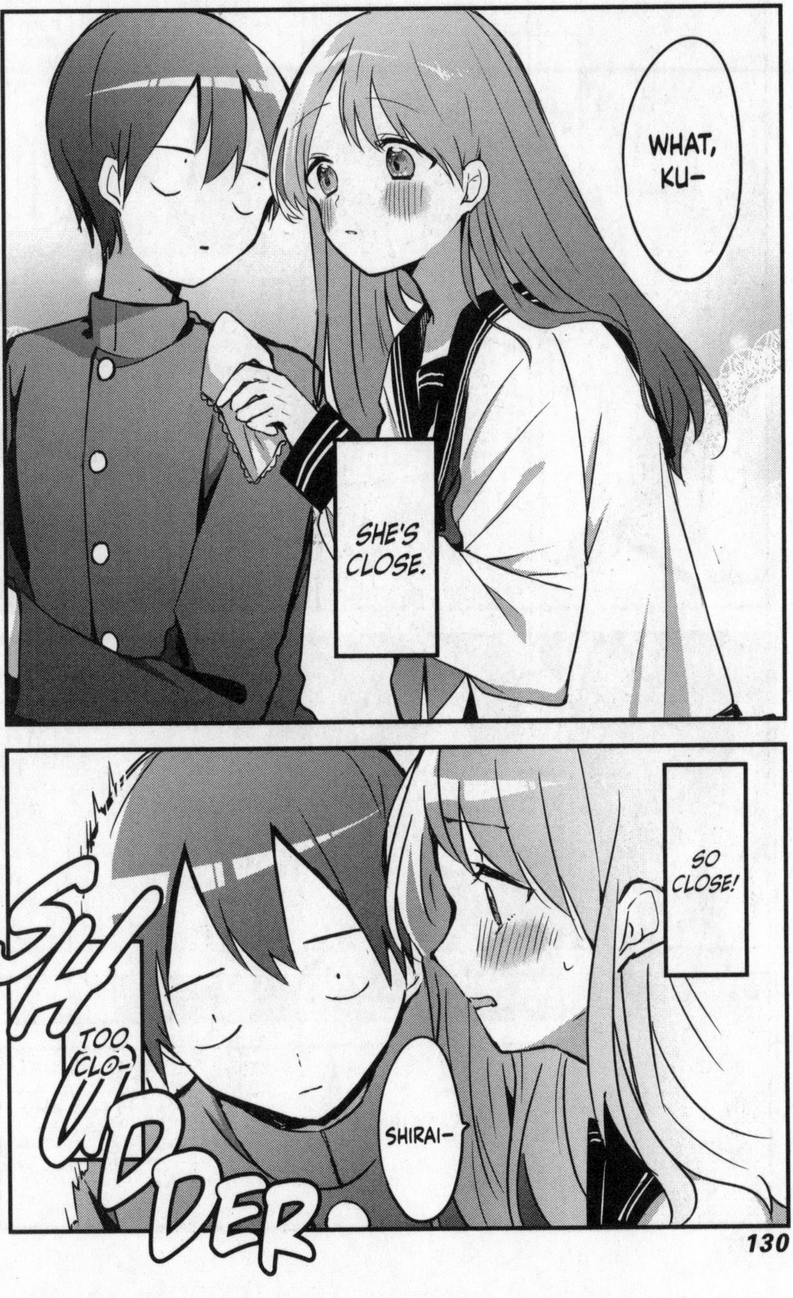
WHAT, KU-
SHE'S CLOSE.
SO CLOSE!
TOO CLO-
SHIRAI-
SHUDDER

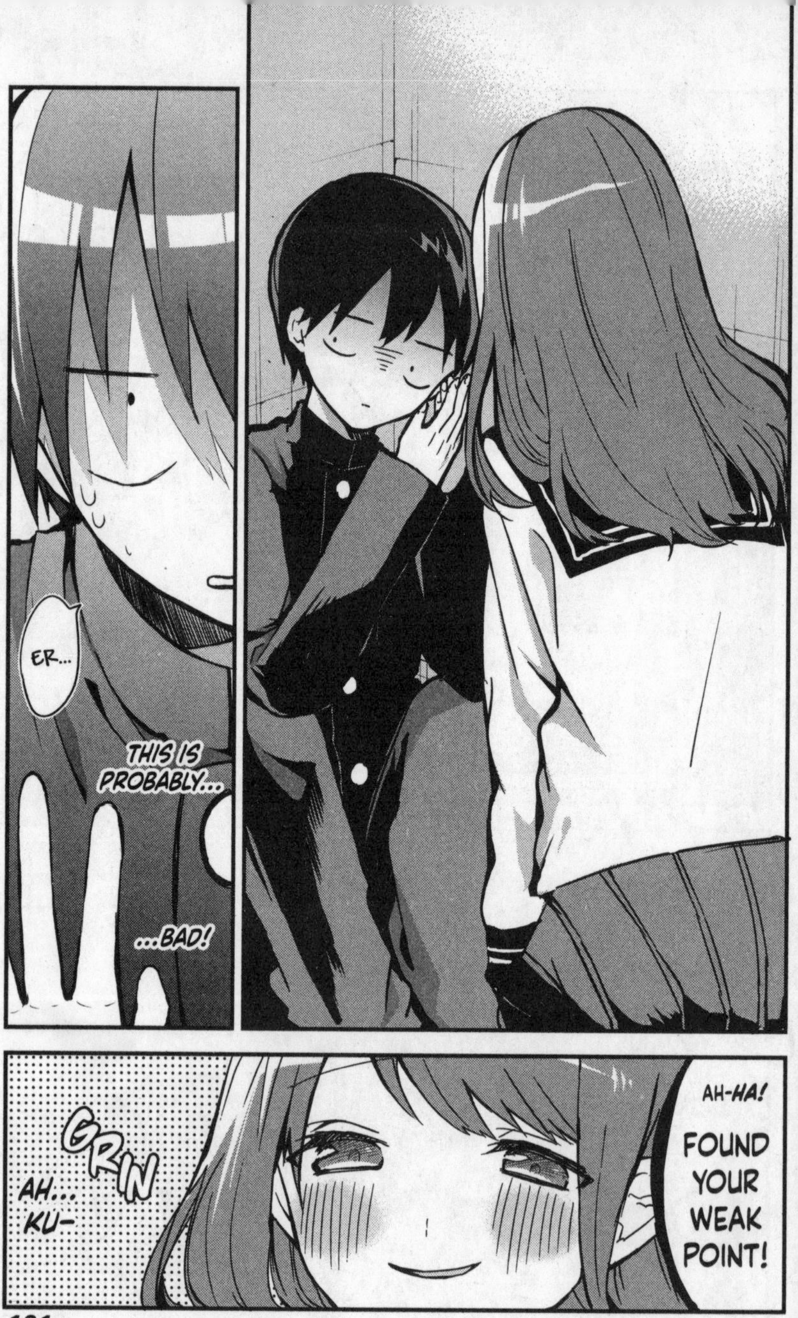
ER...
THIS IS PROBABLY...
...BAD!
AH-HA!
FOUND YOUR WEAK POINT!
GRIN
AH... KU-

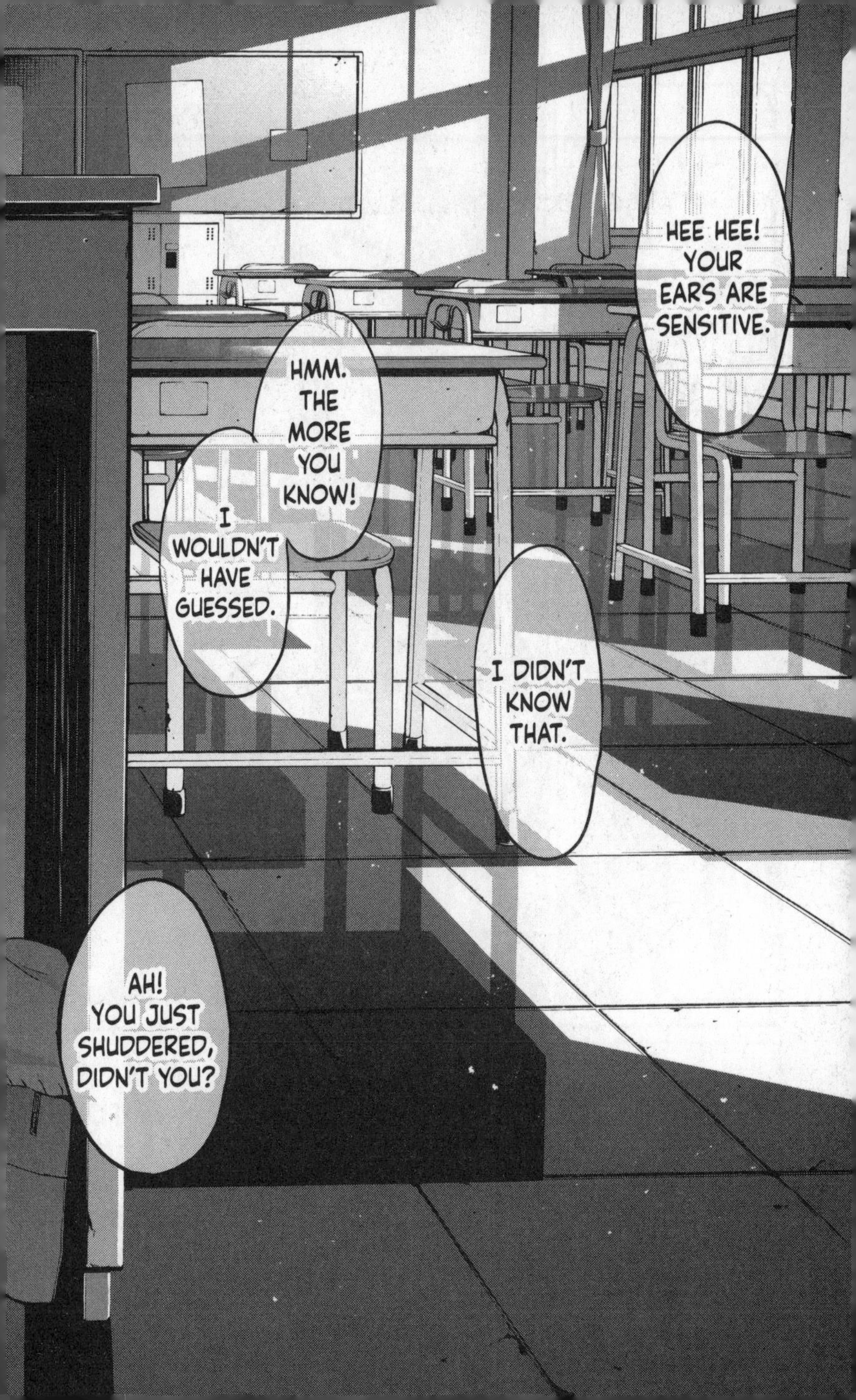
HEE HEE! YOUR EARS ARE SENSITIVE.
I DIDN'T KNOW THAT.
HMM. THE MORE YOU KNOW!
I WOULDN'T HAVE GUESSED.
AH! YOU JUST SHUDDERED, DIDN'T YOU?

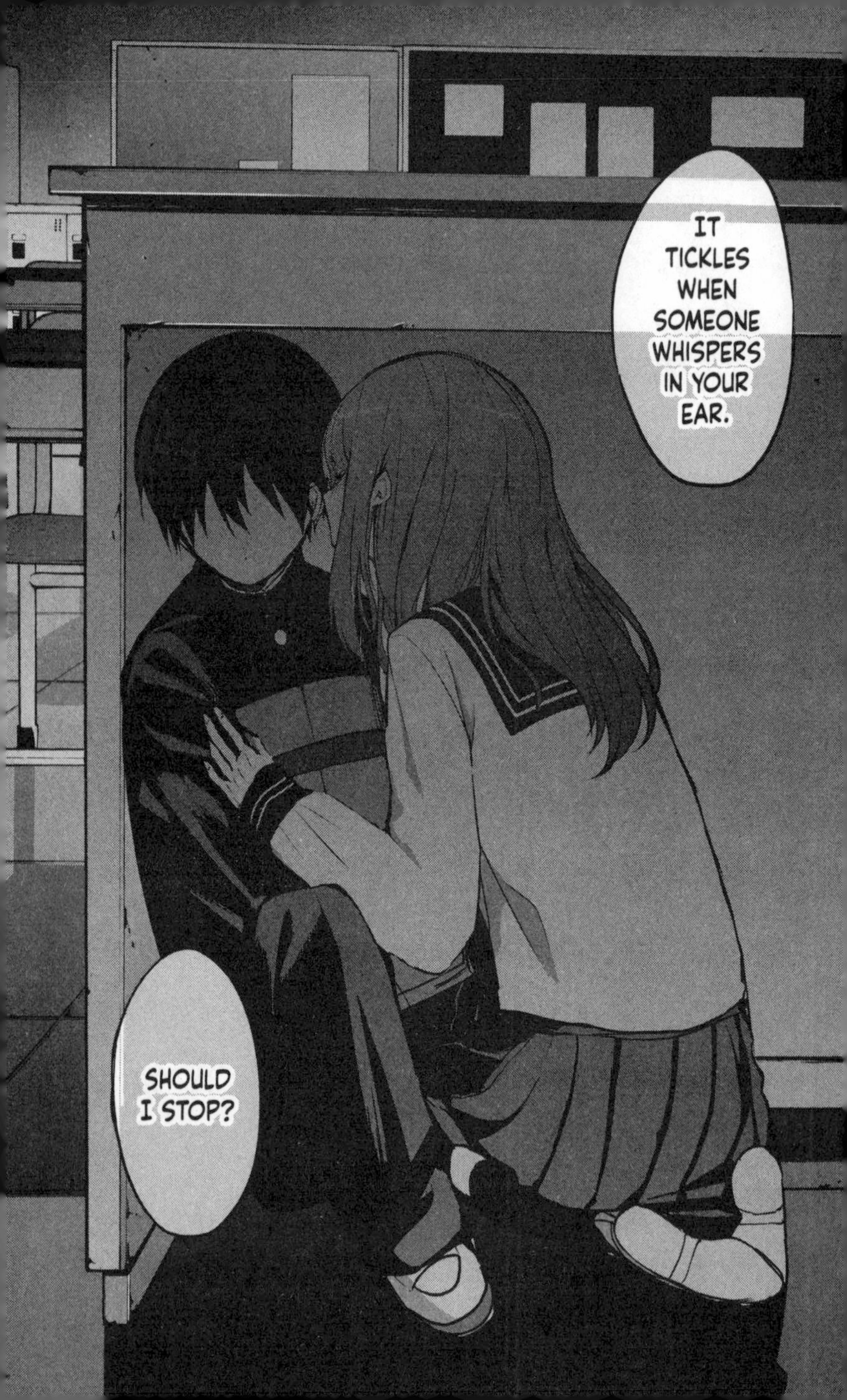
IT TICKLES WHEN SOMEONE WHISPERS IN YOUR EAR.
SHOULD I STOP?

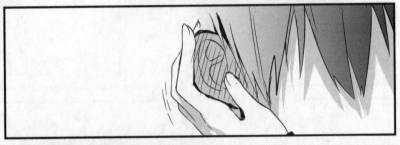

YOU KNOW YOU LIKE IT.

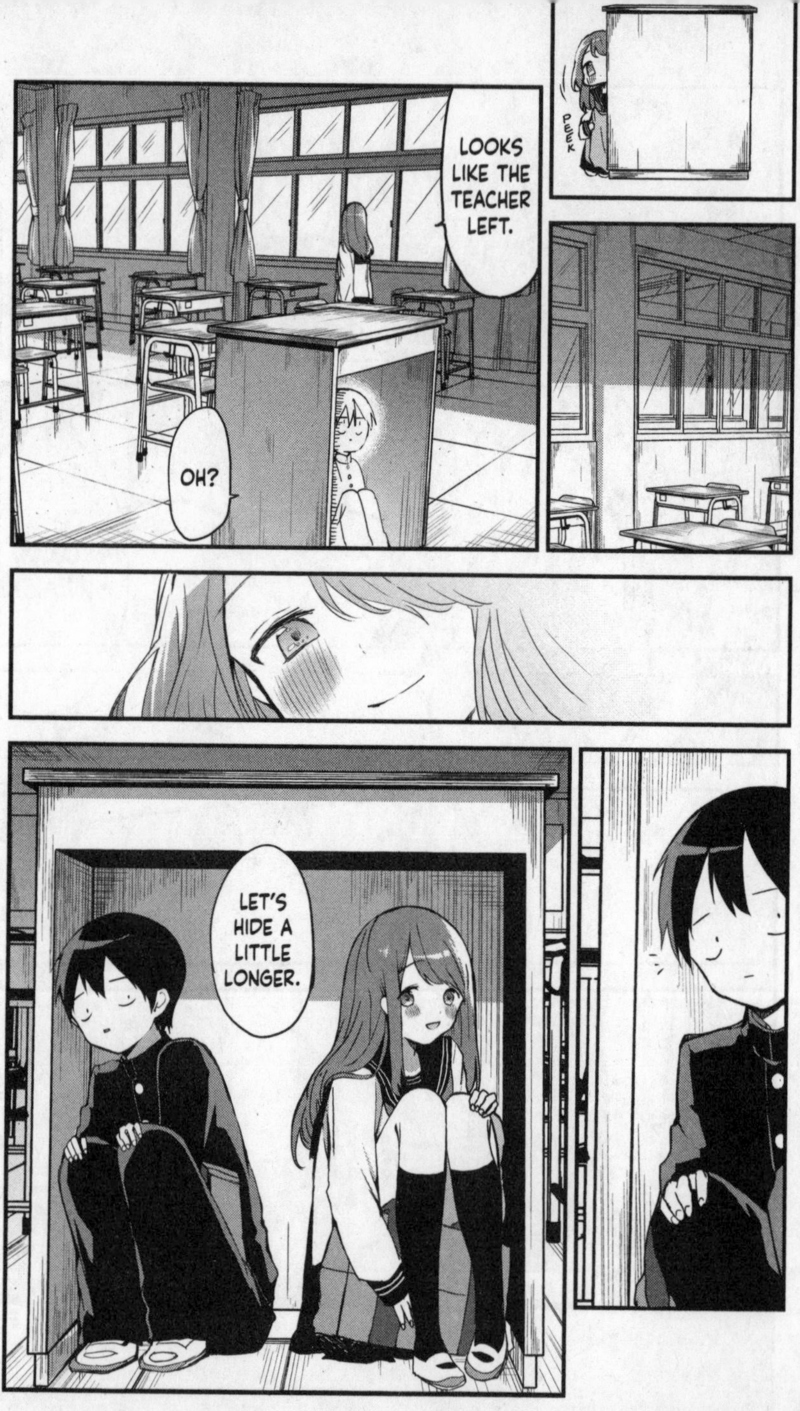
PEEK
LOOKS LIKE THE TEACHER LEFT.
OH?
LET'S HIDE A LITTLE LONGER.

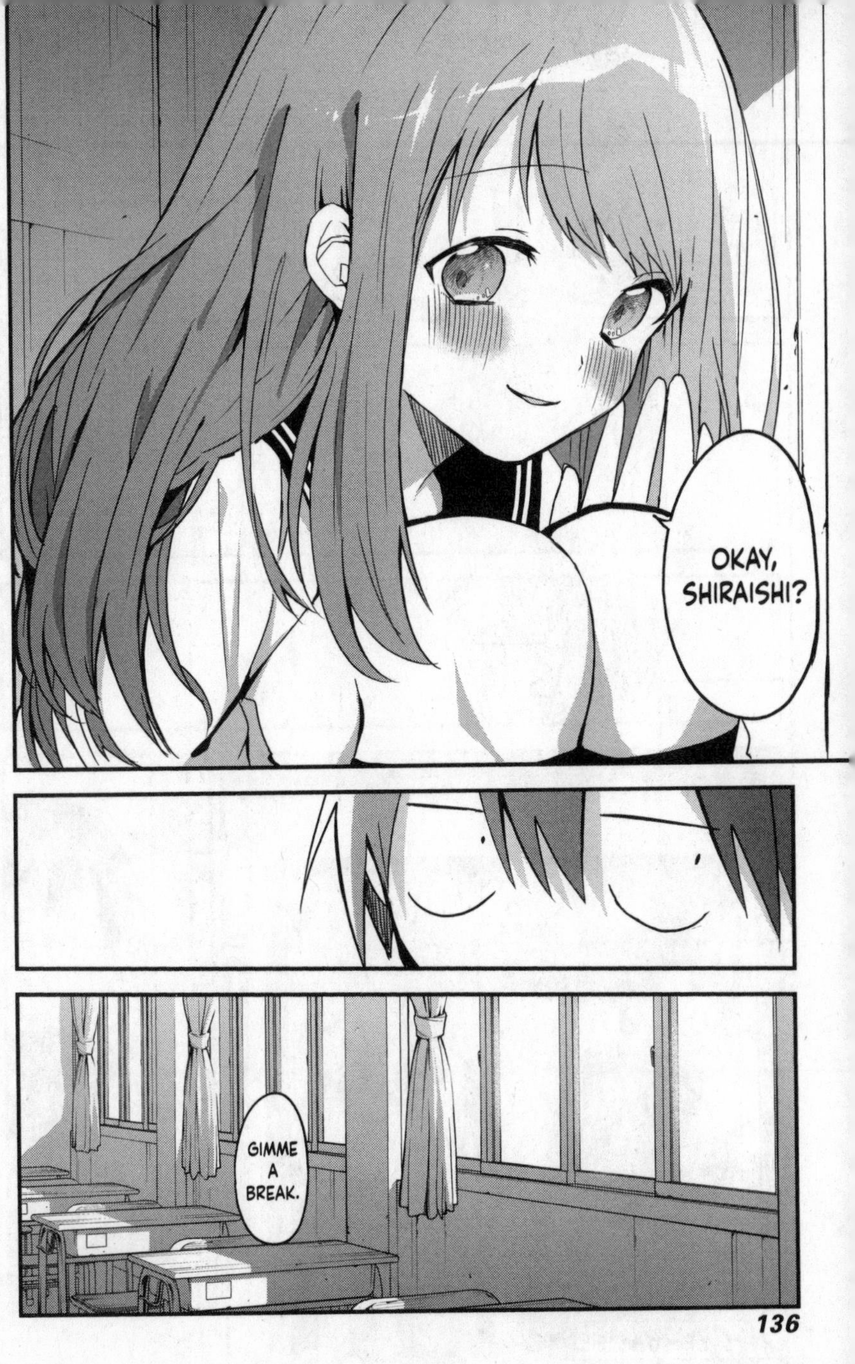
OKAY, SHIRAISHI?
GIMME A BREAK.

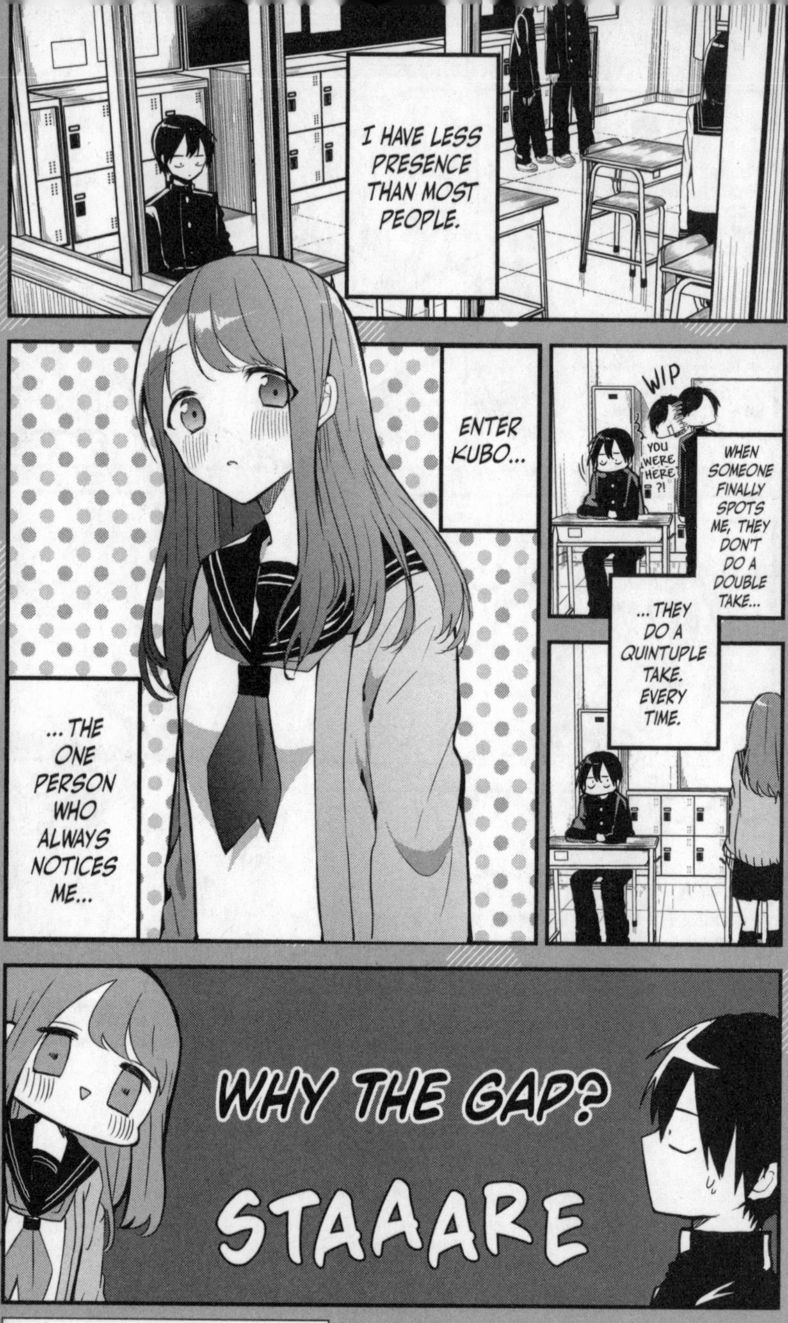
I HAVE LESS PRESENCE THAN MOST PEOPLE.
WIP
YOU WERE HERE?!
WHEN SOMEONE FINALLY SPOTS ME, THEY DON'T DO A DOUBLE TAKE...
...THEY DO A QUINTUPLE TAKE. EVERY TIME.
ENTER KUBO...
...THE ONE PERSON WHO ALWAYS NOTICES ME...
WHY THE GAP?
STAAARE

extra episode BED HEAD

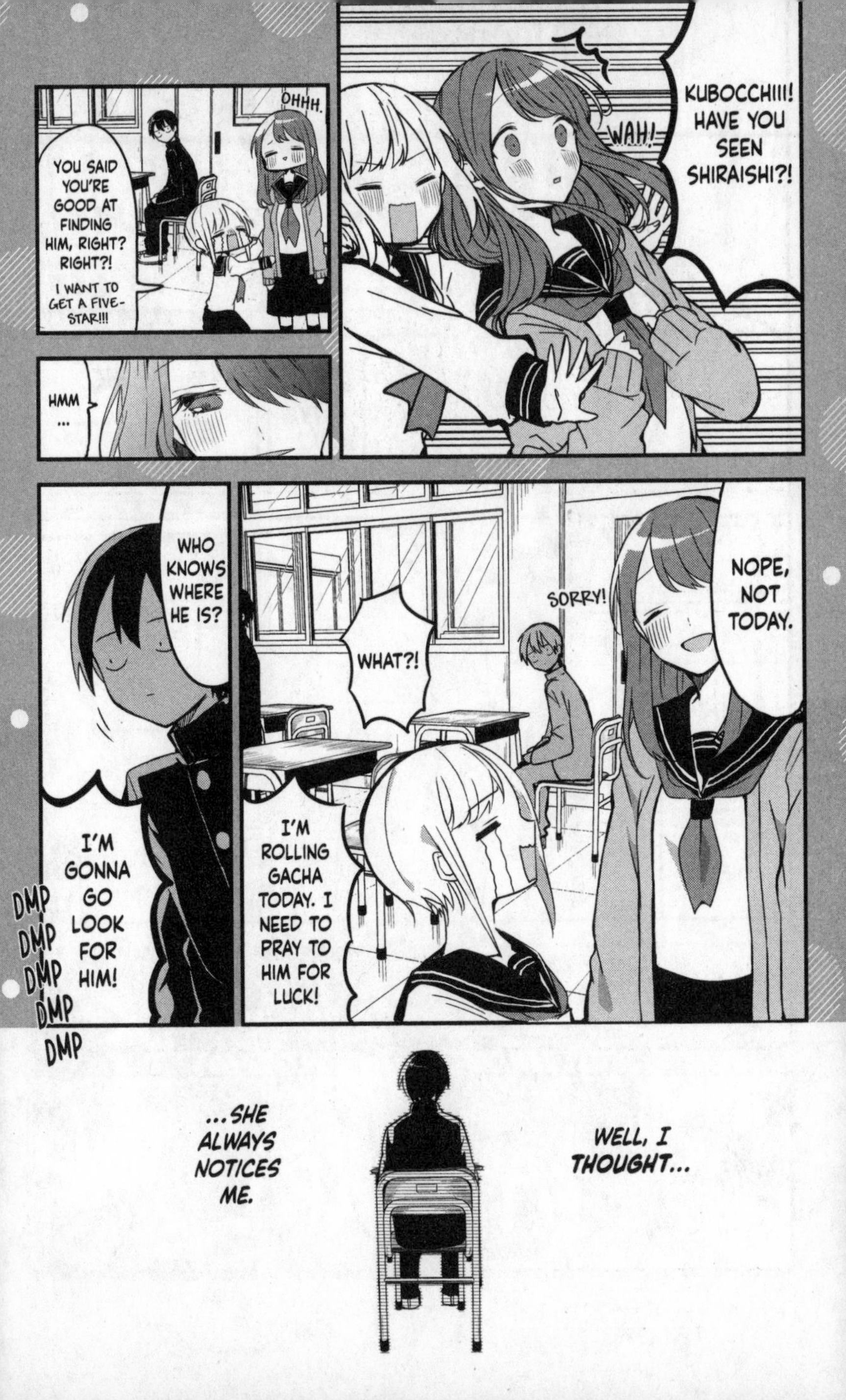
KUBOCCHIIII! HAVE YOU SEEN SHIRAISHI?!
WAH!
OHHH.
YOU SAID YOU'RE GOOD AT FINDING HIM, RIGHT? RIGHT?!
I WANT TO GET A FIVE-STAR!!!
HMM ...
NOPE, NOT TODAY.
SORRY!
WHAT?!
I'M ROLLING GACHA TODAY. I NEED TO PRAY TO HIM FOR LUCK!
WHO KNOWS WHERE HE IS?
I'M GONNA GO LOOK FOR HIM!
DMP DMP DMP DMP DMP
WELL, I THOUGHT...
...SHE ALWAYS NOTICES ME.

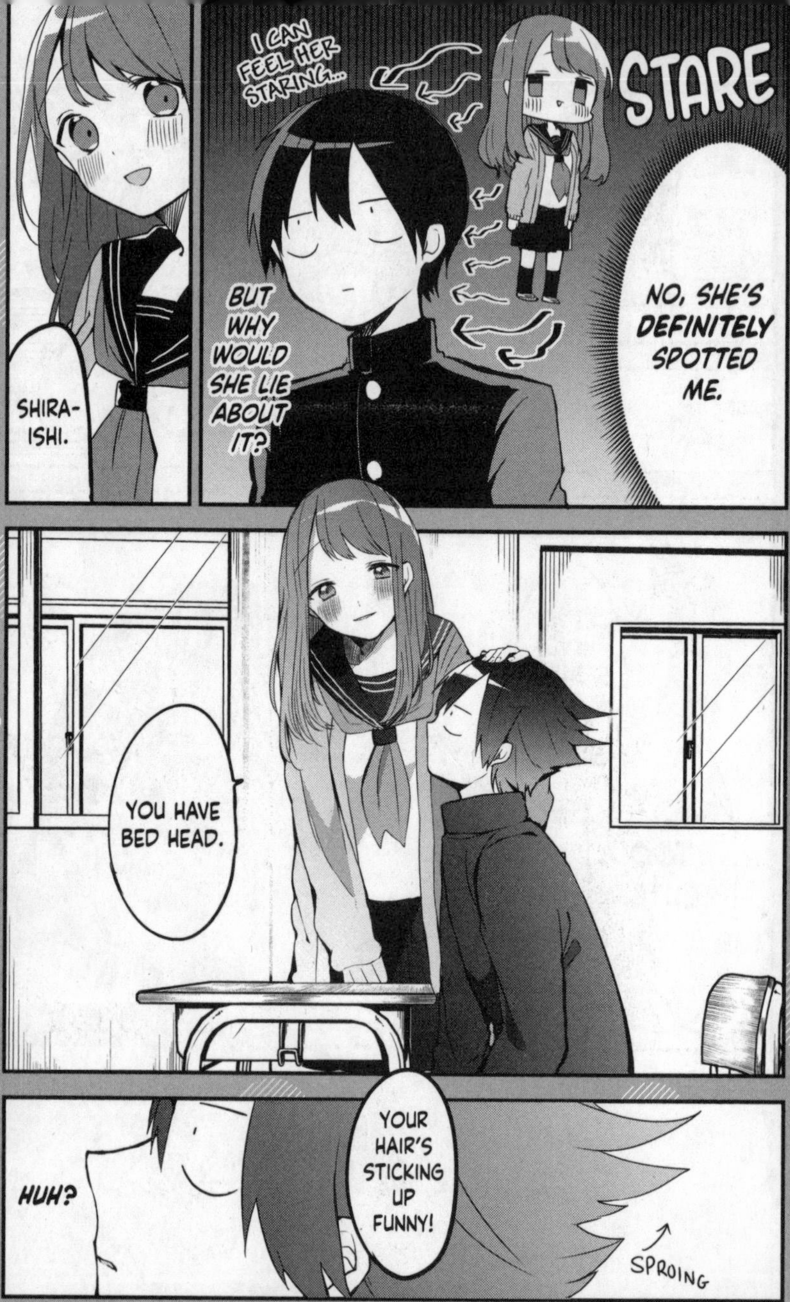
STARE
I CAN FEEL HER STARING...
NO, SHE'S DEFINITELY SPOTTED ME.
BUT WHY WOULD SHE LIE ABOUT IT?
SHIRA-ISHI.
YOU HAVE BED HEAD.
YOUR HAIR'S STICKING UP FUNNY!
SPROING
HUH?

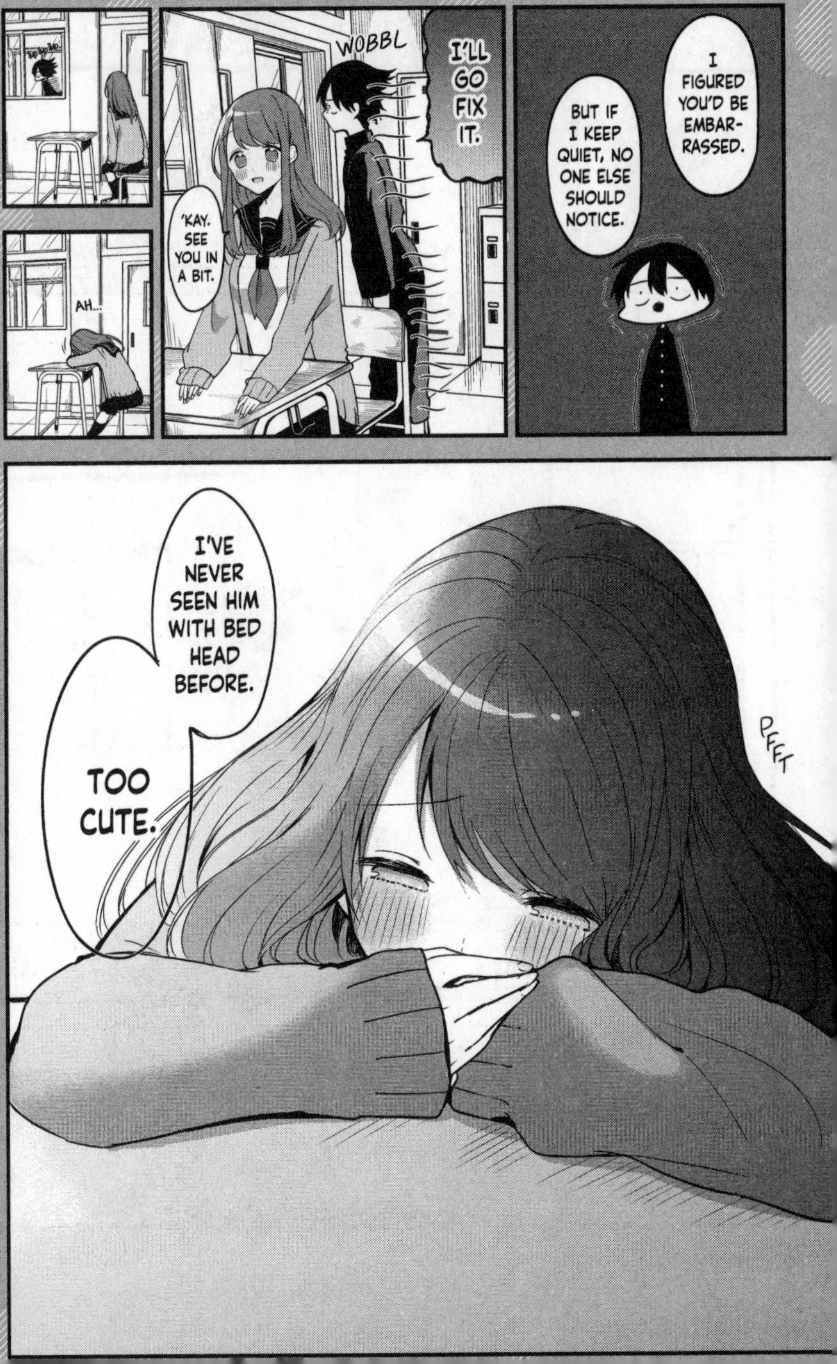
I FIGURED YOU'D BE EMBARRASSED.
BUT IF I KEEP QUIET, NO ONE ELSE SHOULD NOTICE.
I'LL GO FIX IT.
WOBBL
'KAY. SEE YOU IN A BIT.
AH...
I'VE NEVER SEEN HIM WITH BED HEAD BEFORE.
TOO CUTE.
PFFFT

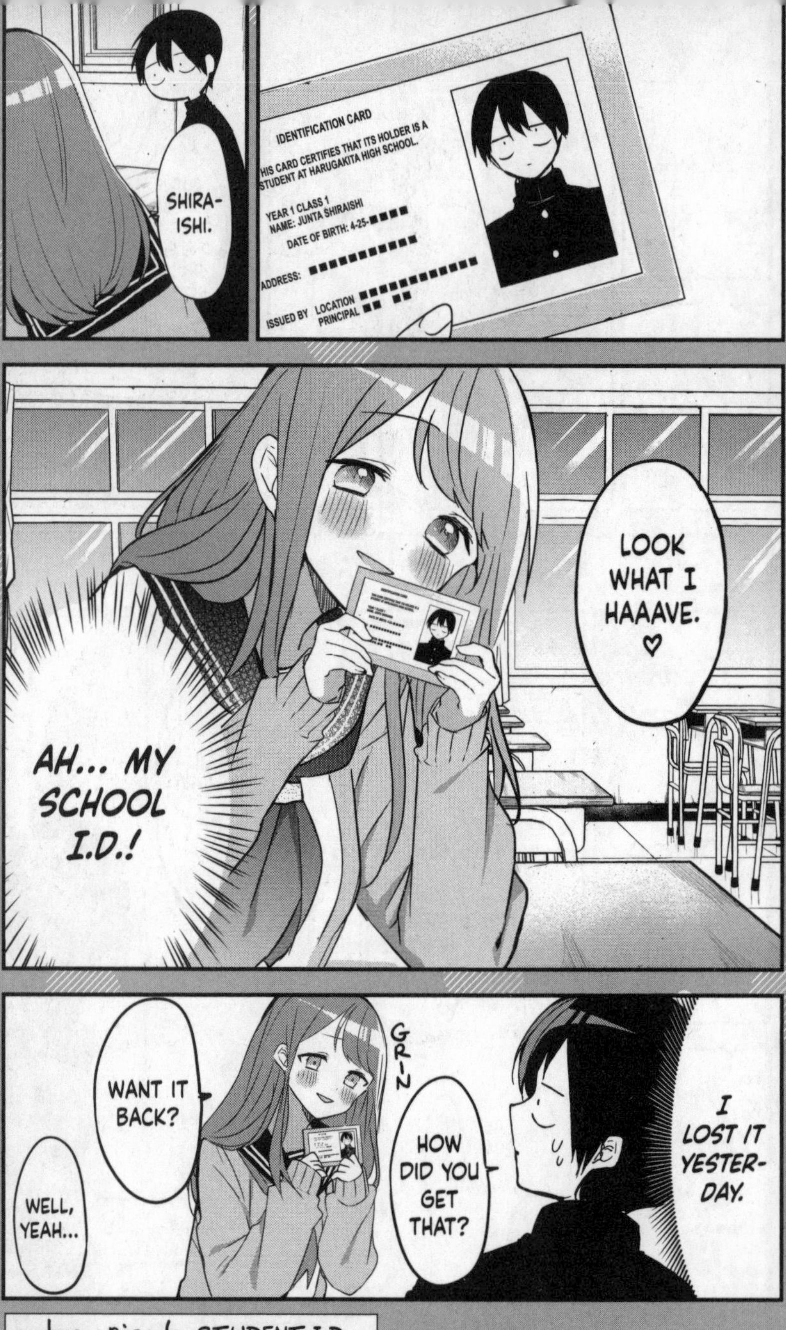
IDENTIFICATION CARD
HIS CARD CERTIFIES THAT ITS HOLDER IS A STUDENT AT HARUGAKITA HIGH SCHOOL.
YEAR 1 CLASS 1
NAME: JUNTA SHIRAISHI
DATE OF BIRTH: 4-25-[redacted]
ADDRESS: [redacted]
ISSUED BY LOCATION [redacted]
PRINCIPAL [redacted]
SHIRA-ISHI.
LOOK WHAT I HAAAVE. ♡
AH... MY SCHOOL I.D.!
I LOST IT YESTER-DAY.
HOW DID YOU GET THAT?
GRIN
WANT IT BACK?
WELL, YEAH...

extra episode STUDENT I.D.

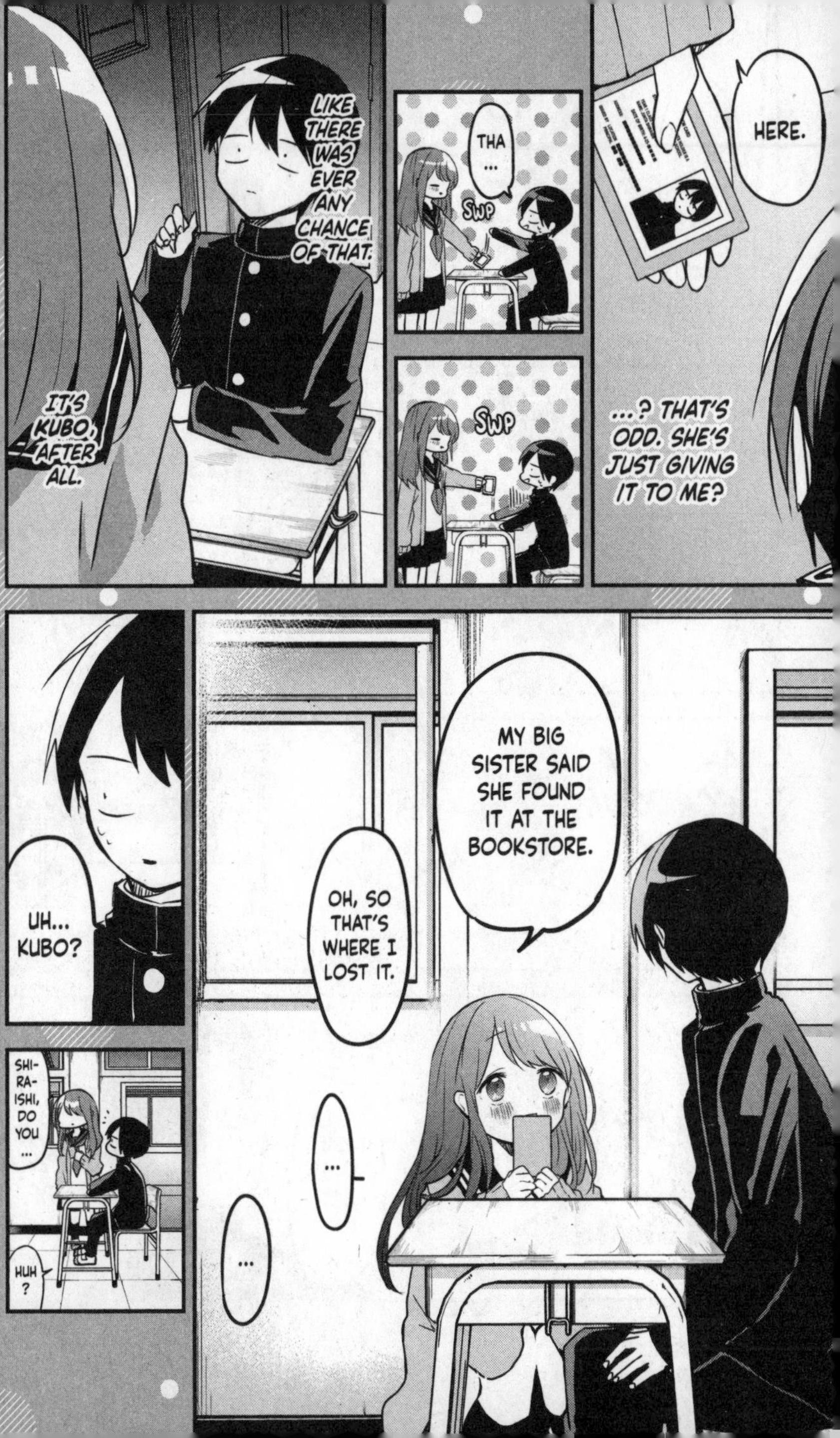

HERE.
...? THAT'S ODD. SHE'S JUST GIVING IT TO ME?
THA ...
SWP
SWP
LIKE THERE WAS EVER ANY CHANCE OF THAT.
IT'S KUBO, AFTER ALL.
MY BIG SISTER SAID SHE FOUND IT AT THE BOOKSTORE.
OH, SO THAT'S WHERE I LOST IT.
...
...
UH... KUBO?
SHI-RA-ISHI, DO YOU ...
HUH ?

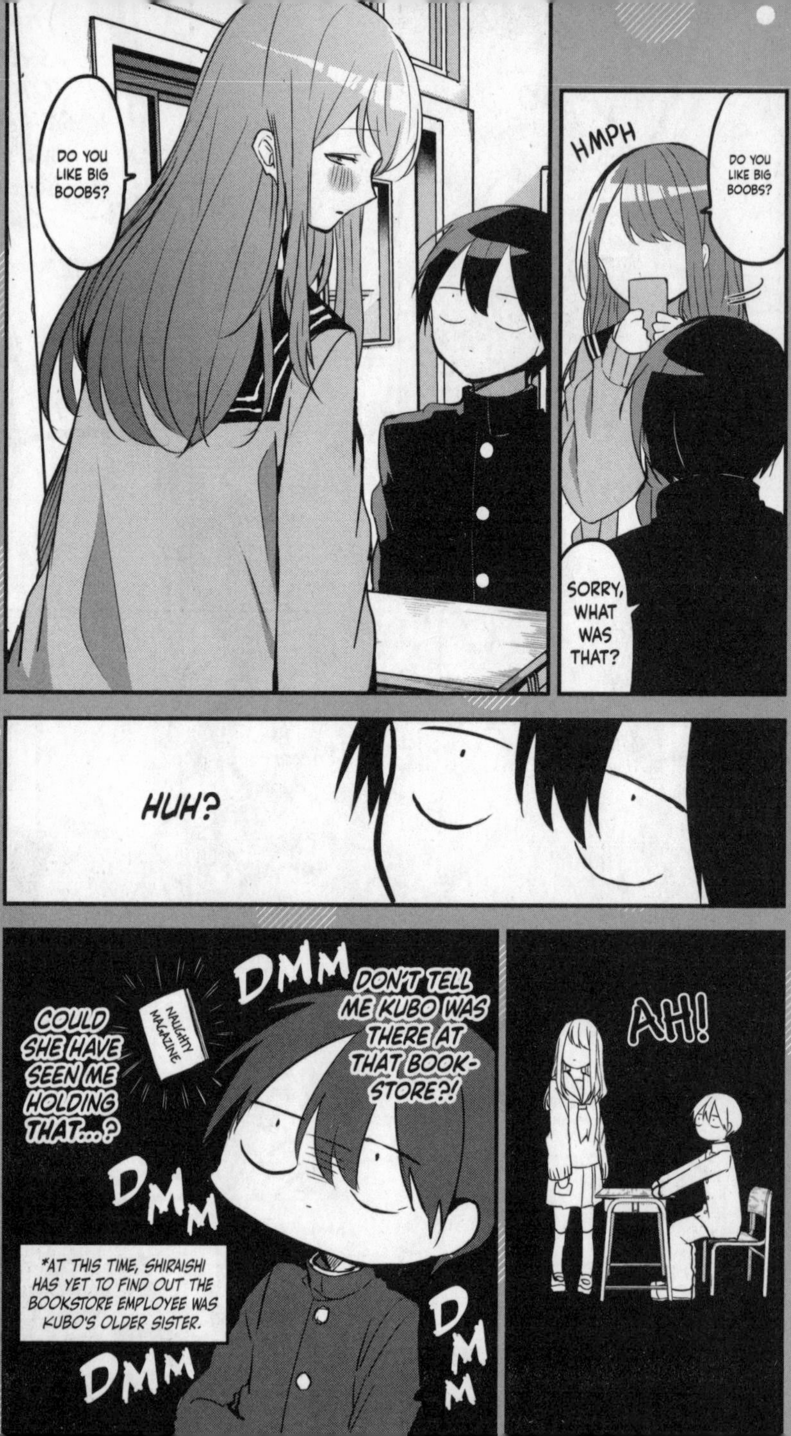
HMPH
DO YOU LIKE BIG BOOBS?
SORRY, WHAT WAS THAT?
DO YOU LIKE BIG BOOBS?
HUH?
AH!
DMM
DON'T TELL ME KUBO WAS THERE AT THAT BOOK-STORE?!
NAUGHTY MAGAZINE
COULD SHE HAVE SEEN ME HOLDING THAT...?
DMM
DMM
*AT THIS TIME, SHIRAISHI HAS YET TO FIND OUT THE BOOKSTORE EMPLOYEE WAS KUBO'S OLDER SISTER.
DMM

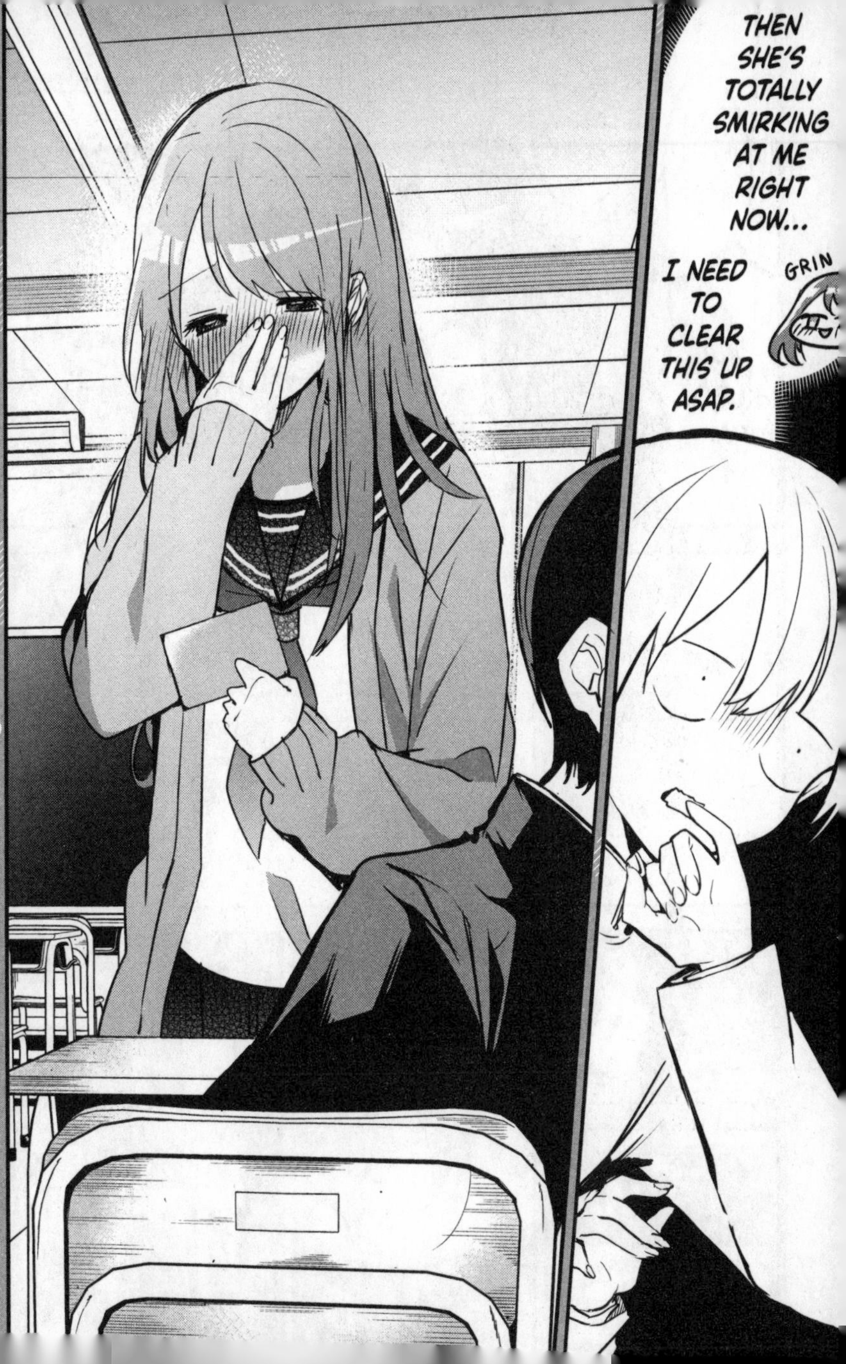
THEN SHE'S TOTALLY SMIRKING AT ME RIGHT NOW...
I NEED TO CLEAR THIS UP ASAP.
GRIN

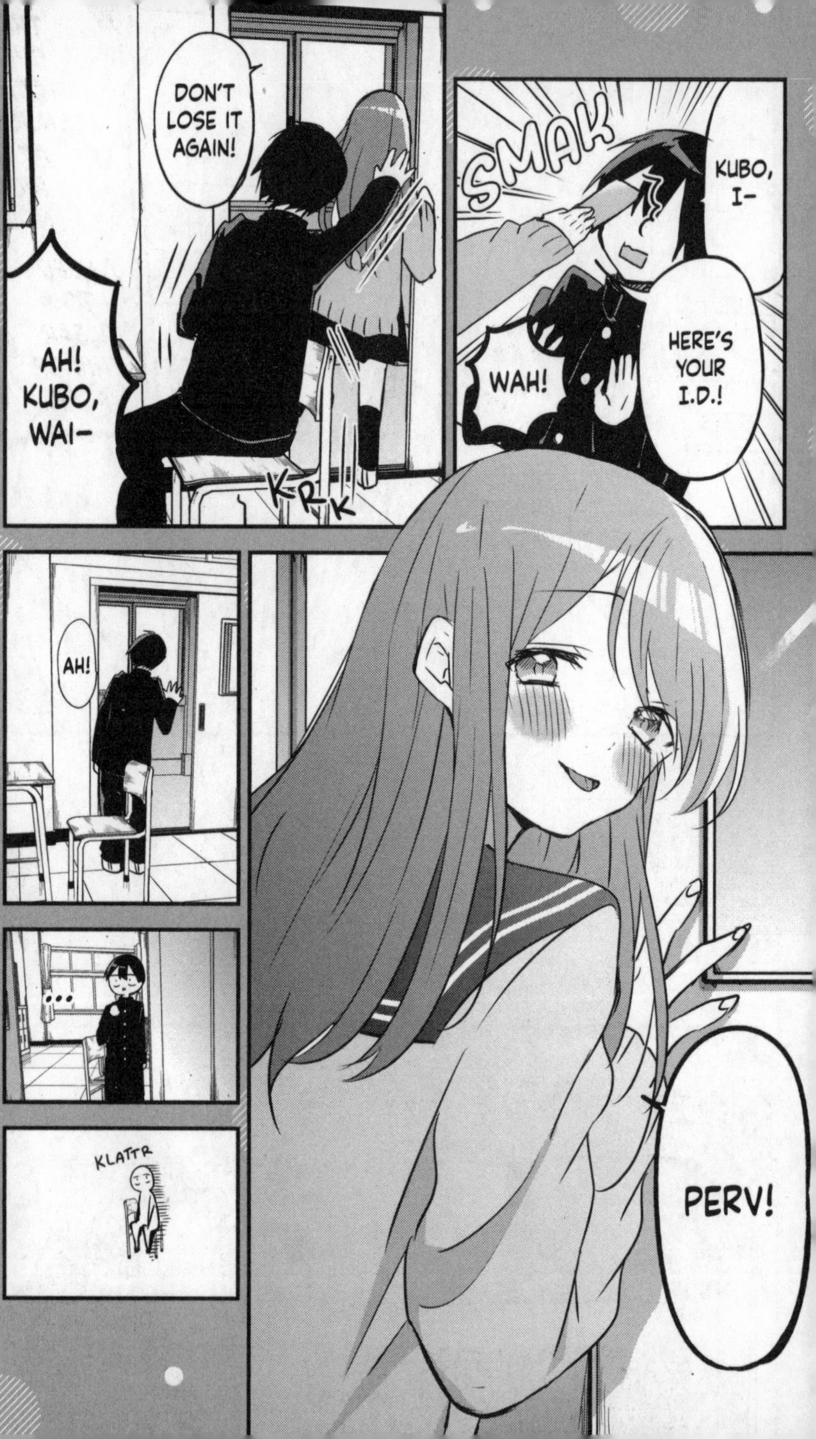
KUBO, I–
SMAK
HERE'S YOUR I.D.!
WAH!
DON'T LOSE IT AGAIN!
AH! KUBO, WAI–
KRK
PERV!
AH!
...
KLATTR

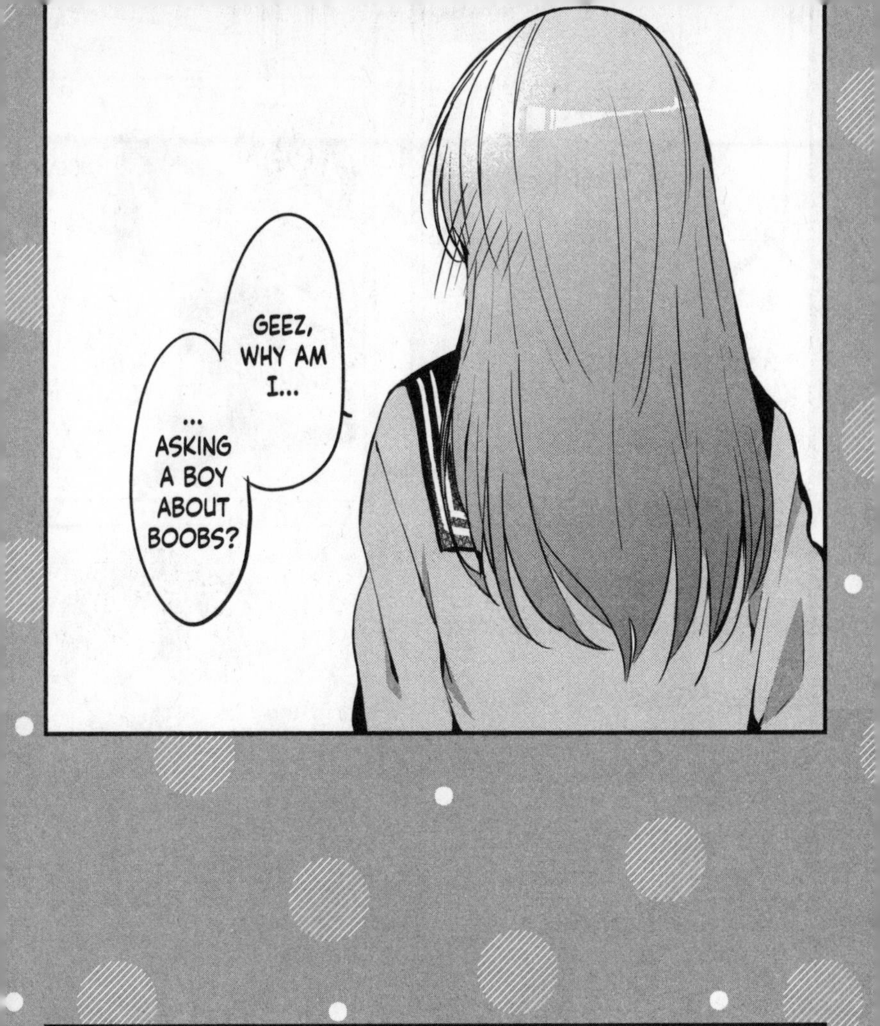
GEEZ, WHY AM I...
... ASKING A BOY ABOUT BOOBS?

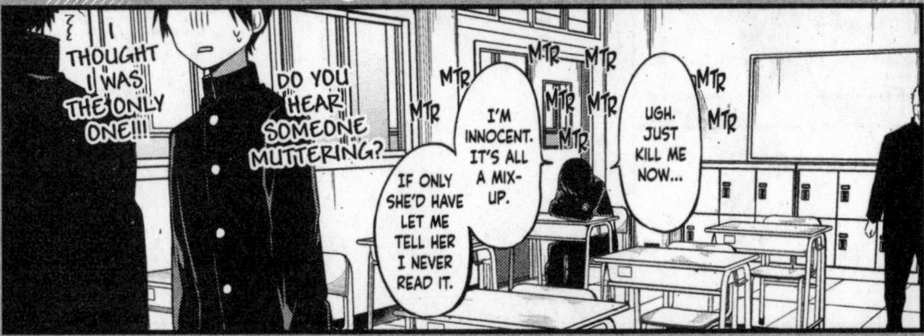
MTR MTR
UGH. JUST KILL ME NOW...
MTR MTR MTR MTR MTR
I'M INNOCENT. IT'S ALL A MIX-UP.
MTR MTR
IF ONLY SHE'D HAVE LET ME TELL HER I NEVER READ IT.
DO YOU HEAR SOMEONE MUTTERING?
I THOUGHT I WAS THE ONLY ONE!!!

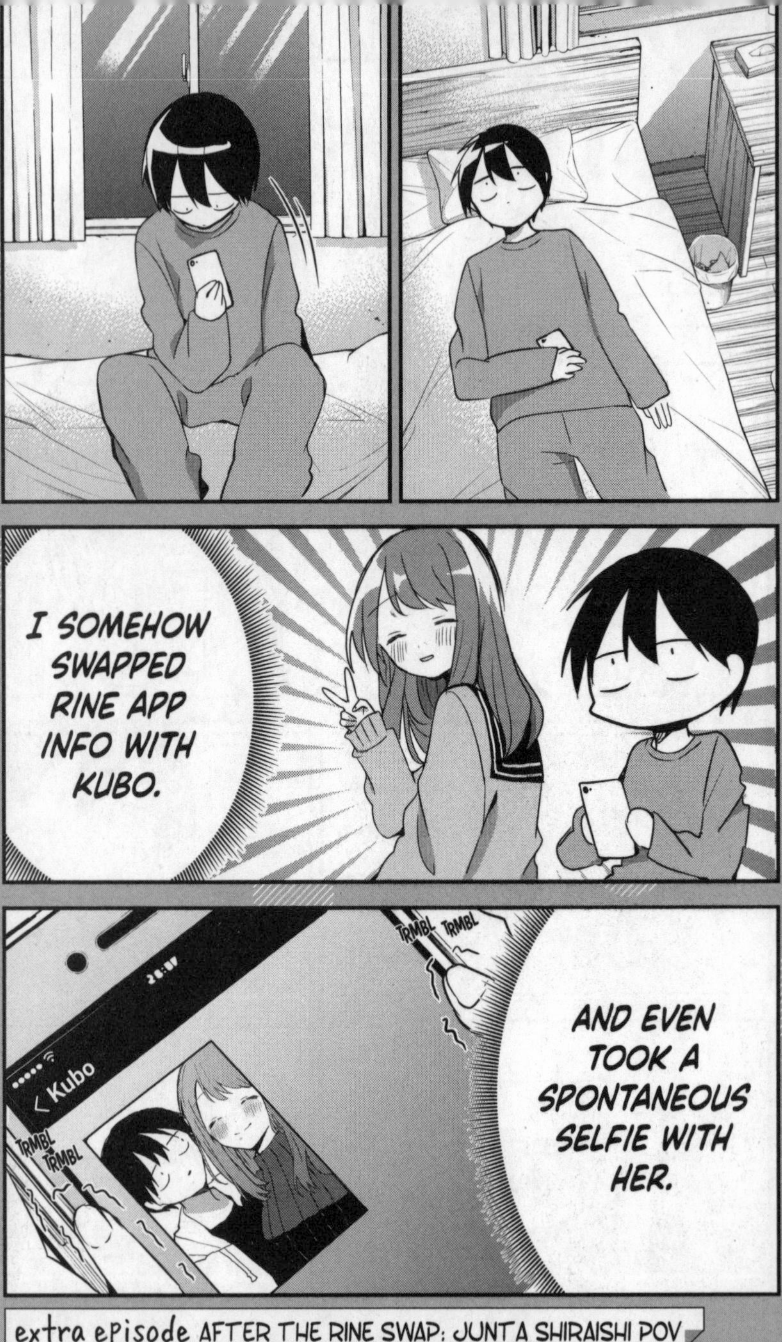
I SOMEHOW SWAPPED RINE APP INFO WITH KUBO.
TRMBL TRMBL
AND EVEN TOOK A SPONTANEOUS SELFIE WITH HER.
Kubo
TRMBL TRMBL

extra episode AFTER THE RINE SWAP: JUNTA SHIRAISHI POV

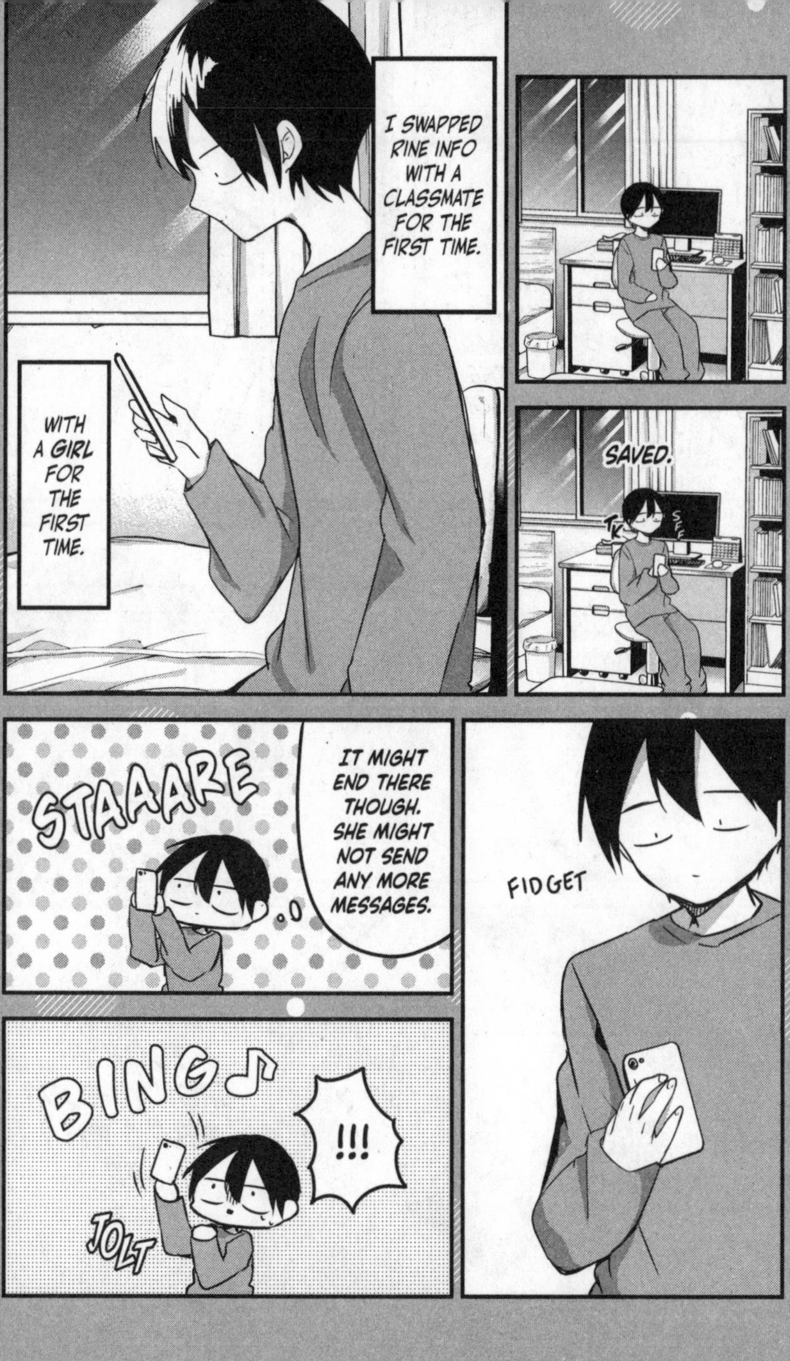
SAVED.
TK
SFF
I SWAPPED RINE INFO WITH A CLASSMATE FOR THE FIRST TIME.
WITH A GIRL FOR THE FIRST TIME.
FIDGET
STAAARE
IT MIGHT END THERE THOUGH. SHE MIGHT NOT SEND ANY MORE MESSAGES.
BING♪
!!!
JOLT

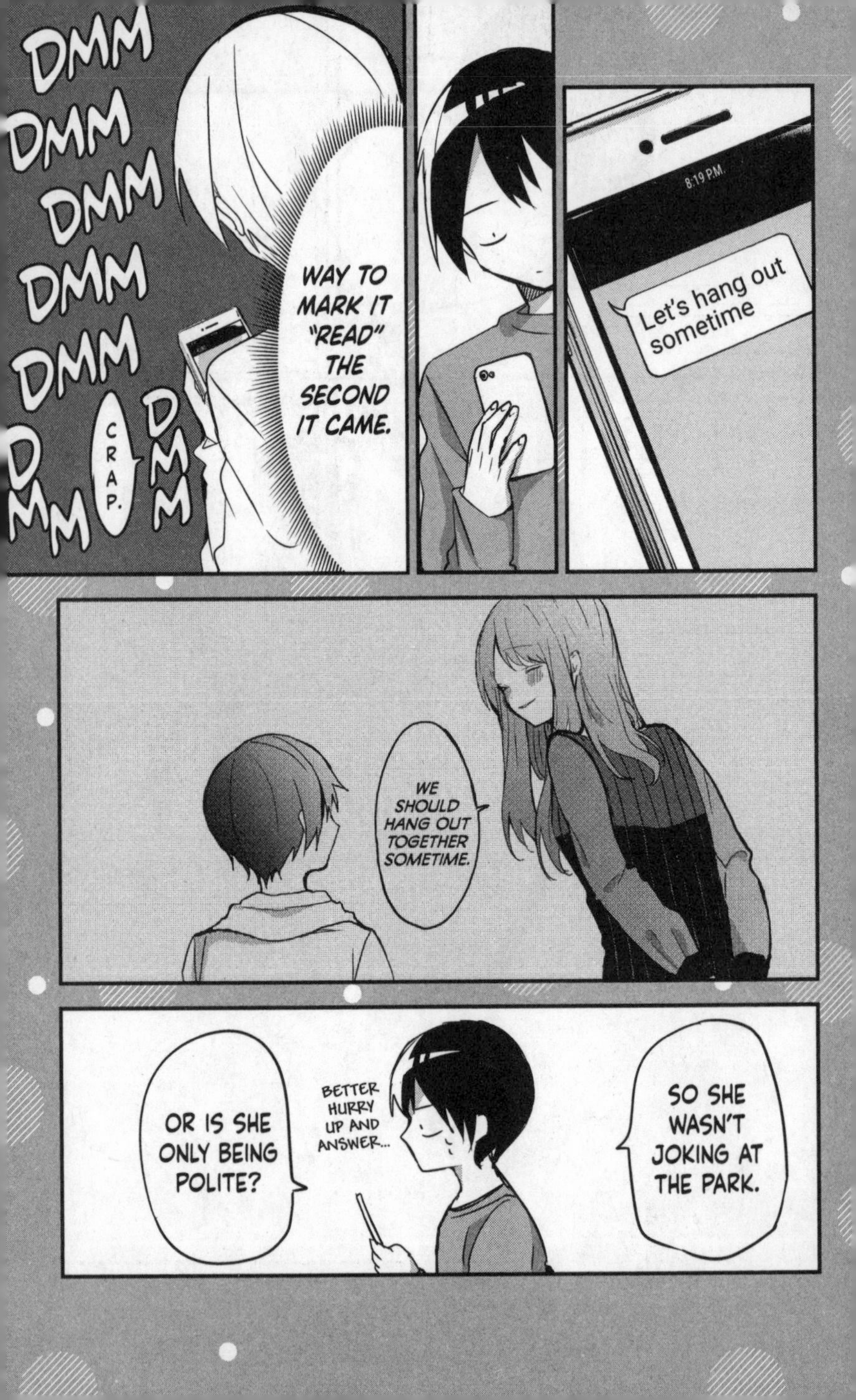
8:19 P.M.
Let's hang out sometime
WAY TO MARK IT "READ" THE SECOND IT CAME.
DMM DMM DMM DMM DMM DMM DMM
CRAP.
DMM
WE SHOULD HANG OUT TOGETHER SOMETIME.
SO SHE WASN'T JOKING AT THE PARK.
BETTER HURRY UP AND ANSWER...
OR IS SHE ONLY BEING POLITE?

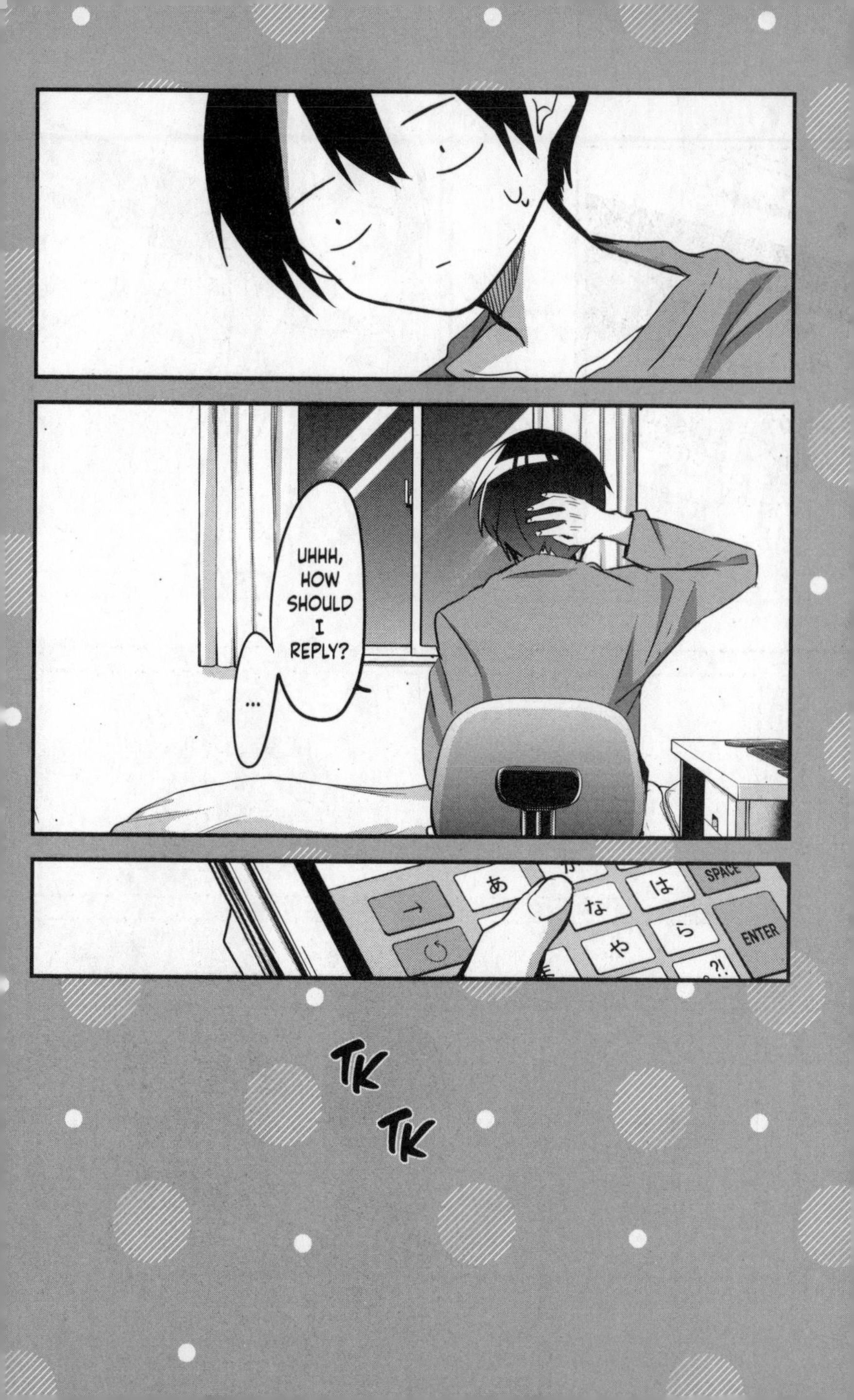
UHHH, HOW SHOULD I REPLY?
...
あ
は
な
ら
や
SPACE
ENTER
?!
TK
TK

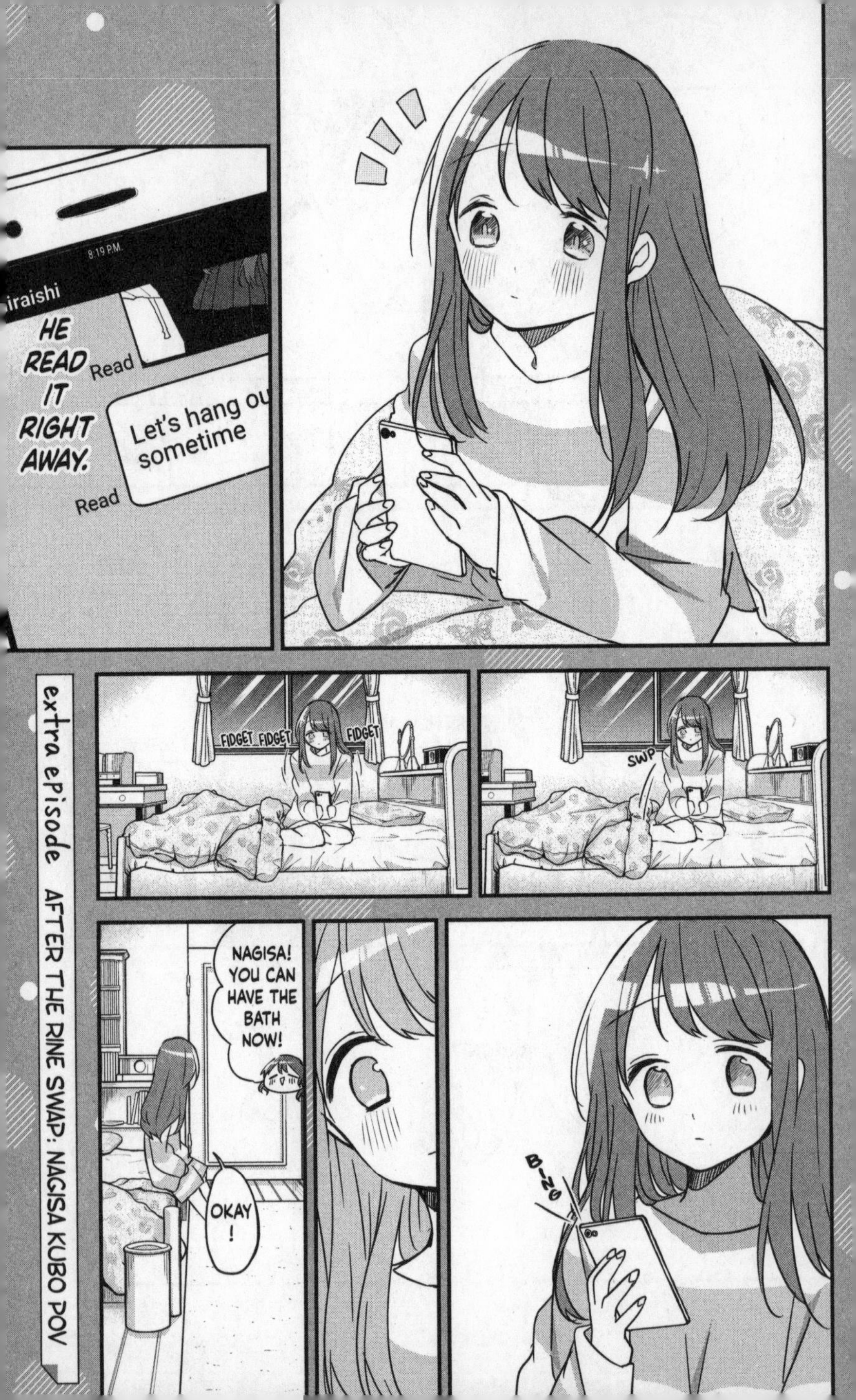
8:19 P.M.
iraishi
Read
Let's hang ou sometime
Read
HE READ IT RIGHT AWAY.
SWP
FIDGET FIDGET FIDGET
extra episode AFTER THE RINE SWAP: NAGISA KUBO POV
BING
NAGISA! YOU CAN HAVE THE BATH NOW!
OKAY!

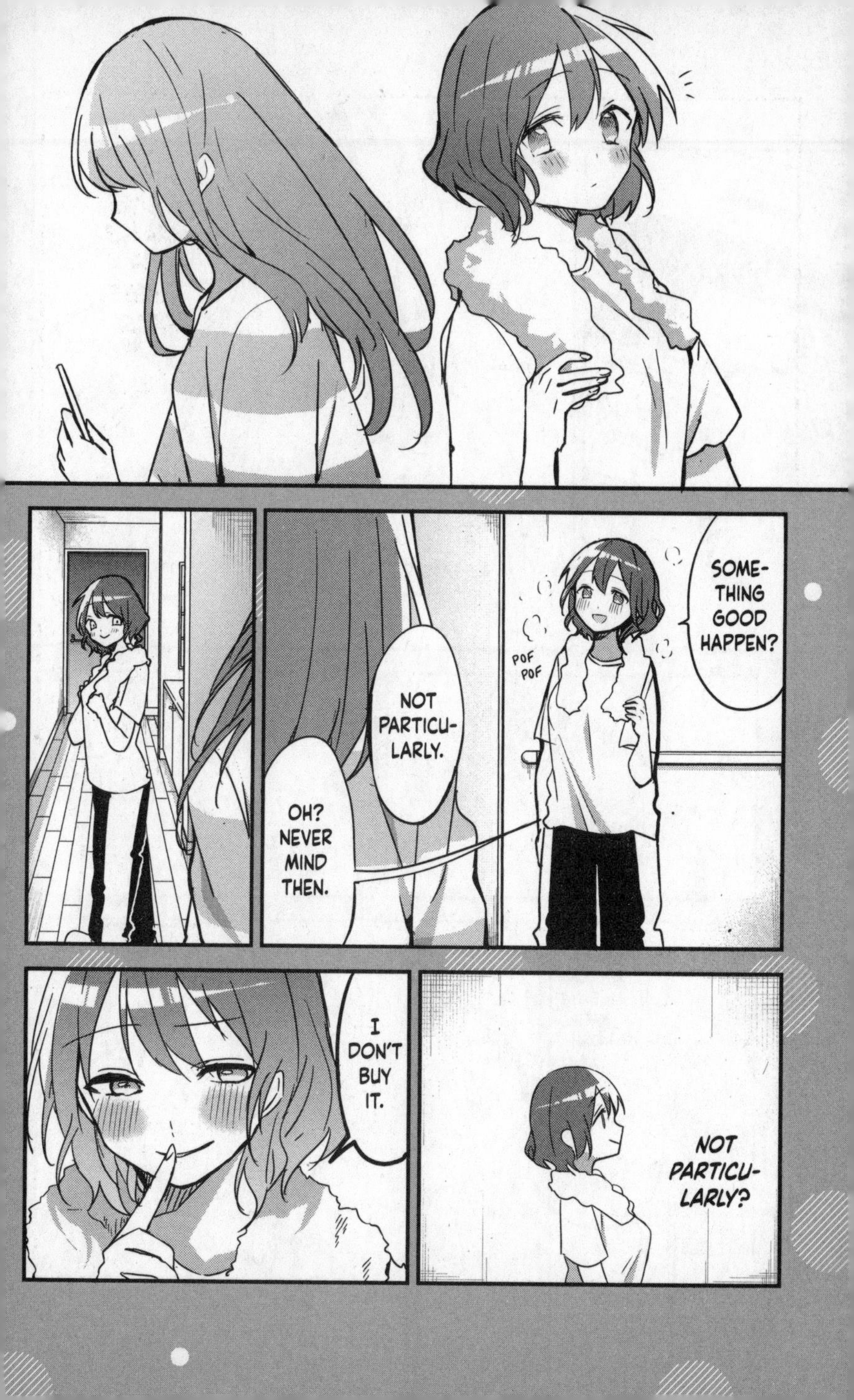
SOME-THING GOOD HAPPEN?
POF POF
NOT PARTICU-LARLY.
OH? NEVER MIND THEN.
NOT PARTICU-LARLY?
I DON'T BUY IT.

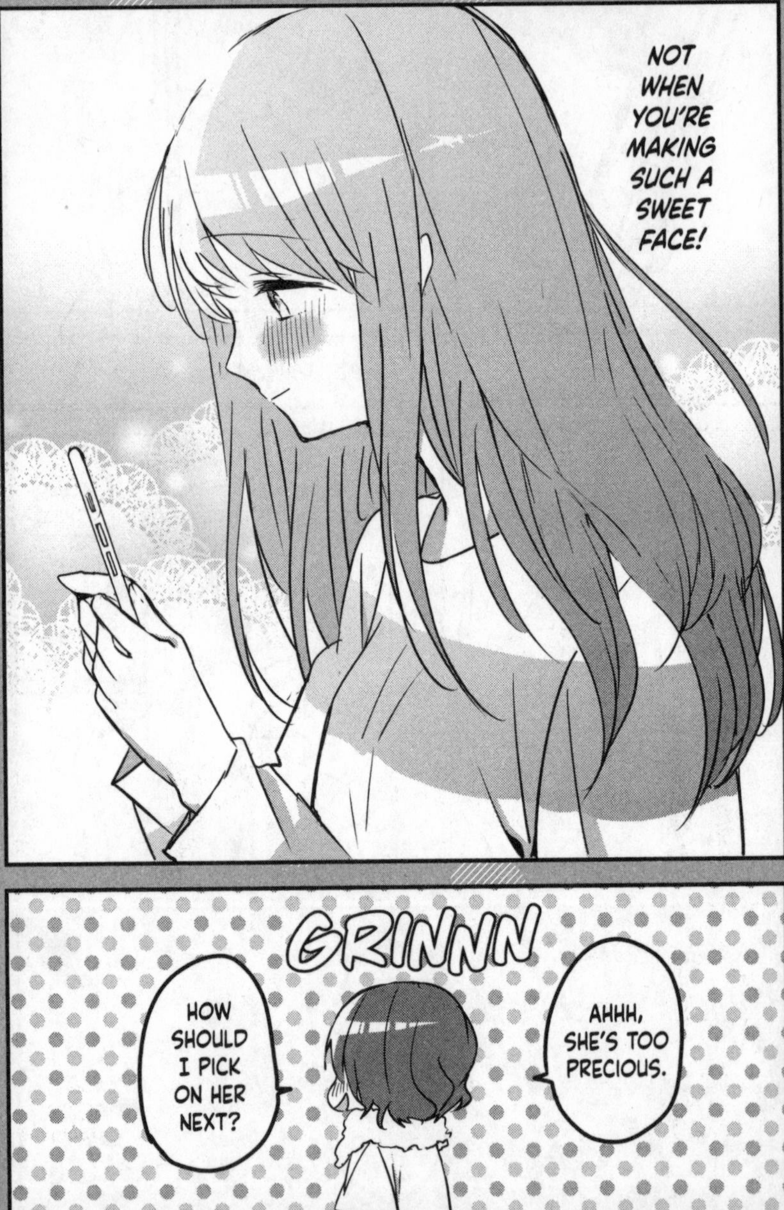
NOT WHEN YOU'RE MAKING SUCH A SWEET FACE!
GRINNN
AHHH, SHE'S TOO PRECIOUS.
HOW SHOULD I PICK ON HER NEXT?

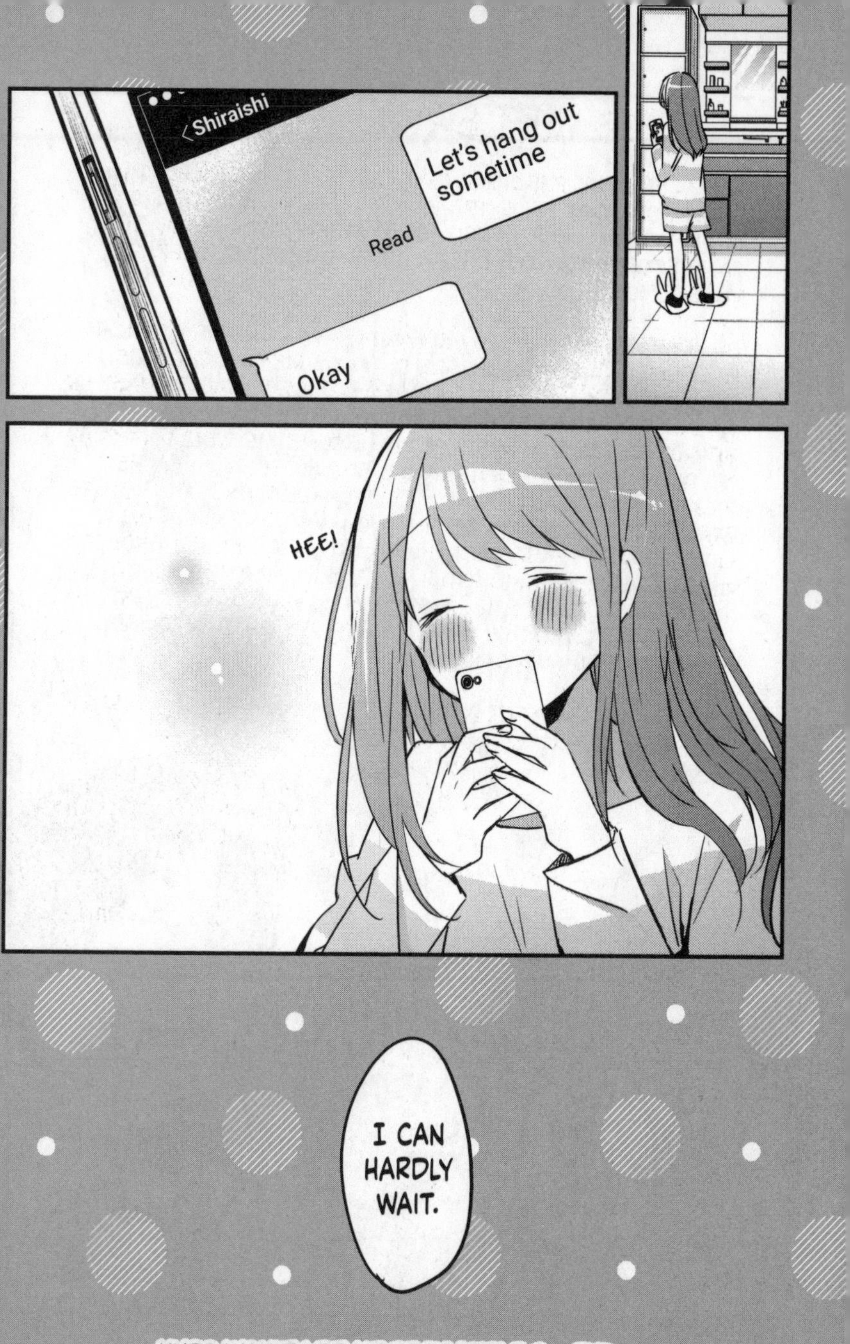
Shiraishi
Let's hang out sometime
Read
Okay
HEE!
I CAN HARDLY WAIT.

KUBO WON'T LET ME BE INVISIBLE 2 - END

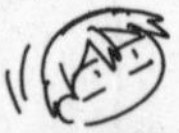

AFTERWORD

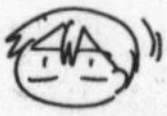

THANK YOU FOR PURCHASING VOLUME 2! I'M SO GLAD! THE FIRST BOOK GOT AN EXTRA PRINTING... I'M INDEBTED TO SO MANY PEOPLE... THANK YOU SO, SO MUCH! THANKS FOR THE FAN LETTERS TOO. I'LL CHERISH THEM. THEY'RE MY PRIZED POSSESSIONS.

OH YEAH, I'M PLAYING *FINAL FANTASY VII REMAKE*. GOSH, IT'S FUN. AND SO NOSTALGIC. IT TAKES ME BACK TO WHEN I WOULD WATCH MY DAD PLAY VIDEO GAMES. *FINAL FANTASY VII* WAS ONE OF THE GAMES HE'D PLAY AT THE TIME, AND AFTER HE GOT TO THE INFAMOUS AERITH SCENE, HE WOULDN'T PLAY IT FOR AN ENTIRE MONTH. I WAS SO SAD. THEN WHEN HE PICKED IT UP AGAIN, I WAS LIKE, "FINALLY!" ONLY FOR HIM TO START OVER FROM THE BEGINNING... LOOKING BACK ON IT NOW, IT MUST HAVE GIVEN HIM QUITE THE SHOCK. I BROUGHT UP GAMES IN VOLUME 1 TOO—ACTUALLY, I'M PRETTY INTO THEM. WHEN I WAS STILL A STUDENT, I WOULD GET UP AT 2 A.M. AND PLAY VIDEO GAMES UNTIL IT WAS TIME TO GO TO SCHOOL. SO MANY MEMORIES.

LASTLY, I HOPE I MEET A FUTURE YOU WHO HAS READ VOLUME 3! THANKS FOR ALL THE SUPPORT! SEE YOU!

NENE YUKIMORI
4/28/2020

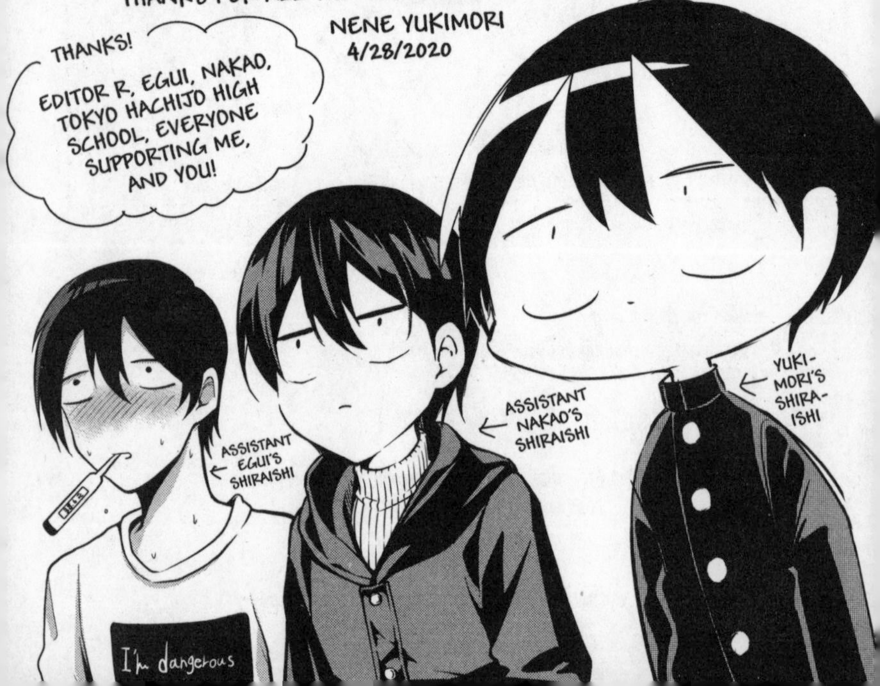
YUKI-MORI'S SHIRA-ISHI
ASSISTANT NAKAO'S SHIRAISHI
THANKS!
EDITOR R, EGUI, NAKAO, TOKYO HACHIJO HIGH SCHOOL, EVERYONE SUPPORTING ME, AND YOU!
ASSISTANT EGUI'S SHIRAISHI
I'm dangerous

I'll leave behind the meanings of the words
and synchronize with the wavelengths of your life.

Don't say "the secret ingredient is love" like it's simple.
Love is the hardest ingredient of all to add.

I have no idea how many questions there are,
how long the answer section is.
Still, I'll overcome
the tough questions wrenching my heart.

Editor R's Very Best Title Page Poems

Vol. 2

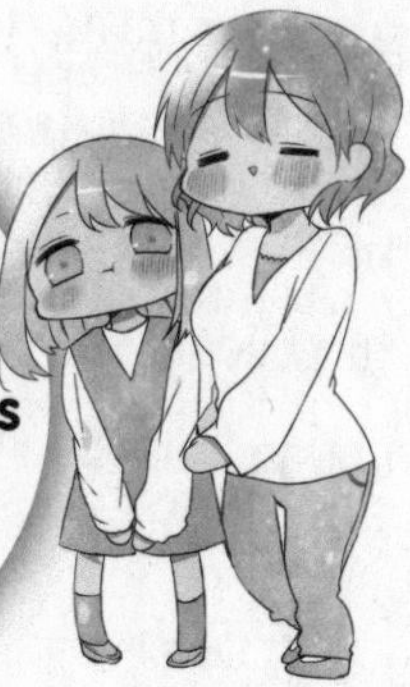

360 days a year, I hope for the status quo.
Sometimes, when I start to want a different tomorrow, I attempt some small resistance.

Height, 5'4", weight, about 117 pounds.
My god looks surprisingly unreliable.

You think I'm strong.
I'll never ever show you my vulnerability.

I link the fragments within me together with a line in second-person perspective,
give it your name without asking, and make a new constellation.

The brand-new notebook I got for you is still blank.
The things I want to jot down are all things I can't put into words.

The other side of a crystal lens.
You look more beautiful than usual,
but smaller than usual,
and I still don't know the formula to make that distance zero.

We make every moment into a save point
because we know we'll stop being able to catch up one day.

"Youth" – like a food sample on the other side of glass, my longing for it transparent.
I put a single piece in my mouth, still not ready to chew.

This is round two of my editor's finest poems. Congratulations.

I was glad I suggested using them for the first volume because it made the editor in chief and deputy editor in chief laugh.

When volume 1 went on sale, people here and there said they wanted to see my poetry, so I wrote a single poem for the table of contents.

I hope you enjoyed it along with these.

Nene
Yukimori

Nene Yukimori

I won't forget where I came from. I want to remember that I am who I am today because of the people supporting me.

Nene Yukimori earned the right to serialize *Kubo Won't Let Me Be Invisible* in *Young Jump* after the manga's one-shot version won the magazine's Shinman GP 2019 Season 5 contest. The manga then began serialization in October 2019. The work is Yukimori's first to receive an English release.

Kubo Won't Let Me Be Invisible

2

SHONEN JUMP EDITION

STORY AND ART BY
NENE YUKIMORI

TRANSLATION
AMANDA HALEY

TOUCH-UP ART & LETTERING
SNIR AHARON

DESIGN
ALICE LEWIS

EDITOR
JENNIFER SHERMAN

Printed in Canada

Published by VIZ Media, LLC
P.O. Box 77010
San Francisco, CA 94107

10 9 8 7 6 5 4 3 2 1
First printing, July 2022

ratings.viz.com RATED T+ OLDER TEEN

PARENTAL ADVISORY
KUBO WON'T LET ME BE INVISIBLE is rated T+ for Older Teen and is recommended for ages 16 and up. This volume contains suggestive themes.

VIZ MEDIA
viz.com

SHONEN JUMP

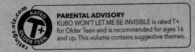

STOP!

YOU MAY BE READING THE WRONG WAY!

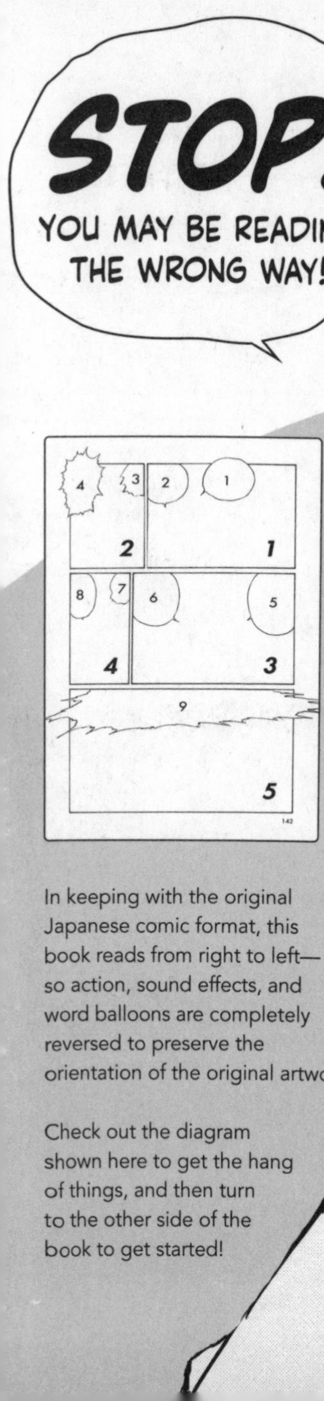
1
2
1
3
4
2
5
6
3
7
8
4
9
5
142

In keeping with the original Japanese comic format, this book reads from right to left—so action, sound effects, and word balloons are completely reversed to preserve the orientation of the original artwork.

Check out the diagram shown here to get the hang of things, and then turn to the other side of the book to get started!

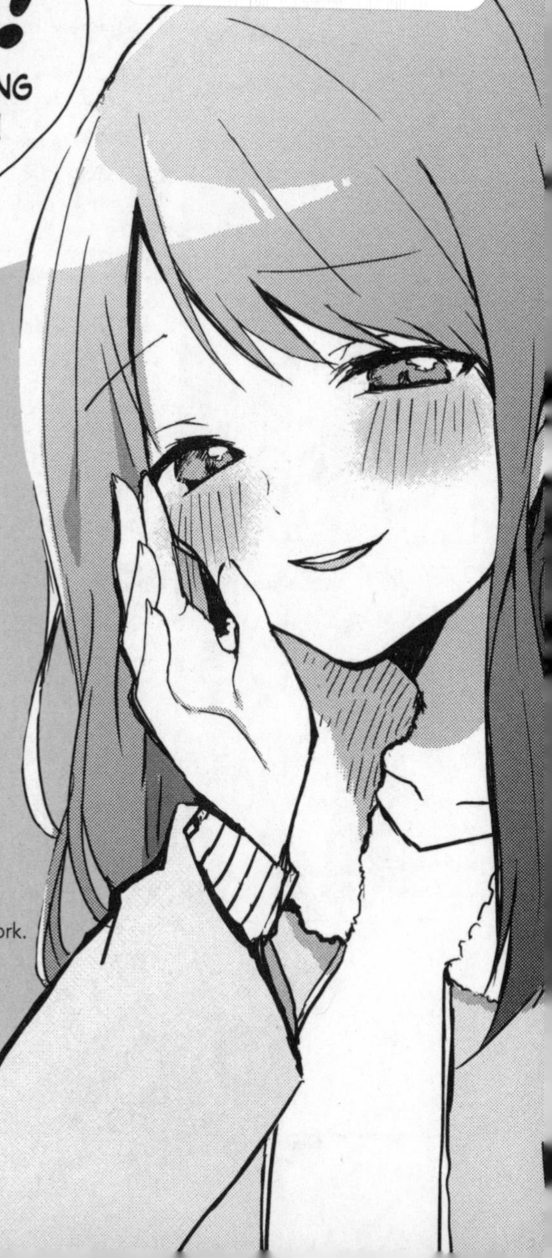